SILVER CITY

SILVER CITY

and Other Screenplays

Volume 1

JOHN SAYLES

NATION
BOOKS

SILVER CITY AND OTHER SCREENPLAYS

Compilation © 2004 by John Sayles
Silver City © 2004 by John Sayles
Sunshine State © 2002 by John Sayles
Passion Fish © 1992 by John Sayles

Published by
Nation Books
An Imprint of Avalon Publishing Group
245 West 17th St., 11th Floor
New York, NY 10011

AVALON
publishing group incorporated

Nation Books is a co-publishing venture of the Nation Institute and Avalon Publishing Group Incorporated.

Library of Congress Cataloging-in-Publication Data is available

ISBN 1-56025-631-1

9 8 7 6 5 4 3 2 1

Book design by Paul Paddock
Printed in the United States of America
Distributed by Publishers Group West

CONTENTS

SILVER CITY

BY

JOHN SAYLES

Introduction

I THINK IT WAS THE SLAUGHTERHOUSES that got me into it. I'd been in the Meat-packers (just making sausage, not the heavy breakdown) in the mid-1970s, and I remember getting lectures during cleanup about asses being in slings if things weren't right and the inspectors popped in. There was usually a bit of warning on the day, but they rotated inspectors back then to avoid overfamiliarity, so you never knew who you'd get, and they actually did seem to poke their nose into just about everything. Plus we did the cleanup ourselves, the union guys, blasting away with steam hoses at the end of every shift. They didn't subcontract anything; the locals would have had a shitfit. So years later when I start to read things about the fast-food business, start to see items in the paper about accidents and illegal immigrants getting hurt and killed in packing houses and construction sites, it feels like we're going backwards. What gives? And then digging into the whole mythic creation of *competitiveness* and *deregulation*, of the super-patriotic captains of industry exporting jobs and importing Third World wages and working conditions—and the mainstream media treating it like a *phenomenon*, like a forest fire caused by lightning or a heavy snowfall—it seemed like a clear call to make a film that connected a few dots. Yes, Shit Happens, but a lot of it happens thanks to highly organized campaigns of disinformation and influence-buying.

And if ours are the best politicians money can buy, as they say, then the American dollar doesn't pack the wallop it used to.

So—*Silver City*. The research wasn't hard. Every slab of hypocrisy I turned over revealed a thriving colony of rot beneath it, and I decided to base the central metaphor of the story on my own interpretation of the famous trickle-down theory so chipperly introduced by Ronald Reagan. I read a bunch about the methods, historical and present-day, of separating gold and silver from baser materials, and about where those toxic leftovers go when the shiny stuff is spirited away, and got to use the word "lixiviant" in a screenplay. The hero of the piece, if he can be said to be that, is a guy who has been sleepwalking through his life for some time, convinced that the inequities of his community are beyond fixing, and that complaint itself is a waste of breath. He may be right, and the important lesson to be learned from the trickle-down theory may be to make sure it doesn't trickle down on *you*, but the story presented is more hopeful, maybe even "romantic,"and the challenge of writing it was more about trying to balance anger, honesty, and hopefulness rather than the working out of who does what to who.

I've often said that a screenplay is the first draft, shooting the second, and editing the third and final draft of a movie story, and that holds true here. The cast and crew were assembled and came together to bring their talents and hard work to the movie, the part where I get to be audience as well as author. We got lucky when we decided to have Danny be a bit of a Hamlet, to dress him and only him in black or near-black. In the editing room, when I felt some serious juggling of time scheme and scene order would improve the sense and flow of the story, there weren't a lot of blatant costume discontinuities to flag the attention of the audience. For the record, the completed film goes Scene 1, 3, 4, 5, 15, 6, 8, 9, 11, 10, 12, 13, 7, 14, 16, 17, 18, 20, 22, 23, 25, 26, 27-33, 42, 35, 34 part 1, 24, 35 part 2, 36, 37, 38, 39, 21, 19, 40, 41, 46, 43, 44, 45, 48, 47, 52, 53, 54, 49, 57 part 1, 56, 57 part 2, 58, 59, 55, 40, 60-86, 88, 87, 89–97. What you'll read here is the shooting script we went into production with. Only Scene 2, at the interior climbing face, bit the dust completely— good scene, didn't need it. Everything else got shuffled and reshuffled, interrupted, trimmed, and rebalanced for emphasis—you always hope it gets better. When I'm writing a movie I'm going to direct I don't put a lot of physical description or internal character motivation or explanation of how exciting it's going to be into the text of the screenplay. A lot of what makes a movie a movie gets worked out with the director of photography and production designer and actors and composer and all your other allies, and I prefer to go into detail with them in person rather than sludge the script up and make potential investors think it's any longer than it actually is. So this is a working document, a plan that a story was built from. Raw meat, if you will, but produced under fair and sanitary working conditions.

And remember—look for the union label.

Disclaimer: Any similarities between characters portrayed in *Silver City* and officials of the Bush administration are unavoidable.

SILVER CITY

1   EXT. ARAPAHO LAKE — MORNING

DICKIE PILAGER, a bland-looking man in a fishing vest, stares into the camera, a blue lake at the base of a steep mountain behind him—

> **DICKIE**
> I always turn to Nature when I need to sort things out in my mind, to make sense of the world. But our environment is under siege—

He hesitates, unsure, looks past the camera—

> **DICKIE**
> Under siege, under fire, under attack—?

CHUCK RAVEN, Dickie's multi-tasking campaign manager, walks past with a cell phone up to his ear—

> **CHUCK RAVEN**
> It's not <u>under</u> anything, it's en<u>dan</u>gered.
> (into phone) So buy ten of the twenty second spots and put a hold on a dozen more—

We TRACK to FOLLOW Chuck through various CAMPAIGN WORKERS and VIDEO CREW MEMBERS who are prepping for a shoot on the shore of the lake—

> **DICKIE**
> But our endangerment is under— dammit— But our environment—

> **CHUCK RAVEN**
> (into phone) We're shooting the bucolic fishing thing and then we've got press coming in a hour for a photo op and a couple position quotes—

                    DICKIE
—is endangered by those who believe only the
elite deserve to share in its bounty—

                  CHUCK RAVEN
Be ready with the helicopter on my signal.
They start getting pushy we'll whisk him
away—

He has reached LLOYD, a junior campaign flunky who is
inexpertly attaching a Day-Glo fishing lure to the hook
on a rod—

                  CHUCK RAVEN
Can't you find anything less garish? It looks
like a French tickler—

                    LLOYD
It's supposed to attract the big ones—

                  CHUCK RAVEN
We're trying to attract voters, not fish. Put
that shiny one on.

                    LLOYD
(near whisper) Can he actually cast without
snagging the cameraman?

                  CHUCK RAVEN
Dickie grew up on this stuff.

                    LLOYD
Hey, if he can hunt, it's almost elk season.
We could—

                  CHUCK RAVEN
No dead animals. This isn't Texas.

Dickie comes to join them, a MAKE-UP WOMAN powdering his
nose as he walks—

                   DIRECTOR
(calling out) Okay, folks— let's set up for
a rehearsal!

> **DICKIE**
> (sees lure) Listen, Director-guy, the perch
> are gonna spit that thing right out—
>
> **DIRECTOR**
> We just want you to go through the action,
> nice and smooth, so we can get the camera
> movement down. We'll deal with the props
> later—

MONITOR

We look at the VIDEO MONITOR SCREEN over the shoulder of
the DIRECTOR. Dickie is taking the rod from Lloyd, who
backpedals nervously—

> **LLOYD (VIDEO)**
> Lemme just get out of your way—
>
> **DIRECTOR**
> Okay, we start tight on the hands—

The video camera ZOOMS IN tight on Dickie's hands—

> **DIRECTOR**
> —and action!

CLOSER, VIDEO SCREEN

The video camera PANS rapidly back and forth with Dickie's
hands as he casts, then SWISH PANS out to get to a patch
of water just before PLOP! the hook and lure hit the
surface—

> **DICKIE (O.S.)**
> You know, I've always turned back to Nature—

The camera PANS back to a heroic profile of Dickie as he
ruminates—

                              DICKIE
         —to sort things out in my mind, to make sense
         of the world. But our environment dammit—

DICKIE, OTHERS

Dickie is frowning, tugging at the rod—
                          CHUCK RAVEN
         "Our environment is endangered—"
                              DICKIE
         No, I'm snagged on something here—
                              LLOYD
         Here, let me—
                              DICKIE
         No, I can get it. I think I hooked a Russian
         submarine—

LAUGHTER from the campaign workers and crew. Lloyd sits
on the bank and starts to take off his shoes and socks as
Dickie cranks the handle—
                              DICKIE
         It's a whopper, whatever it is— oh God—

Dickie stops reeling in, mouth agape—

VIDEO CREW, CAMPAIGN WORKERS

All stare in disbelief at what has come up to the surface—

POV — HAND

The fishing line is taut, holding a human HAND just above
the surface, bluish, swollen fingers curled around the
lure in its palm!

JOHN SAYLES

SHORE

Everybody gaping silently. The OPERATOR pans his camera
out toward it, but Chuck breaks the spell, pushing the
lens away—

> CHUCK RAVEN
>
> Turn that off. Now! (into cell phone) Donna?
> We're gonna scramble here—(to LESLIE) What
> was our backup location for this?

> LESLIE
>
> Wilson's Creek—

> CHUCK RAVEN
>
> (into cell phone) We're changing location to
> Wilson's Creek, track down the press people,
> get the chopper in here immediately! You
> got me?

He takes the rod from Dickie, still staring out at the
water—

> CHUCK RAVEN
>
> Dickie, you're in the chopper— go!

Dickie is led away, annoyed—

> DICKIE
>
> Somebody's messing with us, Chuck—

> CHUCK RAVEN
>
> I'll deal with it—

> DICKIE
>
> You find out who it is, you cut em off at the
> knees!

> CHUCK RAVEN
>
> I'm on top of it, just go! Folks, we're going
> to reconvene, I want this whole circus on the
> road, you'll follow Leslie to Wilson's Creek—
> (to Lloyd) Hold this—

The crew begins to pack up, confused. Chuck is already moving away with Leslie dogging his heels—

CHUCK RAVEN
(to Leslie) None of these people get out of our sight before I give them a thorough debriefing.

LESLIE
Should I call the police?

CHUCK RAVEN
I'll handle that.

Lloyd, still holding the hand taut on the fishing line in the background, realizes he's being left behind—

LLOYD
Sir? What do I do with this?

CHUCK RAVEN
(without turning) Don't reel it in and don't let it get away.

2. EXT. ROCK CLIMBING FACE — DAY

DANNY O'BRIEN stands at the foot of a practice rock-climbing face, notebook and pen in hand, looking up at KIT, who clings precariously several feet above him. Danny is mightily bored by his job—

KIT
He'll give em the chair.

DANNY
This is only a civil lawsuit, but that's good to know—

KIT
He's the kind of guy, you're playing handball or something, he can't just _beat_ you he's gotta des_troy_ you.

DANNY

(writing) Competitive.

KIT

"Vindictive" is the word I'd use.

DANNY

And you worked with him how long? I'm sorry, you're dangling—

Kit is lifting himself by his arms alone—

KIT

(struggling) Three years, it was like a life sentence. So this jury he might be on— you checking him out for the defense or the prosecution?

DANNY

(sighs) You know, I'm not really sure. We just collect the information

3   EXT. ARAPAHO LAKE — DAY

SHERIFF JOE SKAGGS peers down at a BODY being laid out on a pop-up gurney by an EMT SQUAD. A few DEPUTIES are out wading in the lake behind him—

SKAGGS

This boy's been through the wringer.

CHUCK RAVEN

You understand how much we'd appreciate a low profile on this, Sheriff. I've already spoken with Captain Fox at the State Patrol—

SKAGGS

You have, have you?

CHUCK RAVEN

Hey, you do your job, and I'm certain you're very good at it, and I have to do mine—

DEPUTY DAVIS

(from water) I found something!

They turn to see young DEPUTY DAVIS holding up a rubber
SWIM FIN—

> ### SKAGGS
> I'd don't think that's what killed him,
> Davis! Keep looking.

Skaggs turns back to Chuck Raven—

> ### SKAGGS
> Enthusiastic kid— just hired him—

> ### CHUCK RAVEN
> So do you have any guess as to—

> ### SKAGGS
> (sees) Here's Henry. He's in charge of guess-
> work on the cold ones.

We PAN to see HENRY, the county coroner, making his way
toward the bank, waving to various people he knows. He's
still wearing his golf clothes—

> ### HENRY
> These people insist on floating to the sur-
> face on my day off—

Chuck hurries to intercept him, holding out his hand—

> ### CHUCK RAVEN
> Henry, hey— Chuck Raven, we met at the fund-
> raiser for Clark Hodges?

> ### HENRY
> (suddenly wary) Oh, right— you're Dickie
> Pilager's—

> ### CHUCK RAVEN
> We were about to shoot an environmental spot,
> beautiful setting, beautiful day, and then
> this— (indicates the body)

Henry notices the hook and lure still imbedded in the corpse's hand—

                         HENRY

    Surprised you caught anything with this lure.

                      CHUCK RAVEN

    You understand that discretion is the watchword
    here. If you're asked in an official capacity,
    of course, there's the truth, but we'd prefer
    it if there were no public statements—

Henry turns the dead man's head to one side, already doing his job—

                         HENRY

    (distracted) I am the soul of discretion.

4   INT. SEE - MORE DETECTIVE AGENCY

Danny walks in through the various desks of the See-More Detective Agency—

                         DANNY

    Kermit, my man, what's shakin?

KERMIT is a dedicated computer hacker who never looks up from his rig, even when Danny waves a hand in front of his eyes. He calls to Lupe, the office cleaner, who is vacuuming a few feet away—

                         DANNY

    You might want to run the DustBuster over him
    while you're at it, Lupe.

HILARY, the secretary-receptionist, looks up from her magazine—

                       HILARY

    Boss wants to see you.

Danny reaches his little work area—

                    DANNY
        Just need to fill out my time sheet—

                    HILARY
        She wants me to let her know the minute you
        come in.

Danny smells danger—

                    DANNY
        What'd I fuck up this time?

MORT SEYMOUR, a graying glad-hander, strides out of the
boss's office—

                    MORT
        Danny Boy! My favorite snoop.

                    DANNY
        Hey, Mort. How's the real estate moving?

Mort winks as he passes—

                    MORT
        Got a big one on the hook, Danny. Just got
        to land her. Later, folks!

Nobody waves goodbye, accustomed to Mort blowing in and
out of the office—

                    DANNY
        (mutters) Mort the Mogul. He's had a big one
        on the hook since the day I met him—

                    GRACE
        Danny—

GRACE SEYMOUR, the boss, stands in the doorway of her
office, having heard this last dis of her husband. She

gently closes the door behind her, approaches, and speaks
to Danny in a hushed voice—

> **GRACE**
>
> I have a client in my office who has brought
> a lot of business to this firm over the
> years. I need you to be on your best be—

> **DANNY**
>
> I promise not to pee on your carpet, Grace—

> **GRACE**
>
> That means none of your witticisms. And your
> language—

> **DANNY**
>
> It's some religious guy?

> **GRACE**
>
> No, no, he's—

> **DANNY**
>
> Some, like, political hack who needs us to do
> some dirty w—

> **GRACE**
>
> Stop. Take a breath. Be a good boy.

5   INT. GRACE'S OFFICE

Chuck Raven wanders around the office, poking into this
and that, as Danny sits in the chair across from Grace's
desk watching him—

> **CHUCK RAVEN**
>
> Obviously we at the campaign can't seem to be
> too interested. We'd rather not be associated
> in the public mind with—

> **DANNY**
>
> Why not just walk away from it?

> **CHUCK RAVEN**
>
> That's what I intend to do. These things get
> stuck in people's minds, distract them from

the message. Gerald Ford falling down the stairs, Carter whacking that rabbit with his paddle. I don't want my candidate remembered—

CHUCK RAVEN

—as the guy who hooked a stiff in Arapaho Lake.

CHUCK RAVEN

Exactly. There's also the remote possibility that this was not a coincidence.

Danny perks up a bit at this, shooting a look to Grace—

CHUCK RAVEN

I don't think I'm being paranoid to consider the possibility that one of our—our opponents had something to do with this—

DANNY

You mean they threw a dead body into the lake as a prank?

CHUCK RAVEN

I'm not accusing the other side, but when you play the game to win you're bound to step on a few toes—

DANNY

Twist a few arms—

CHUCK RAVEN

There are always a few loose cannons on the deck, people who hold grudges—

DANNY

Who'd hold a grudge against Dickie Pilager? Unless it's like some hazing incident from his fraternity days—

He stops as he catches the warning glare from Grace—

CHUCK RAVEN

Look, I'm the best at what I do because I've

got the best in<u>te</u>lligence, because my candidates are never caught with their pants down—

                    DANNY
So to speak—

Chuck hands Danny a slip of paper—

                  CHUCK RAVEN
Here are three names. These are people I feel might be unstable enough and vindictive enough to— well.

                    DANNY
And you want them investigated?

                  CHUCK RAVEN
I want them con<u>front</u>ed. Let them know they're being watched. Don't be subtle—

                    DANNY
I'm incapable of subtlety—

Another warning look from Grace. Chuck smiles with hard eyes—

                  CHUCK RAVEN
A good stiff warning but nothing actionable. And the press, of course, never hear a whisper of this—

                    DANNY
Hey, I don't even <u>read</u> the newspapers.

Chuck looks to Grace for reassurance—

                    GRACE
Totally confidential.

                  CHUCK RAVEN
(smiles) I'll expect a progress report by Thursday. Happy hunting.

Chuck exits.

> **GRACE**
> I ought to put a muzzle on you.

> **DANNY**
> Sorry.

> **GRACE**
> You're off the jury prep and you're on this.
> Don't worry about expenses or overtime—

> **DANNY**
> I appreciate your confidence, Grace—

> **GRACE**
> Don't. Peters is still in Grand Rapids
> chasing the trust fund kid and Kelly is stuck
> in court for the next two weeks.

> **DANNY**
> Oh.

> **GRACE**
> Seriously, Danny, this is a big deal for us.

> **DANNY**
> Hey, I'll work it high and low. Find out how
> the deceased got into the lake, lean on these
> people on his shit list, see if there's any
> connection—

> **GRACE**
> What I want to know is can I trust you?

Danny gives her his most disarming grin—

> **DANNY**
> With your life.

6   EXT. CAPITOL PLAZA

Dickie Pilager stands surrounded by REPORTERS, the CAPITOL
DOME visible in the BG. He seems a little lost, eyes
searching past the reporters for help—

REPORTER 1

With the amount of federal money coming to the state decreasing drastically—

DICKIE

I'm not raising taxes.

REPORTER 1

But the shortfall for social programs—

DICKIE

I repeat— I'm not raising taxes. We can't just keep throwing the taxpayers' hard-earned money at these perceived— and some of them I admit are real— so-called social problems. We have to get our priorities straight. Education is a priority. Affordable housing for our working people is a priority. Health care is a priority. Our economy is a priority. The environmental the whole environmental— arena that's a big priority. Building new roads and maintaining the present— keeping the infrastructure in place, where it belongs, that's a priority—

NORA

What isn't a priority?

DICKIE

(stumped) What's not a priority— is those matters which are of less of a— not that they're not important but— if you're going to have a front-burner which is where you want your priorities, like, <u>cook</u>ing, there needs to be something sitting on the back one. And that's where your other organizations, your church people and your— organizations formed to help these things, will be happy to pitch in if only government would get out of their way.

A tiny moment of silence as the reporters try to unscramble this. Chuck Raven swoops in to the rescue—

> **CHUCK RAVEN**
> Press conference is at two o'clock, people!
> No fair hijacking my candidate when we're
> late for a meeting—

He has Dickie's arm and is spiriting him away to cries of Mr. Pilager! Mr. Pilager! from the reporters—

> **DICKIE**
> Where were you?

> **CHUCK RAVEN**
> Gridlocked. Don't ever get caught out in the
> open like that—

> **DICKIE**
> Who's the chick with the red blouse again?

> **CHUCK RAVEN**
> "Newswoman"—

> **DICKIE**
> Whatever—

> **CHUCK RAVEN**
> Nora Allardyce. Writes for the *Dispatch*.

> **DICKIE**
> She wouldn't get off my DWIs. All this stuff
> from ten years ago—

> **CHUCK RAVEN**
> Give it a few days, she'll back off. We've
> got something in the works—

7   INT. MORT'S REAL ESTATE OFFICE — SILVER CITY SCALE MODEL

We are in a 3-D plastic SCALE MODEL of a vast condo village— curving, tree-lined streets dotted with houses that come in three architecturally-compatible sizes—

MORT (O.S.)

With a planned community you know what you're
getting.

WIDER

Mort is showing off the scale model to CHANDLER TYSON, a
slick corporate lobbyist in his early forties. The walls
of Mort's little real estate office are plastered with
idealized SKETCHES of the proposed development—

                    MORT
People own their houses, they own shares in
the amenities, but the corporation calls the
shots. This whole section here will be
assisted living—

                   CHANDLER
The lake is a nice attraction.

                    MORT
The lake is the key. Half these people they
don't fish, they don't boat, they can't
climb a flight of stairs, much less a mountain, but knowing it's there, just around
the bend—

                   CHANDLER
To live in the Rockies.

                    MORT
We're selling a dream. Now of course a few
regulations need to be—

                   CHANDLER
The Developers' Association—

                    MORT
Which I pay into—

Chandler begins to idly pick up loose houses and trees and
play with them, making Mort a little nervous—

CHANDLER

The Association has some general legislation
they want to concentrate on. Individual cases—

MORT

You talk to Chuck Raven—

CHANDLER

On a daily basis. And he is, let's face it,
the brains behind our future governor.

MORT

You need examples, specific instances, for
your general legislation, right? Silver City—

Chandler begins to wander around the room perusing the
drawings on the wall—

CHANDLER

That wouldn't be fair to the other members of
the Association. Showing favoritism—

MORT

But—

CHANDLER

But— if you were to retain me as your lobbyist on an individual basis—

MORT

Oh—

CHANDLER

There's no reason I couldn't honestly serve
both clients equally during my talks with the
future governor and his staff.

MORT

Retaining— I'm— so much of my cash is tied up
with—

CHANDLER

I could probably work on a commission basis.

MORT

You mean like a piece of the action?

Mort is clearly not enthusiastic about this possibility—

> **CHANDLER**
> Mort— the regulatory legislation the governor
> is going to go to bat for? I'm <u>writing</u> it.
> You think the Association pays me just to
> suck up to these people?

Mort indicates a tiny gap with his fingers—

> **MORT**
> We're only that far from qualifying for an
> economic initiative subsidy. Timberline
> County is on the ropes. And if the state was
> to relax the soil standards just a—

> **CHANDLER**
> No reason we can't raise the river and lower
> the bridge at the same time.

Mort, intrigued, takes the bait—

> **MORT**
> How big a piece of the action would this be?

8   INT. DANNY'S APARTMENT — NIGHT

Danny enters his apartment through the kitchen—

> **DANNY**
> Debbie? Debbie? You home?

We FOLLOW Danny into his LIVING ROOM. He absently flicks
on the TV SET, which is playing a campaign ad for Dickie
Pilager, and continues to call into the bedroom—

> **DANNY**
> Debbie?

No response. Danny comes back, glances at the TV, then
frowns. Something is wrong. He turns, stares at an empty

space. A rectangle of un-vaccuumed carpet dirt indicates what is missing—

> DANNY
>
> There was a couch here.

We FOLLOW Danny back to the KITCHEN—

> DANNY
>
> Debbie?

He looks around the kitchen, concerned now, till he lights on the wall calendar. He crosses to check it out—

CALENDAR

Various things written on the October page. On today's square, in bold letters, Debbie has written— **D-DAY!!!!**

DANNY

Danny runs his finger back over the days, reads—

> DANNY
>
> "Call movers." She's been planning this for fucking <u>weeks.</u>

He turns and finds a NOTE attached to the refrigerator—

> DANNY
>
> (reads) "Sorry but I had to do this— don't try to find me— I'll call you when you calm down."

Danny sits at the kitchen table with the note in front of him, thinks for a moment. He snatches up the sugar bowl and SMASH! hurls it against the wall! He sits for another long moment, staring forlornly at the note—

                              DANNY
            I am extremely calm.

                                              FADE TO BLACK.

9   INT. COUNTY MORGUE — MORNING

Danny walks into the morgue with Henry the coroner—
                              HENRY
            So officially you are not here.
                              DANNY
            The candidate—
                              HENRY
            I got the message from his people—
He lifts sheet from a BODY lying on a table. Danny reacts—
                              DANNY
            Whoah. This guy is seriously dead. Smells
            like— what—?
                              HENRY
            Apricots.
                              DANNY
            Yeah.
                              HENRY
            The CBI sent a pathologist out, took some
            tissue samples— (reading from the chart) "Cause
            Of Death— Deceased suffered multiple fractures
            including trauma to the skull, crushed ribcage,
            and damage to internal organs consistent with
            a fall—
                              DANNY
            A fall from where?
                              HENRY
            That's Manner Of Death— I left that blank so
            far. The pathologist FAXed me this— (reading)
            "A residue of cyanide—"

DANNY

He was poisoned too?

HENRY

"—was found on hair and skin, though none was present in lungs, stomach, or liver." Like he'd been dipped in the stuff. What else? (scanning) "Chlorine in the lungs—"

DANNY

Like from a swimming pool chlorine?

HENRY

Your guess is as good as mine. I'm just a county coroner with a law degree—

DANNY

So you have no idea who he is? Was?

HENRY

(looks at body) Hispanic male, late twenties, early thirties—

DANNY

He's dark but where do you get Hispanic?

Henry reaches down and pulls back the corpse's lips—

HENRY

Check out the dental work. That kind of gold, we're talking Mexico, maybe Guatemala. Probably a manual laborer—

He lifts one of the corpse's hands, turns it palm up. We notice that the fingertips are stained with blue ink—

HENRY

—heavy callousing on the hands. There's where the fish hook snagged him—

DANNY

Any ID in his clothes?

> **HENRY**
>
> (shrugs) Bought his shoes at WalMart. Other than that he's just another Juan Doe.

Henry turns the hand over. There is a red-eyed SCORPION TATTOO on the back of it—

> **HENRY**
>
> This is the only distinguishing feature.

> **DANNY**
>
> Can I take of photo of that?

Henry pulls a snapshot out of his shirt pocket—

> **HENRY**
>
> Have one of mine.

> **SKAGGS (O.S.)**
>
> You—

They look up to see Sheriff Skaggs entering, hard eyes appraising Danny—

> **SKAGGS**
>
> You're the one working for the Pilagers?

> **DANNY**
>
> I'm not here. Officially—

> **SKAGGS**
>
> I'm supposed to keep you in the loop on this—

Danny offers his hands—

> **DANNY**
>
> Danny O'Brien—

Skaggs ignores his hand, looking him over—

> **SKAGGS**
>
> You used to write for the *Mountain Monitor*.

When it existed, yeah. And you're—?

SKAGGS

Timber line County Sheriff. Joe Skaggs.

Danny's warning lights go off at the name—

DANNY

There used to be a Jerry Skaggs who—

SKAGGS

My brother.

DANNY

(faintly) Oh. How's he doing?

SKAGGS

He died a year ago of colon cancer.

DANNY

Sorry to hear that—

SKAGGS

No you're not.

He indicates the body—

SKAGGS

This should be totally routine— so don't go making it complicated.

DANNY

I wouldn't think of it. Any idea who he—?

SKAGGS

CBI has nothing on his fingerprints. The falls we get, it's usually one of our many climbing enthusiasts up from Boulder, wander off the trail to admire the view and step on some loose rock—

DANNY

You could check his stomach for granola.

Skaggs shoots a look at Danny—

DANNY

Sorry.

The Sheriff cocks his head to consider the body on the
slab—

SKAGGS

No— he's got that crossed-the-border-crammed-
in-a-car-trunk look to him. We find a lot
of those boys out in the scrub, never do get
an ID.

He turns his attention back to Danny—

SKAGGS

If you do stumble on anything that pertains
to this case, what's the first call you gonna
make?

DANNY

Timberline Sheriff's Department?

SKAGGS

Anything goes public without I know it first,
I'm coming after your ass. See you, Henry.

With that the Sheriff makes his exit. Danny looks to the
coroner—

HENRY

I don't think he likes you.

10 INT. PILAGER CAMPAIGN OFFICE

Chuck Raven moves through the crowded, busy campaign
office—

CHUCK RAVEN

No, I don't think it's overkill! Fifteen

points is not what I call comfortable— we're talking scorched earth or nothing. A lot can happen in four years, I want them dead in the water!— If, when this is over he can still show his _face_ in the state of Colorado, we've failed in our mission. Just get on it!

He clicks the phone off and falls into step with Leslie—

CHUCK RAVEN

How did it go with our friends from Cherry Hills?

LESLIE

I think they get it. They can finance the attack campaign—

CHUCK RAVEN

"Public information outreach"—

LESLIE

—as long as it's limited to phone calls and print material financed directly through the educational committee they set up. And we provide them—

CHUCK RAVEN

Ad_vise_ them—

LESLIE

—advise them on which agency to hire, on the content of the print material, and the text for the phone message, we give them voter lists, home and work numbers—

CHUCK RAVEN

(distracted) Stephanie, get me Jim Wilkinson at the _Defender_— and put my call from Washington through as soon as it comes— (back to Leslie) When will we have the ads ready for them?

11 INT. RADIO STATION — CU NEWSPAPER

We start on an ECU of a NEWSPAPER ARTICLE in the *Denver Defender*—

BODY DISCOVERED

The body of an unidentified man was found in Arapahoe Lake this morning. Timberline County Sheriff Joe Skaggs, in charge of the investigation, stated that the cause of death has not yet been determined.

As we read we hear a RADIO TALK SHOW over a SPEAKER SYSTEM—

> **CLIFF CASTLETON (O.S.)**
> Okay, Russell, Russell— I can sense your frustration, but what's your point?

> **RUSSELL (O.S.)**
> What ever happened to "To the victor go the spoils?"

ANTEROOM — DANNY

Danny sits looking at the paper just outside the glass-fronted BOOTH where CLIFF CASTLETON sits broadcasting—

> **RUSSELL**
> (ON RADIO FEED) We go in and kick their butts, run their dictators out of the country, and now it's our responsibility to pay for recon-struction? Hey, if I have Terminix come over to get rid of some vermin, they hand me the bill, not the other way around.

> **CLIFF CASTLETON (O.S.)**
> I'm with you a hundred percent, my friend. It's the price of democracy and it's only fair they're the ones to pay it.

Cliff grimaces, takes a big gulp from the bottle of pink bismuth (as in Pepto-Bismol) he keeps beside him—

BOOTH

We cut in tighter on Cliff as he wipes his mouth and signs off—

CLIFF CASTLETON
Listen, we're out of time, but I appreciate all your calls today, especially that wingnut from Boulder— eat some red meat, buddy, your brain needs the protein. This is Cliff Castleton and you've been listening to *The Hot Seat* on KQRY, the Free Voice of the American Rockies.

Cliff gathers up his papers and his bottle of antacid and we TRACK to lead him out to where Danny is sitting. Danny jumps up to his feet—

DANNY
Mr. Castleton? Danny O'Brien, I called—

CLIFF CASTLETON
Talk to me.

Cliff does not even slow down as he passes. We FOLLOW the two of them as Cliff leads Danny through a MAZE of radio station HALLWAYS, snatches of other right-wing TALK SHOWS drifting out from other studios as they go by—

DANNY
I'm here sort of— on behalf? of the Pilager campaign—

CLIFF CASTLETON
Dickie didn't send you over, his little pit-bull did.

DANNY
That would be Mr.—?

CLIFF CASTLETON

Chuck Raven.

DANNY

You and Mr. Raven know—?

CLIFF CASTLETON

Chucky and I go back to campus politics. You know the American Students' League?

DANNY

Uhm— with the information tables at the air-port? Something about nuking Jane Fonda?

CLIFF CASTLETON

(smiles) God, we miss her.

DANNY

So you were college buddies—

CLIFF CASTLETON

I was in line to be national president of the ASL—

DANNY

The right wing's answer to Abbie Hoffman.

Cliff gives him a withering look. He has to swallow to keep the bile down as he tells the story—

CLIFF CASTLETON

This was going to be an orderly succession, strict adherence to parliamentary proce-dure, when all of a sudden we start hearing about credentials challenges at the regional chapters.

DANNY

And behind this is?

CLIFF CASTLETON

Chuck Raven. Mr. If-You-Can't-Win-the-Game-Just-Change-the-Rules. We come to the con-vention and we've got two sets of delegates fighting over the seats—bedlam. We had to

---

kick it upstairs to the Party for a ruling—
totally humiliating, this is when the Democ-
rats were riding high and it makes us this
laughing stock. And who happens to be the man
to make the decision?

DANNY

I have no—

CLIFF CASTLETON

Judson Pilager—

DANNY

The Senator—

CLIFF CASTLETON

Who Chuck Raven has been carefully culti-
vating, knowing this would come up, he wrote
his damn <u>the</u>sis on the senator, went on pic-
nics with the family, and I'm not only
screwed in the election I'm persona non grata
in the Party from that moment on. So whatever Chucky wants, tell him he can go—

DANNY

You're being watched.

CLIFF CASTLETON

What?

DANNY

He wants you to know you're being watched.
There's a perception you might have it in for
the candidate in some way—

CLIFF CASTLETON

There's more than a per<u>ce</u>ption, I let the
little snot have it with both barrels at
least once a broadcast. They think they can
get me to back down by in<u>ve</u>stigating me?

DANNY

No, no—

Cliff begins ticking off on his fingers—

CLIFF CASTLETON

He's wishy-washy on right-to-life, he's got no plans for dealing with this alien invasion we're in the midst of, you go to Pueblo and English is the second language if not the third, he's a draft dodger and a mama's boy and a dimwit— if he wasn't running against a known Communist I'd run him out of the state.

DANNY

What I'm saying is, if you were to do anything illegal in order to embarrass—

Cliff stops abruptly, turning to face Danny—

CLIFF CASTLETON

If I were to paste you one in the mouth right now, would that be considered illegal?

Danny holds up his hands for peace—

DANNY

I don't think that will be necessary—

CLIFF CASTLETON

You come into my studio with threats and intimidation—

DANNY

Uhm— thank you for your time, best of luck with your show—

CLIFF CASTLETON

You tell Chuck Raven I'm not one bit afraid of him!

DANNY

(backing toward an exit) I'll pass your sentiments on—

We HOLD on Cliff as he calls after the hastily retreating Danny—

> **CLIFF CASTLETON**
> He wants a piece of me, he knows where to find me! Little prick wouldn't last thirty seconds on the air with me—

12 INT. BACKSTAGE, AUDITORIUM

Chuck Raven hurries down a corridor in the auditorium hosting the press conference. He sees Lloyd standing uncomfortably guarding a door—

> **CHUCK RAVEN**
> Where the hell is he?

> **LLOYD**
> He's in with his— uh— spiritual advisor?

> **CHUCK RAVEN**
> Oh Christ.

> **LLOYD**
> He may be in there too.

13 INT. ROOM

Dickie sits with REVEREND BILLY TUBBS, a televangelist with a solid-state hairdo and a thick Bible parked on his lap—

> **REV. TUBBS**
> We're talking about murder. The murder of innocents.

> **DICKIE**
> There's a limit to what I can do on this, Billy. It's the kind of issue that attracts a lot of people to the polls who wouldn't ordinarily vote, and—

> **REV. TUBBS**
> But if you were to take leadership on the issue, throw the full weight of your office behind it—

DICKIE

If you could get it on a referendum—

REV. TUBBS

I honestly don't think it would pass, not in the secular climate we live in. But when Moses found the children of Israel prostrate before a golden calf, did he call for a referendum? No, he—

Chuck Raven sticks his head in—

CHUCK RAVEN

Excuse me, Reverend Tubbs— we need him.

REV. TUBBS

We were just discussing the Sermon on the Mount.

CHUCK RAVEN

We must obey the Eleventh Commandment— "Thou Shalt Not Keep the Press Waiting."

14 INT. AUDITORIUM

The state political PRESS has gathered, including NORA ALLARDYCE, the print reporter in her early forties we first saw out in front of the capitol. Dickie is at a podium fielding questions while Chuck Raven sits to one side sweating it out—

DICKIE

In the case of capital offenses I am absolutely in favor of the death penalty. You hear stories about frontier justice— you can bet that the wrongdoers, the folks who couldn't play by the rules, had some respect for that. And there was no— it didn't cost the taxpayer— if they had had taxpayers back then, those were the good old days, I suppose— and all you needed was a good strong rope and a tree to hang it from.

Chuck Raven winces at the mention of a rope—

REPORTER 1

So you'll be proposing tougher criminal legis—

DICKIE

My message to criminals is this— straighten up or get out. There's no place for you in our state. You do the crime, and by God, you're gonna have to face your lumps.

NORA

But the majority of those serving time for possession of dru—

DICKIE

You want to change the behavior, you stiffen the consequences.

NORA

There are reports, Mr. Pilager, that before you became involved in politics you had con-siderable experience with—

DICKIE

(quickly) Look, if you're up in a helicopter, airplane, something that flies, you don't want your pilot intoxicated with drugs, do you? And it's that way with our schoolchildren— Junior can't read if he's high on crack. The air is thin enough up here, (points to another reporter) Yes?

REPORTER 2

So you support mandatory sentencing?

DICKIE

Not only mandatory but predetermined and strict and with uh—

Chuck Raven holds his breath, willing Dickie through the syntactic minefield—

                            DICKIE

        —fixed and serious lengths of time attached.
        Colorado is not a halfway house for criminal
        offenders— you're either all the way or— or you
        hit the highway.

15 EXT. OFFICE BUILDING — BACK ENTRANCE

MITCH, about the same age as Danny but a good bit more
unkempt, finishes a cigarette break—

                            DANNY
        I always picture you in some smoky hole-in-
        the-wall hunched over a computer, spewing
        your bile at the military-industrial
        complex.

                            MITCH
        It is a hole-in-the-wall but I'm surrounded
        by a bunch of anti-tobacco fascists.

Mitch puts the butt out and we FOLLOW them down into a
basement WEBSITE OFFICE, various young staffers working
computers and telephones—

                            DANNY
        I think we say "pro-oxygen" these days.

                            MITCH
        Bunch of vegans and computer nerds.

KAREN, a very young staffer with jewelry in her face, does
an exaggerated COUGH and phlegmy THROAT-CLEARING as Mitch
passes—

                            MITCH
        Half of them don't know dick, but they at
        least don't buy the official story. You're
        some kind of investigator now?

MITCH

Yeah, some kind.

MITCH

Maybe you could do some snooping for me— for
the Website.

DANNY

What's it pay?

MITCH

What do you think? Bupkes.

DANNY

I don't really do politics anymore— Debbie
said it was bad for my mental health. And
hey, there's nothing I can do about it
anyway. (uncomfortable with Debbie talk)
Listen, can I run some names by you?

They've reached Mitch's disaster-area of a work station.
Danny hands him the paper Chuck Raven gave him—

MITCH

(reading) Cliff Castleton— neo-fascist radio
crackpot—

DANNY

I've already spoken with Mr. Castleton—

MITCH

Very big with the crowd that thinks our form
of capital punishment isn't _painful_ enough.
Casey Lyle— he was a big cheese in one of the
Health and Safety agencies a couple adminis-
trations back—

DANNY

An unstable personality?

MITCH

What, compared to you?

DANNY

Thanks—

MITCH

(reading on) Speaking of unstable personalities—
Madeleine Pilager, the nympho nut case sister—

DANNY

Is she local?

MITCH

Lives outside of Vail, comes in to hit our
so-called club scene now and then. What is
this you're working on?

DANNY

Something that if one detail of it ends up
here on Kill-the-Rich-dot-com I get fired.

MITCH

You're no fun anymore.

DANNY

I've had the fun pretty much knocked out of
me. This here— your Website— for you this is
a natural progression, you never wanted to be
a mainstream news guy—

MITCH

Neither did you.

DANNY

Of course I did. If you hadn't talked me into
pushing that fucking kickback story on Jerry
Skaggs—

MITCH

We were set up.

DANNY

You could have triple-checked the information. You just wanted to believe it so bad,
wanted another trophy—

MITCH

You're working for them now, aren't you?

DANNY

(defensive) Them who?

                              MITCH

          (points outside) Them who run the whole deal.

                              DANNY

          Suppose I am? Listen, what do you know about
          the Pilager family?

                              MITCH

          (grins) You want the *USA Today* version or
          full graphics?

COMPUTER SCREEN — VARIOUS GRAPHICS

PHOTOS from newspapers and magazines and an occasional bit
of downloaded VIDEO appear on the screen as Karen runs the
computer and narrates. We start on a screen emblazoned
with "GREED INCORPORATED—THE PILAGER DYNASTY"

                          KAREN (O.S.)

          Jeremiah Pilager who comes here in 1870,
          sells dry goods at cutthroat prices to the
          pickers and panners, accepts a land deed as
          payment from one poor sourdough, which turns
          out to be the Pilager Seam—

                              DANNY

          So the lone-wolf prospector legend—

                              KAREN

          Is a crock. Boomtown money, big mansions,
          extravagant lifestyle— but when the silver
          bubble bursts in 1893 Jeremiah has already
          diversified and he comes out richer than
          ever. These days the family fortune has
          shifted from mining to agricultural waste.

A GRAPHIC of a pile of cowshit appears on the screen—

                          KAREN (O.S.)

          Cow pies. More than you can possibly imagine.
          If somebody doesn't dispose of these from

time to time, the stock would be up to its
sirloins in shit—

> **DANNY**
> This is the family business—

> **KAREN**
> The flagship, so to speak. The real money comes
> from their association with this gentleman—

A PHOTO of a well-heeled rancher, WES BENTEEN appears—

> **MITCH**
> You know the name Wes Benteen—

> **DANNY**
> As in Benteen Ranch—

> **KAREN**
> As in Benteen Realty, Benteen Medical Asso-
> ciates, Gold Mine Communications, DenAgra,
> which produces the doo-doo the Pilagers clean
> up, Bentel Stadium—

> **DANNY**
> He's the Bentel Corporation.

> **KAREN**
> Founder and CEO—

> **DANNY**
> A big money guy.

> **KAREN**
> Mega.

> **MITCH**
> A real piece of work. During the Iran-
> Contra thing he sent Oliver North's boys a
> set of cargo planes. He used blacks and
> Chicanos to bust the union in his slaugh-
> terhouses and then he fired half of them
> and brought in migrants without papers and
> has never once been hit on by the immigra-
> tion service—

                              DANNY
And he and the Senator—

                              KAREN
When Richard, the son, fondly known by his frat-
mates as "Dim Dickie," sinks his inheritance
into Silver City, a ghost town with an abandoned
mine that turns out to have been abandoned for
good reason, who bails him out by purchasing it
at six million above its original value?

Another PHOTO of Wes Benteen, shaking hands with a younger
Dickie Pilager—

                          DANNY (O.S.)
Wes Benteen. So— a personal favor—

                              KAREN
One contributor putting up over half the
money for a senate run that outspends the
opposition five-to-one looks fishy—

                              MITCH
Unless it comes from within the family. So
Dickie Pilager, not a public official yet—

                              DANNY
—serves as a front for Benteen bankrolling
his father's campaign. And in return?

                              MITCH
Benteen is in real estate, he's in cattle, he's
in publishing, media, mining utilities, waste
disposal— how much federal regulation you think
that entails?

                              KAREN
When Benteen wanted to get rid of the safety
and health inspections at his meat processing
plants, Senator Jud led the charge.

                              DANNY
So now he wants a man in the governor's mansion. Somebody corruptible—

> MITCH
>
> There's not a corrupt bone in Dickie Pilager's body. He's just— what— user-<u>friend</u>ly. Guys like Wes Benteen and Chuck Raven say whatever they think will get them what they want. Dickie's a true believer.

DANNY AND MITCH

Danny stares at the screen, the clout of his employers hitting home—

> MITCH
>
> These are the people you're working for, pal.

> KAREN
>
> I wasn't even born when most of this happened, and it still pisses me off.

> DANNY:
>
> It's not like I'm helping to get him elected or anything. It's—

> MITCH
>
> Sure, you're just paying the rent like everybody else. Any dirt you can spare, though

> DANNY
>
> Come on, Mitch. I got professional ethics—

> MITCH
>
> Chickenshit.

An awkward pause. Mitch looks Danny over as he stares glumly at the computer screen—

> MITCH
>
> You seen Nora lately?

The name is like an electric shock—

                              DANNY
Nora? (uncomfortable) No, I— I see her byline
now and then.

                              MITCH
I hear she's engaged to some guy.

                              DANNY
(a jolt) Oh. Terrific.

16 EXT. RESTAURANT

We APPROACH the ENTRANCE of a downtown Denver RESTAURANT—

                              MORT
The roads are there, the scenery is there—

17 INT. RESTAURANT—DAY 17

Mort Seymour sits with PHIL ROSS, ELLIE HASTINGS, and
FREDDY MONDRAGON, three rural county commissioners who
are very impressed to be in the capitol's power-lunch
eatery. Mort has the Silver City scale model out on the
table in front of them—

                              MORT
—we've got this jewel of a lake only a mile
away—

                              ELLIE
But the water quality—

                              MORT
The lake is pristine. Whatever the mining
outfits did in the hills never touched the
lake. The question you have to ask yourself
is do you want your county to be thought of
as one big Superfund site—

                              PHIL
We've got Carbonville—

---

48   **JOHN SAYLES**

                              MORT

Or one big migrant labor camp— (to Freddy) No
offense intended—

                             FREDDY

We can't deny it—

                              MORT

Or do you want Silver City— (indicates scale
model)— emerging like a shining phoenix from
the ashes?

                              PHIL

It's gonna be big as Phoenix?

                             ELLIE

The mythical creature, not the city, Phil.

                              MORT

It will have the potential to grow into whatever you want it to be.

                             FREDDY

Now the land—

                              MORT

We acquired the land at a very reasonable
figure, very reasonable— Bentel Corporation
had no further use for it, and of course,
it's been classified as a degraded habitat—

                             FREDDY

Meaning—?

                              MORT

Meaning the environmental folks won't be
breathing down our necks once we get this
project rolling.

                              PHIL

But the soil is still full of heavy metals.
If you dig a well—

                              MORT

(smiles) We're not digging any wells. We've
got some folks downstate I'm pretty sure will
be happy to sell us their water rights.

SILVER CITY and other Screenplays

ELLIE

Why would they do that?

Mort sees somebody coming up behind the commissioners—

MORT

(smugly) Let's say you grow your crop out on an arid
plain, got to irrigate the hell out of the land, got
to rely on federal price supports— you draw a
hell of a lot of water and barely make a profit.

Mort waves to Chandler, who whispers to Chuck Raven, who
whispers to Dickie Pilager as they head for their table—

MORT

Now you pull that price support out of the
equation— well, there's a bunch of farmers
who'd be thrilled to cash in their chips for
a healthy one-time water settlement.

FRED

How do you know that's going to happen?

MORT

The price support is a line-item pushed into
the federal budget every year by our Senator,
Jud Pilager—

ELLIE

And he's told you that—

MORT

Chuck!

Mort stands just as Chuck Raven comes past with Dickie and
the entourage—

MORT

Hot on the campaign trail—

CHUCK RAVEN

(slapping Mort's back) Mort, how's it going?
You know our man, here—

JOHN SAYLES

                    MORT
Governor—

                    DICKIE
Don't jump the gun.

                    MORT
You're fifteen up in the polls. Hey, I'd like
to introduce you to some of your supporters
out in the trenches—this is the Timberline
County Commission—

                    DICKIE
Don't stand up—

                    MORT
This is Ellie— Phil— Freddy Mondragón—

Dickie leans in to shake their hands. They are thrilled
to meet the future top man—

                    ELLIE
It's such a pleasure—

Dickie sees the plastic town on the table—

                    DICKIE
Hey, where's your electric train?

                    MORT
(laughing) This is Silver City.

                    DICKIE
No kidding? I owned a patch of land out where
that used to be. Pretty near lost my—

Chuck steps in, giving Dickie's arm a squeeze—

                  CHUCK RAVEN
Mort's spearheading some development in that
part of the state. Nothing like the private
sector taking a little initiative.

> **DICKIE**
>
> Right— hey, you folks in Timberline could use a shot in the arm. And he—

> **CHUCK RAVEN**
>
> Mort—

> **DICKIE**
>
> Mort's the fella who could do it for you. Have a nice lunch.

The power party moves away, Mort giving a wink and thumbs-up thanks to Chandler Tyson as he goes. He sits back down across from the thrilled commissioners—

> **MORT**
>
> Terrific guy, Dickie, he'll make a hell of a governor. Now, as I was saying, I have it on very good authority that this year Senator Pilager is not—

ANOTHER TABLE

Nora Allardyce sits at a table writing in her notebook—

> **DANNY (O.S.)**
>
> Still writing in restaurants.

She looks up to see Danny. She is more surprised than happy to see him—

> **NORA**
>
> Danny—

Danny sits across from her—

> **DANNY**
>
> I hear all the big pols hang out here.

> **NORA**
>
> And the humble reporters who cover them. How's Debbie?

                    DANNY

She, uh— she moved out. From where she was
living with me— took most of the furniture.

                    NORA

Oh— sorry.

                    DANNY

I should have been suspicious when she
bought all those boxes at Staples.

                    NORA

You were having problems?

                    DANNY

Apparently. We weren't, uhm— she maybe wanted
somebody a little more predictable.

                    NORA

You're totally predictable, Danny. You get
involved in something positive and then find
a way to fuck it up.

Danny just smiles at this—

                    DANNY

And you're—?

                    NORA

I'm fine. They've got me assigned to the governor's race—

She points to the table where Dickie, Chuck, and the
staffers have just been seated, Chandler lingering to chat—

                    DANNY

Listen, Nora, there's a work thing—

                    NORA

You still a private eye?

                    DANNY

Investigator, yeah— that friend of yours who
did health care with the migrants—

NORA

NORA

Rebecca Zeller.

DANNY

Zeller, right. She's still in town?

NORA

In the phone book.

Nora looks up as Chandler comes over—

CHANDLER

Hey, babe, sorry I'm late. (indicates the power table) Greasing the rusty wheels of government.

NORA

Chan, this is Danny I told you about? Danny— Chandler Tyson—

Danny realizes he's in Chandler's seat and gets up to shake hands—

CHANDLER

Danny the ex-boyfriend from hell?

DANNY

I know you—

CHANDLER

I don't think so.

DANNY

On TV?

CHANDLER

Oh—that was a while back. The public state- ments when I was handling—

DANNY

You're a tobacco lobbyist.

CHANDLER

One of our clients—

DANNY

You said there was no scientific evidence that smo—

　　　　　　　　　　　　　　　　　　　　　　JOHN SAYLES

CHANDLER

(smiling) I see myself as a sort of champion of the underdog. Every point of view, no matter how politically incorrect, deserves an advocate in the court of public opinion.

Danny turns to Nora, makes a face—

DANNY

Wow. I heard you were with somebody new, but hey, a champion of the underdog.

NORA

It was nice to see you, Danny.

DANNY

Yeah, right—

NORA

Rebecca Zeller.

Danny gives Chandler a thumbs-up as he backs away—

DANNY

Keep up the good fight.

18 EXT. MUNICIPAL PARK — DAY

A very OLD MAN painstakingly makes his way through a PARK as CHILDREN play in the BG—

REBECCA (O.S.)

They cut the program.

We PAN back to see REBECCA ZELLER, keeping an eye on the old man as she talks with Danny—

DANNY

The Feds. But you're still in health care—

She indicates the old man—

REBECCA

Visiting nurse. They discontinued the outreach funds, disqualified the majority of my
people for insurance—

DANNY

When the program was up, did you get out to
Timberline County?

REBECCA

That was half my caseload. Of course getting
dentists to see Medicaid patients was never any
picnic, and then the migrants, they'd rather
chew aspirin for the rest of their lives than—

DANNY

Who hires undocumented workers out there?

REBECCA

Who doesn't? Nice cheap labor who can't complain to the authorities if they're ripped
off or mistreated— to the left, Mr. Scarpa.
Left— that's it—

DANNY

Do you have like a list? Of employers?

REBECCA

It's six months old. And a lot of these characters, the little construction outfits and
whatnot, they move around.

DANNY

It's a place for me to start.

Rebecca looks him over—

REBECCA

You really blew it, you know? With Nora.

DANNY

Tell me about it.

REBECCA

She was devastated after she left you.

> DANNY

(a ray of hope) Yeah? I mean she seems pretty happy with this Chandler guy—

> REBECCA

Mercenary little prick.

Danny beams—

> DANNY

So— you've met him—

19 INT. DANNY'S KITCHEN — NIGHT — ANTS

A work detail of ANTS streams between the pile of spilled sugar still on the kitchen floor and the baseboard—

> MITCH (O.S.)

First you have to plant the seed of doubt.

> DANNY (O.S.)

The seed—

We begin to TRACK toward the living room, following the trail of ants for a ways—

> MITCH (O.S.)

We run something on the site, information we've gotten, and we connect the dots. And the guilty parties pretend to ignore it. If they sue us certain documents could be entered into a court of law, where if they deny things it's perjury—

The camera reaches the living room entrance and we see Danny and Mitch, sitting on the floor where the couch used to be, watching TV with the sound turned off. Dickie's press conference is being excerpted on the late news. They are surrounded by empty beer cans and take turns dipping

Ritz crackers into a jar of peanut butter. Both have had a lot to drink—

> DANNY
>
> Gotta have the documents—

> MITCH
>
> It's amazing what things blow in under the door and end up on my desk.

> DANNY
>
> So you plant the seed—

> MITCH
>
> And the mainstream guys— he print journalists— they bring it to their editors and the editors say cool your jets, this is too far out, we don't have the resources, we don't have the <u>balls</u> to go after this kind of thing. But track the story and if it ever breaks—

> DANNY
>
> No balls.

We CONTINUE TRACKING toward Mitch and Danny—

> MITCH
>
> And we keep accumulating the facts till the story is screaming out so loud it's impossible to ignore and they run a little test item on page six that says "allegations have been made."

> DANNY
>
> Allegations.

> MITCH
>
> It's beneath their dignity to quote some cellar-dweller Website in their hallowed journal, but the bastards in power have to publicly deny those allegations and then they're fair game. First it's the columnists taking potshots and when they've got

politicians on the run they use our legwork
and our ideas to write outraged exposés and
win Pulitzers and gang up like a pack of
jackals—

                    DANNY
—on a wounded wildebeest.

Danny is in a somber mood. He opens another can of beer—

                    DANNY
Only thing I watch anymore— animal snuff
videos.

                    MITCH
But somebody has to plant the seed.

                    DANNY
The seed of doubt.

They watch Dickie fielding questions for a long moment—

                    DANNY
He seems a lot more gubernatorial with the
sound off.

                                        FADE TO BLACK.

20 EXT. CONSTRUCTION SITE — MORNING — SIGN

We start on a SIGN posted in front of an empty lot where
a foundation is being built. MEXICAN WORKERS dump cinder
blocks and bags of concrete from the back of a truck.
The SIGN has the usual permit information under a big
BENTEL CORPORATION logo—

                    FOREMAN (O.S.)
Can't help you, Chief.

SITE

Danny follows the site FOREMAN, a wiry Anglo guy, as he meas-
ures boundaries and taps in stakes to mark the property—

>   **DANNY**
> I'm working for— this is strictly confiden-
> tial, by the way— I'm working for a very
> close friend of your employer.

Danny points to the BENTEL sign—

>   **DANNY**
> The uh— Pilager family?

The Foreman looks at him suspiciously—

>   **DANNY**
> I only want to know if any of your workers
> are missing.

>   **FOREMAN**
> What, these guys? (indicates Mexicans)
> They're <u>all</u> missing. They don't exist, right?

>   **DANNY**
> Illegal—

>   **FOREMAN**
> Undocumented, whatever. This is a prep crew—
> the foundation, the frame, roof— I don't get
> into citizens until the plumbing and wiring
> go in.

>   **DANNY**
> This is standard practice?

>   **FOREMAN**
> If you want to stay competitive it is. I'm a
> subcontractor, okay? Bentel hires somebody
> who hires me, and I hire a guy who rounds up
> these trabajeros on a job-by-job basis. I ask
> him no questions—

>   **DANNY**
> So if somebody doesn't show up for work—

FOREMAN

My labor contractor makes sure there's another one to take their place. I don't know the language, I don't learn their names— it's like—"Yo! Amigo—" and then you show em what you want.

DANNY

The Immigration—

FOREMAN

(grins) Funny thing, working for Bentel, we don't seem to have any trouble from them. Way down on the border they play hide and seek, but up here—(shrugs) There's a few contractors— marginal characters— who'll call in the INS on their guys just before a big payday, nail 'em where they live and get them deported, but I don't play that shit.

DANNY

So if the police were looking for somebody—

FOREMAN

Their own families don't know where these guys are half the time.

DANNY

And the man who hires them for you—

FOREMAN

He drives over to Carbonville, strolls into El Rincón, says he's paying six bucks an hour and has to beat them off with a stick.

21 INT. GYM — DAY

Mort and Grace, wearing matching sweatsuits, sit on EXER-CYCLES next to each other, grinding away the pounds—

MORT

I've never been so close before.

GRACE
I know how much it means to you.

MORT
The County Commission went off walking on air. When Chuck brought Dickie Pilager to the table—

GRACE
That was a nice thing for him to do.

MORT
Nice? I'm paying him a fortune.

GRACE
(worried) A fortune?

MORT
A slice of the pie. But they were star-struck, Gracie. The zoning is in the bag, these people will bend over backwards—

GRACE
You've worked so hard—

MORT
If we were a little bit more liquid I'd sink every dime we have into this thing.

GRACE
(more worried) Like you did with the stock market that time—

MORT
Hell, it's more than the money. I'm building a city, Grace. A <u>city.</u>

Grace looks over. Her husband is glowing with excitement. She smiles—

22 EXT. STREET, CARBONVILLE — DAY — BAR SIGN

CARBONVILLE is an old mining town struggling to survive.

FIESTA MUSIC spills out as we TRACK toward the doorway of the EL RINCON bar—

> **DICKIE (TV, O.S.)**
> *Cuido mucho para nuestros ciudadanos latinos.*
> *Necesitamos trabajar—*

23 INT. EL RINCÓN

We start on a TV SET, playing a political ad in which Dickie sits surrounded by small LATINO SCHOOL KIDS, speaking to the camera in badly-pronounced but well-rehearsed SPANISH—

> **DICKIE (TV)**
> *—juntos por un futuro mejor para nuestros niños.*

We PAN away to see Danny working his way through the bar crowded with temporarily-unemployed MEXICAN WORKERS, showing each the photo of the dead man's hand—

> **DANNY**
> Uh— sabe un hombre con esto en su mano?

Danny's Spanish is worse than Dickie's—

> **DANNY**
> Excusa mi— sabe un hombre con esto en su mano?

Blank looks and shaken heads till he comes to VINCE ESPARZA, a hard-looking vato nursing a beer—

> **DANNY**
> Excusa mi—

> **VINCE ESPARZA**
> *No comprendo.*

Vince barely looks at the photo—

                              DANNY
        Este— photo? Sabe un hombre—

Now he gives Danny a stone-hard look—
                         VINCE ESPARZA
        *No compren*do.

Danny picks up on the hostile vibe and disengages, heading
for the bar—
                              DANNY
        Right.

He sits at the bar, gets the bartender's attention—
                              DANNY
        Corona?
                              TONY
        It's *"conoce."*

Danny turns to see the man sitting at the next stool, TONY
GUERRA—
                              DANNY
        Huh?
                              TONY
        You don't say *"sabe"* when you're askin about
        a person. It's *"conoce"*. *"¿Conoce a un hombre
        con esto en la mano?"*
                              DANNY
        It's not *'el mano'*?
                              TONY
        It's irregular. Like a gringo coming in to
        this bar askin questions. Irregular.
                              DANNY
        Right.

                              TONY
          So what's his name, this *tipo* you lookin for?

                              DANNY
          I don't know.

                              TONY
          Tough to find somebody, you don't know his
          name.

                              DANNY
          He has this on his— (shows photo)— on la mano.

                              TONY
          And there's a reward for this information?

Danny hadn't thought of that yet—

                              DANNY
          Uh— there could be—

                              TONY
          How much?

                              DANNY
          (calculates, raises his voice) One hundred
          bucks to whoever can give me a name that goes
          with this tattoo.

                              TONY
          Tony Guerra. That's the name. (holds out his
          hand) *Entrégame la lana, ese*—

                              DANNY
          Who's Tony Guerra?

                              TONY
          Speaking.

He turns his hand over to show the SCORPION TATTOO on the
back of it. The other BAR PATRONS laugh—

                              TONY
          Twenties if you got em.

SILVER CITY and other Screenplays   65

Danny realizes he's blown it, pulls out his wallet, and starts shucking bills on the counter—

                    TONY

So what you want with me? I gotta warn you, man, I'm a citizen. I don't have to take no shit—

                    DANNY

You're not the guy.

                    TONY

How you know that?

                    DANNY

You're breathing. Where'd you get that tattoo?

                    TONY

Oh, me and the *lavaplatos* from my kitchen went out one night, I got a little *borracho*—

                    DANNY

You're a cook—

                    TONY

I am a <u>chef</u>— *por favor.* Up in Vail for the ski bunnies. We talkin blue corn polenta with a *mango-chipotle salsa,* free-range sage hen stuffed with chestnut—

                    DANNY

The tattoo—

                    TONY

I saw it on the wall in this place we went, I liked the way it looked and I asked the dude to lay it on me. (admiring the tattoo) *Qué padre, ¿no?*

24 EXT. MOUNTAIN VALLEY — DAY

A pair of RIDERS move through a beautiful mountain valley—

                    BENTEEN (V.O.)

You take a good look, Dickie.

CLOSER

Wes Benteen and Dickie Pilager ride their horses at a slow walk, side by side—

                    BENTEEN

What do you see?

                    DICKIE

Uh— mountains?

                    BENTEEN

I see a big sign that says "No Americans Allowed."

                    DICKIE

You do?

                    BENTEEN

You look at a map, they got half the West under lock and key.

                    DICKIE

They—?

                    BENTEEN

Bureau of Land Management, Forest Service, National Parks, the state—

                    DICKIE

Right.

                    BENTEEN

It's like a treasure chest waiting to be opened, only there's a five-hundred pound bureaucrat sitting on it.

                    DICKIE

I'm a small-government man—

                    BENTEEN

That's why we chose you, son.

                    DICKIE

Of course, the people—

                    BENTEEN

The people got to be grabbed by the horns and

<u>dragg</u>ed to what's good for em. The people—
you remember the shale oil?

                    DICKIE
Over in Parachute—

                    BENTEEN
Big oil companies say they're gonna squeeze
oil out of rock, and the people come flocking
like a damn herd of sheep. Thought they were
all gonna get rich quick, like with every
other mineral strike in the history of this
state. But who's left holdin the shiny stuff
when all the dust clears?

                    DICKIE
Uhm— who?

                    BENTEEN
The folks that see the big picture.

                    DICKIE
Right.

                    BENTEEN
And that's me and you, son. We're lookin at
it right now, all around us.

                    DICKIE
Right.

                    BENTEEN
Couple weeks Imonna have to call you
Governor.

Dickie grins—

                    BENTEEN
You know what the big picture is, don't you,
Dickie?

                    DICKIE
Uhm— it's—

                    BENTEEN
Privatization. The land was meant for the

citizens, not for the damn pencil pushers in Washington.

                    DICKIE
Like this Silver City deal—

                    BENTEEN
(shakes his head) That's just a pile of mine debris I'm trying to unload. Son, we got resources here you wouldn't be<u>lieve</u>, untapped resources. And you and your dad are the point men in the fight to liberate those resources for the American people. Aspen, Vail, that ain't shit compared to what I could build if they opened this up to somebody with some ideas, with some knowhow. We got rivers, lakes, forest— and that's just what's on top of the ground.

                    DICKIE
I understand—

                    BENTEEN
And the <u>people</u> won't get it done, not by a long sight. They'll get distracted worrying about some postcard idea of the Rockies, some black-footed ferret or endangered tumble-weed. But if a man of vision were to come along—

                    DICKIE
I can see it.

Dickie has a visionary expression on his face as he gazes out on the beautiful valley. Benteen lets him feel the rapture for a moment—

                    BENTEEN
How's that saddle feeling?

Dickie wriggles uncomfortably—

                              DICKIE
        Oh, it's— coming along.

                             BENTEEN
        (smiles) We'll make a cowboy out of you yet.

25 INT. TATTOO PARLOR

We PAN along the various DESIGNS on the wall, ending with
the SCORPION—

                          PREACHER (O.S.)
        I have em sign when they come in, check their ID—

We reach Danny, looking over the shoulder of PREACHER, the
tattoo artist, as he digs through an account book—

                             PREACHER
        —if they look underage. Redeye Stinger— "Tony
        Guerra"— he was pretty drunk, this guy—

                              DANNY
        Not him. Try earlier—

                             PREACHER
        I only done one other stinger this year—

                              DANNY
        You remember anything about him? The other one?

                             PREACHER
        Another Mexican, I think. (shakes his head)
        I get so many bean-eaters in here— I was
        probably just glad it wasn't her again—

He points to a four-color VIRGIN OF GUADALUPE on the wall—

                             PREACHER
        I could do that tat with my eyes closed. This
        like a cop thing?

                              DANNY
        I imagine they'll get around to you pretty soon.

Preacher stubs his finger down on a name—

PREACHER

Here he is. "Lázaro Huerta."

26 EXT. PILAGER HOUSE—AFTERNOON 26

Chuck Raven and SENATOR JUDSON PILAGER walk the grounds in front of the senator's beautiful mountainside house, mighty mountain peaks surrounding them—

CHUCK RAVEN

These people have raised the bulk of our war chest, and since we can't invite them to the governor's mansion yet—

SENATOR PILAGER

It's the least I can do.

CHUCK RAVEN

The caterer will be coming pretty early—

SENATOR PILAGER

I get up with the sun. How's my— how's the candidate holding up?

Chuck calculates how honest he should be—

SENATOR PILAGER

Give it to me straight.

CHUCK RAVEN

Well— he doesn't have your head for policy—

SENATOR PILAGER

(grins) I'd like to see him try to get through the appropriations bill— he's never been much of a reader—

CHUCK RAVEN

We break it down and feed to him— bite-sized—

SENATOR PILAGER

Impatient. He was always impatient—

CHUCK RAVEN

He's knuckling down. You can be proud of him.
Publicly he's—

SENATOR PILAGER

He's a fucking disaster when he goes off the
script.

CHUCK RAVEN

Oh— I don't think we have to worry about him
straying too far. As long as nothing comes
flying in from left field—

SENATOR PILAGER

(concerned) What would that be?

27 INT. KITCHEN — DANNY'S APARTMENT — NIGHT

Danny paces while on the PHONE with Sheriff Skaggs,
pulling a nukable plastic dish of leftovers from the
fridge—

DANNY

In Carbonville— right next to the Everything-
for-a-Buck store. Lázaro, yeah— there's eighteen
Huertas in the county phone book, I called them
all— shit!

He stands before the empty spot where the microwave used
to be—

DANNY

No, no, I— I seem to be missing a microwave
oven— Yeah, if I get anything more, I'll
check in with you, Sheriff— okay—

He pushes the hangup button, stands staring glumly at the
unnuked food, then grimaces as he steps on something—

Danny bends to pick up a large SHARD of the sugar bowl

he smashed the first night. He tosses it where the
microwave used to be. He opens a little closet and
reaches in— the DUSTPAN hangs on a hook, but there is
nothing on the hook beside. Danny turns back to stare
glumly at the floor—

> DANNY
> Leaves the dustpan but she takes the broom.
> Story of my life.

He impulsively dials another number, sends, heading for
the living room—

> DANNY
> (pacing) Nora? Hey, it's— yeah, it was great
> seeing you the other day.

Danny has written in Magic Marker all over the wall behind
where the couch used to be—

28 INT. NORA'S BEDROOM

Nora sits on the edge of the bed with the phone. We see
a LIGHT from the bathroom and TEETH-BRUSHING NOISES—

> NORA
> (lowers her voice) You looked good, Danny.
> Listen, if this is about me and Chandler—

29 INT. DANNY'S APARTMENT — LIVING ROOM

> DANNY
> No, this is business, actually, I— I could
> use some background on the Pilager family,
> and since you're covering the—

The name "Lázaro Huerta is surrounded by other names— the
suspects, the Pilager family, Chuck Raven and Wes Benteen—
with lots of arrows and question marks in between them—

30 INT. NORA'S BEDROOM

                    NORA
        I'm going to this function at the Senator's
        house tomorrow— a thank you for their big
        fundraisers. If you promise to be on your
        best behavior—

31 INT. DANNY'S APARTMENT — LIVING ROOM
                    DANNY
        Hey, that would be great, Chandler wouldn't
        mind? Okay, I'll meet you— You know, I've
        been thinking about you a lot lately— even
        before Debbie I——

32 INT. NORA'S BEDROOM

This isn't as easy for Nora to say as she expected—
                    NORA
        Danny, that's— it's too late, all right? It's very
        sweet of you, but we've both moved on, haven't we?

She shoots a look toward the bathroom as the brushing
SOUNDS STOP—
                    NORA
        (sadly) We're yesterday's news.

33 INT. DANNY'S APARTMENT
                    DANNY
        Right. Yeah. Sorry to bother you at this
        hour— Goodnight.

A wave of depression hits Danny. He lays the cell phone on
the floor. He reads the writing on the wall.
                              FADE TO BLACK.

----

34 INT. MINE — MORNING

BLACKNESS. We are in the SHAFT of a MINE. One by one, eight or nine HEADLAMPS appear in the distance, bobbing as people move toward us—

> CASEY
>
> They'd be lowered in the man-skip down to the section they were working, and in the early days this is pretty much what you'd see— Everything around you is ore— we got silver, some lead, copper— but gold was the primary focus of this mine. The ore you're looking at assays out to about an ounce and a half per ton—

The group reaches us with CASEY LYLE, looking like a veteran miner, leading the tour—

> CASEY
>
> —which can be worth your while depending on what it costs to get it out of the ground. Knock it down with dynamite, throw it in one of these carts, then upstairs they'd run it through all the crushers and chemicals to separate the valuable stuff from the tailings.

Casey flicks OVERHEAD LIGHTS ON and we see old MINING EQUIPMENT around us—

> CASEY
>
> Now if you'll move up under the stope just ahead and look up to the left, you'll see what every miner was hoping for— a vein of almost-pure yellow stuff. You can all fit in there— I'll join you in a minute.

The TOURISTS move past him. Casey flicks his headlamp off, sits on a barrel to rest while the others check out the stope—

                    DANNY

So were you a miner?

Casey is surprised to see that Danny has hung back—

                    CASEY

Mining engineer. Till I went to work for the
Feds. Got interested in how to do the job
better and safer— this is under Carter, they
put some teeth in the rules.

                    DANNY

What's your beef with Dickie Pilager?

Casey gives him an evaluating look—

                    CASEY

You're not here just for the tour.

                    DANNY

I have to inform you— you're being watched.

                    CASEY

Is that right?

                    DANNY

There was a— an incident on the campaign
trail the other day, and your name came up as
a potential— uhm—

                    CASEY

Perpetrator?

                    DANNY

Something like that.

                    CASEY

It's the old man whose guts I hate.

                    DANNY

The senator?

                    CASEY

And his pal Benteen. You remember the Rocky
Flats deal?

                    DANNY

Something for nuclear—

                    CASEY

Plutonium triggers. The outfit that was
making them was so sloppy and so blatant
about covering up the mess they'd made we got
the FBI to raid the place. Fines, indict-
ments, cover-ups— the whole nine yards.

                    DANNY

And the clean-up—

                    CASEY

Seven billion dollars and counting. Your tax
dollars at work.

                    DANNY

So you helped shut Rocky Flats down.

                    CASEY

We'd done so well with that one I went after
the second biggest hazard in the state— the
Silver City mining operation.

                    DANNY

Owned by Dickie Pilager.

                    CASEY

The land was his then, but Benteen was
leasing the mineral rights. They're hand in
glove, the Benteens and Pilagers—

                    DANNY

They were still digging—

Casey picks up a handful of loose rock from the floor—

                    CASEY

You had acres and acres of tailings piled up
from Silver City's glory days. Looks like a
pile of trash rock, but it's already been
spread out on the <u>surface</u> for you and if you
can process it on a large enough scale— I'm

---

talking bulldozers the size of battleships—
you can make a fortune.

> DANNY

Providing jobs to an economically depressed
area—

Casey heads down the tunnel to join the tourists, Danny
following along—

> CASEY

A few, sure. But we started getting nasty PH
readings from the watershed all around them,
we started getting fish die-off, heavy-metal
residues— which the company claimed was from
the old shaft mines in the mountains all
around them, nothing they could do about it.

> DANNY

Not true?

> CASEY

They were concentrating the gold in these
huge leach piles— you dump a cyanide solution
over them, the chemicals do their work and—

> DANNY

They use cyanide?

> CASEY

Sodium cyanide as a lixiviant— basic chem-
istry. Smells like apricots for miles around.

> DANNY

(remembering) Apricots—

> CASEY

(nods) I had an inside informant, or at least
I thought I did. Fella named Esparza—
(thinking)— Vincent Esparza, foreman on their
clean-up crew. He said they were just pushing
all the contaminated material to one side—no
treatment, no containment— left it out to the
elements and that's what was getting into our

water system. He even helped me plan my surprise inspection.

He stops a bit short of the group of tourists to finish
his story. This is a painful memory—

                    CASEY
          But when we hit the site there was just a
          bunch of big craters and a workforce with
          their lips buttoned. I looked like an idiot—
          I'd brought press, photographers—

                    DANNY
          And your inside man? Esparza?

                    CASEY
          Gone with the wind— they said he'd been fired
          months earlier.

                    DANNY
          You got sandbagged.

                    CASEY
          Benteen, of course, doesn't take any pris-
          oners. His pal Senator Pilager appoints a new
          guy up top whose only mission was to castrate
          the agency. Who's the first man fired?

                    DICKIE
          Bureaucracy—

                    CASEY
          Then came the allegations of misuse of funds,
          all the public hints about a drinking
          problem—

                    DANNY
          Hardball politics—

                    CASEY
          When I tried to go back to work as an engineer
          I found out I was pretty much unhireable in
          the industry. And then— well, I figured if I
          was accused of a drinking problem, I might as
          well develop one.

An uncomfortable silence. Danny has to do his job—

                    DANNY
        But even with all that, you wouldn't—

                    CASEY
        The Pilagers don't have to worry any about
        me. I know when I'm licked.

35 EXT. EXHIBITION MINE — DAY

We start looking up at a towering GOLD MILL, a wooden
structure built into the side of the steep mountain—

                    CASEY (O.S.)
        It rains like the dickens in these mountains
        but you won't find any streams running down
        them. So where does the water go?

We begin to TILT down the mountainside—

                    CASEY (O.S.)
        What you're looking at is honeycombed with
        hundreds, maybe thousands of mine shafts. You
        stop pumping the water out, over time all
        those holes will fill up, top to bottom, till
        there's nowhere else to go and a huge amount
        of pressure builds up— looking for an outlet.

The camera reaches Casey, finishing off his tour out in
front of the mine museum—

                    CASEY
        In 1947 four miners broke a pick-hole through
        a wall to an adjacent area that hadn't been
        worked for twenty years.

Casey points to a spot on the side of the mountain—

                    CASEY
        Water exploded through that wall, blasted

those fellas and all their equipment back
through the shaft they'd dug, back into the
main tunnel Mr. Newhouse had built to service
the mines; water blew out through the opening
of that tunnel and shot clear across the
river to the other side—

We PAN to follow Casey's wave, seeing the rapidly-flowing
RIVER and the buildings of the TOWN on the other side.
Danny and the tourists are suitably impressed—

                    CASEY
Three days the water blasted out of that
mountain— timbers, track, loose rock, half-
ton ore cars flying through the air like they
were toys.

Casey is dead-serious as he turns back to his audience—

                    CASEY
We think we can wound this planet, we think we
can cut corners and stick the money in our
pockets and just walk away from it.

DANNY

The words sinking home—

                 CASEY (O.S.)
But some day the bill comes due. It's only a
matter of time.

36 EXT. PILAGER HOUSE — LATE DAY

A crowd of well-dressed SUPPORTERS have descended on the
mountainside mansion, spilling out onto the deck and
yard—

SENATOR PILAGER (V.O.)
I suppose if there's one thing that all of
you good folks have in common—

37 INT. MANSION

A cocktails-and-buffet function is in progress, well-to-
do GUESTS in expensive casual wear (lots of classy Western
duds) all turned toward Senator Jud as he addresses them
in front of the huge fireplace—

SENATOR PILAGER
—it's that you know a good investment when
you see one.

Dickie stands beaming at his dad to one side, with Chuck
Raven hovering nearby—

SENATOR PILAGER
We've gotten a lot of our agenda rolling on
the federal level, and it's about time we had
somebody running this state who is 100 percent with the program.

DANNY

Danny, uncomfortable, scans the crowd for a familiar face—

SENATOR PILAGER
And that has required a good deal of financial and time commitment from each and every
one of you. But despite the attack on our
rights represented by Amendment twenty-seven—

Some comic BOOING from the guests—

SENATOR PILAGER
—you've gone out and shook the money tree
like never before!

JOHN SAYLES

The guests APPLAUD for themselves—

SENATOR, DICKIE

> **SENATOR PILAGER**
> And so ladies and gentlemen— I present to
> you—our next governor— a young man who's
> almost as good-looking as his father—

LAUGHTER from the guests—

> **SENATOR PILAGER**
> —Richard Pilager! Dickie, say a few words to
> these folks.

Dickie steps forward, acknowledging the warm APPLAUSE—

> **DICKIE**
> I know none of you came here to listen to
> another speech— but I'd just like to say how
> much I appreciate—

NORA

Nora stands a little apart from the crowd, scanning the
room—

> **DICKIE (O.S.)**
> —your support in this— effort we've got going
> to— to bring sober, responsive government—

POV

We PAN with her gaze across various guests till we stop
on Chandler, then RACK FOCUS beyond him to see Danny over
by the bar—

—back to our great state. And you might as
well pledge some money to my daddy's next
campaign while you're here!

More LAUGHTER and APPLAUSE—

NORA

Nora is uncomfortable with the two men almost side by
side—

DICKIE PILAGER

Dickie waves and smiles, acknowledging the response—

DANNY

Danny grabs a drink from the bar, recognizes WES BENTEEN,
who is surveying the crowd—

                    DANNY
        So— Mr. Benteen—

Benteen looks at him warily—

                    DANNY
        How's it look for the Prospectors this year?
                    BENTEEN
        You a fan?
                    DANNY
        Sure.
                    BENTEEN
        Why?

Danny wasn't expecting his motives to be questioned—

DANNY

Uh— (shrugs)— they're uhm— fun to watch—

BENTEEN

But more fun when they win than when they lose.

DANNY

Sure—

BENTEEN

Nothing to be ashamed of. Basic human behavior.

DANNY

Well— you could always pull for the underdog—

BENTEEN

Americans don't have the patience for under-dogs that they used to.

DANNY

They don't?

BENTEEN

Coach goes three seasons without a ring, he's out on his ass. As he should be.

DANNY

Hendrickson has been there for—?

BENTEEN

Hendrickson isn't coming back. You're not a reporter, are you?

DANNY

Me? No—

BENTEEN

Jud said there might be some press here. Use a little colloquialism, tell the wrong kind of joke and the thought police are all over you.

DANNY

Yeah, you gotta be careful.

                              BENTEEN
People want to back a winner, they need to
feel part of something bigger than they are.

                              DANNY
I suppose—

                              BENTEEN
They used to advertise the <u>quality</u> of the
product— tastes great, whitens your teeth,
shaves close, rides like a dream— now what do
they pitch? "America's Number One soft drink."
"Best-selling mid-sized utility vehicle—"

                              DANNY
"The People's favorite corn dog—"

                              BENTEEN
It isn't buy the product, it's join the club.

He indicates a group of the guests lined up to shake
Dickie's hand—

                              BENTEEN
    You make people feel part of a winner,
    they'll follow you anywhere. Are you a
    winner, son?

                              DANNY
    I like to think so.

Benteen gives him a manly whack on the back as he moves
on with his drink—

                              BENTEEN
Good boy.

Danny watches after him, then sees Nora approaching—

                              NORA
    Hey—

                              DANNY
    So Chandler doesn't come to these?

> NORA

He's here somewhere. Working the room.

They stroll through the mansion together—

> DANNY

How's it going at the paper?

> NORA

It's all right. Less time to file these days, less space for hard news—

> DANNY

You're a good writer, you should be doing features.

Nora chooses to take this as a dig—

> NORA

You mean I'm good at telling stories.

> DANNY

That's an insult?

> NORA

As opposed to doing the legwork, digging up the dirt.

> DANNY

I didn't—

> NORA

That was always your specialty.

> DANNY

My specialty was being oblivious to my good fortune.

> NORA

Don't try to suck up to me, Danny. You're really bad at it.

Danny disengages, looks around the room—

> DANNY

Is the sister here?

                          NORA

You'd know it if she was— you'd be staring at
her ass.

                          DANNY

Hot babe?

                          NORA

Too hot for her own good. When she was fifteen she came to her daddy the senator and
announced she was pregnant by a member of the
university's All-American backfield—

                          DANNY

Ooops—

                          NORA

But she wasn't sure which member. I believe your
detective agency took care of the DNA testing.
Very discretely of course. Listen, I've got to
go sweat a few quotes out of the big shots—

                          DANNY

Later—

Nora moves off. Danny watches after her, sees—

TONY GUERRA

Tony Guerra, dressed in his chef outfit, has stepped out
from the kitchen to speak with one of the many Hispanic
WAITERS hustling hors d'oeuvres around—

CHUCK AND CHANDLER

Chuck Raven flips through a multi-page document Chandler
Tyson has just handed him—

                     CHUCK RAVEN

You know, Dickie's not really a fine-print
kind of guy. He's more— intuitive.

                    CHANDLER

My people have whittled the regs down to
where we need them to be. It's pretty simple—

                    CHUCK RAVEN

(reading the title page) "Environmental Her-
itage Initiative"—

                    CHANDLER

(grins) It sounded better than "Developers'
Bill of Rights." You breathe the word "deregulation" and certain parties get all—

                    CHUCK RAVEN

What's he doing here?

Chuck Raven frowns as Danny passes them on his way to the
kitchen—

                    CHANDLER

You know him?

                    CHUCK RAVEN

His agency is uhm— looking into something
for us.

                    CHANDLER

Good luck.

                    CHUCK RAVEN

What's that mean?

                    CHANDLER

He used to be a reporter, O'Brien, till he
screwed the pooch and bankrupted his paper.
Grace Seymour hired him on the rebound.

Chuck is disturbed by this news—

                    CHUCK RAVEN

And when was this?

38 INT. KITCHEN

Danny follows Tony Guerra through the spacious kitchen as he supervises, calling out to various MEXICAN KITCHEN WORKERS as they go—

> **TONY**
>
> *Apúrate con las costillas, Beto. Los necesitamos pronto!* (to Danny) Surprised you could find me, man. You must be some kind of detective.

> **DANNY**
>
> So this Lázaro could have worked in a kitchen—

> **TONY**
>
> They bus them up from Carbonville every day. Resort towns run on *frijole*-power, man. And the richer the *anglos* are the more of *mis hermanos del sur* they got workin for em.

> **DANNY**
>
> So your restaurant caters too?

> **TONY**
>
> I'm moonlighting, man. They doing a big renovation— I got two weeks off starting tomorrow. *Jaime— guarde los Porterhouse! Los prefieren bien cocidos, no quemados!* I figured I go over to Black Hawk, hit the casinos before my ex-wife can get ahold of my paycheck.

> **DANNY**
>
> (thinking) How'd you like to work for me? You know who most of the labor contractors are—

> **TONY**
>
> What's it pay?

> **DANNY**
>
> (guessing) Whatever you get for a day at the restaurant— plus twenty—

> **TONY**
>
> (grins) Private eye, huh?

                    DANNY
Looks good on the resumé.

                    TONY
I'm thinking about the chicks, man. In the
movies those *cabrones* make out like crazy—

                    DANNY
You speak the language, you can get around—

                    TONY
So what happened to this Lázaro Huerta that
he's not breathin no more?

                    DANNY
Oh— multiple fractures, busted skull, punc-
tured lung—

                    TONY
Híjole—

                    DANNY
You still want the job?

39 EXT. PILAGER HOUSE, DECK — LATER

Chandler, troubled, watches Danny and Nora below—

                 NORA (V.O.)
So why'd she dump you?

GROUNDS

Nora and Danny stroll across the grounds, an incredible
view all around them—

                    DANNY
Debbie? (shrugs) Maybe she figured out I was
always going to treat her like the consola-
tion prize—

                    NORA
Danny—

                              DANNY

    I mean, after you, I kind of retired, emo-
    tionally. And we were— I don't know—

                              NORA

    Incompatible.

                              DANNY

    We had some issues—

                              NORA

    She seemed way too— <u>struc</u>tured for someone
    like you.

                              DANNY

    And why did you dump me?

                              NORA

    Oh— you were so down on yourself, so con-
    vinced you were a loser— I started to agree
    with you.

                              DANNY

    I <u>was</u> a loser.

                              NORA

    You lost a job.

                              DANNY

    You were moving up and I was moving down—

                              NORA

    And I didn't quit the paper when you were
    fired. That wasn't loyal.

She sounds a bit regretful—

                              DANNY

    I deserved to be fired. Sort of—

                              NORA

    You were set up. And I was— ambitious.

An awkward pause as Danny doesn't deny this last admission—

                              DANNY

    So you're marrying this guy.

                              NORA

It seems like the mature thing to do.

                              DANNY

That sounds exciting.

                              NORA

Come on, Danny, it's not earthshaking
between, us, but— Romance is for kids. We
like to ski, we like to travel—

                              DANNY

He's a corporate mouthpiece—

                              NORA

And I'm part of the entertainmont business.
What else do you think is out there?

                              DANNY

Look, I hope you're happy with it—

                              NORA

No you don't.

                         CHANDLER (O.S.)

Nora!

They turn to see Chandler calling from the deck—

                            CHANDLER

Come on up! There's somebody I want you to
meet—

Nora gives Danny a pained smile and heads for the
house—

                              NORA

Stay in touch, okay?

Danny watches her go, sadly—

40   EXT. ARAPAHO LAKE — DAY

STRANGE LIGHT as we look at the water's surface. Something appears from below, a shape, gathering definition as it rises toward us— we TIGHTEN as the shape surfaces— it is the decomposing BODY of Lázaro Huerta. We have tightened to a CU and suddenly his eyes pop wide open, staring at us!

41   INT. DANNY'S APARTMENT — LIVING ROOM

Danny wakes with a gasp. He is fully clothed, sitting with his back against the wall, Magic Marker in hand. The TV is on, Reverend Tubbs' holy hour playing—

> **REV. TUBBS (TV)**
> —and the dead shall rise and walk upon the earth and the wicked and righteous shall be judged alike! But that day cannot come unless the children of Israel are within the Holy Land—

Danny gets up, rubs his eyes. He draws arrows from "Casey Lyle" to "Sen. Pilager" and "Wes Benteen," then adds, in parenthesis beneath Casey, "(Vincent Esparza?)"

FADE TO BLACK.

42   EXT. HOUSE — DENVER — MORNING

We're in a nice residential neighborhood. Nora sits sleepy-eyed on the porch of her little house, drinking coffee and watching Chandler don his protective gear to go bicycling—

> **CHANDLER**
> So what did you ever see in him?

> **NORA**
> He was— intense. He cared about things. (smiles) He used to write on the walls—

> **CHANDLER**
> Like graffiti?

                              NORA

In the house. He'd be working on a story and
he'd get so wrapped up in it he'd like Magic
Marker all the names and important facts on
the wall in the living room and then— you
know— try to connect the dots.

                            CHANDLER

So you had to live with this?

                              NORA

The landlord was not thrilled, but Danny
always painted it over. He thought— this was
when we were at the *Monitor* when it was still
political— he thought journalists should
change things, not just report—

                            CHANDLER

He thought he was the referee, not just the
scorekeeper.

                              NORA

I guess.

                            CHANDLER

When I was press liason for Fred Loomis we
had a slogan hung on the door— "Don't Tell
Us How to Stage the News and We Won't Tell
You How to Report It."

                              NORA

(not amused) Terrific—

                            CHANDLER

Power is a locomotive, babe. You either hop
on board or it runs right over you. Sounds
like he laid down on the tracks.

He pops his helmet on and starts to pedal away—

                            CHANDLER

Dinner at La Fonda!

Nora watches him disappear down the street, reflects—

SILVER CITY and other Screenplays   95

                              NORA
        (wistful) He was the love of my life.

43   EXT. VAIL STREET — MORNING

Danny winds through the RESORT TOWN in his beat-up car.
He waits for a bunch of Mexican DAY WORKERS getting out
of a bus to cross the street, the CAR RADIO playing a spot
attacking Dickie's opponent—

44   EXT./INT. MADDY'S HOUSE — DAY

Danny walks across the front lawn of an expensive but
badly-maintained house, through strange ornaments, scattered athletic equipment and a few bewildered PEACOCKS.
ROCK MUSIC blasts out from the house as Danny rings,
then bangs on the front door. The lead guitar drops out
of the mix and suddenly DEWEY, a young man who is at
least part African American, appears at the door with
his guitar in hand—

                              DEWEY
        Whassup?

                              DANNY
        Daniel O'Brien? I called earlier for Mrs.—

                              DEWEY
        She's back in the rink.

Dewey opens the door wider and points through the house.
We FOLLOW Danny in through the LIVING ROOM which is dou-
bling now as a rehearsal hall for Dewey and three musician friends. Dewey crosses to the little mixing board—

                              DEWEY
        Just keep heading straight through.

                              DANNY
        Thanks—

Danny makes his way through, stepping over cables—

> **DEWEY**
> Imonna, play that last one back.

Dewey hits a button on the board and their last take
BLASTS OUT, filling the house—

45 EXT. MADDY'S BACKYARD — SKATING RINK

The backyard is even more cluttered than the front— a
trampoline, lots of non-matching furniture (not all meant
to be left outside) and MADDY PILAGER, forties, pretty and
athletic, who stands inside a small SKATING RINK (no ice
yet), drawing back a bow and *shhhhhht!* planting an arrow on
the edge of the bullseye of a target several yards away. She
pauses to study her shot, then takes a hit from a joint that
has been resting on the arm of a chair beside her—

> **DANNY**
> Nice shot.

Maddy glances over to see Danny coming out from the house—

> **MADDY**
> It bit.

Danny stops a few feet away, nods at the joint—

> **DANNY**
> Training for the Olympics?

> **MADDY**
> Actually, I am. Only sport I'm not already
> too old for.

She offers the joint toward him—

> **DANNY**
> Uh—no thanks—

MADDY

It helps me with the zen aspect. Eventually
the arrow should become one with the bullseye
and release itself, and I'll just be like a
channel.

Danny leans back against the wooden wall of the rink as
Maddy notches another arrow—

MADDY

So you from *Home and Garden* or what?

DANNY

I'm working for Chuck Raven.

Shhhhht! An arrow digs into the wall just inches from
Danny. He freezes. Maddy calmly notches another arrow,
draws and aims it at him—

MADDY

Go on—

DANNY

You're like— really accurate with that, right?

MADDY

Depends on how much dope I've smoked.

DANNY

And how much have—

MADDY

I lost track.

DANNY

He— Mr. Raven—there was an incident that was—
potentially embarrassing to your brother—

MADDY

What, he made a speech without a Tele-
prompter?

DANNY

There was a dead body involved.

                    MADDY
        Anybody I know?

                    DANNY
        Lázaro Huerta?

Maddy shakes her head—

                    MADDY
        I can't place him. Maybe just another skeleton
        out of Daddy's closet.

Maddy nods to the joint on the chair arm—

                    MADDY
        Sure you don't want a hit? You look tense.

                    DANNY
        No, really— it makes me like paranoid—

                    MADDY
        Like somebody's got you in their crosshairs.

                    DANNY
        Something like that.

                    MADDY
        How about a drink, then?

                    DANNY
        Uh— sure—

                    MADDY
        There's a bottle of tequila by your left leg.

Danny shifts his eyes down to see the bottle—

                    DANNY
        You're not going to shoot it out of my hand
        or anything—

                    MADDY
        Relax.

Danny bends and picks up the bottle, not taking his eyes

SILVER CITY and other Screenplays

off Maddy. She keeps the bow drawn without a quaver. Danny takes a pull of the liquor—

MADDY

So you're some kind of campaign lackey—

DANNY

Investigator.

MADDY

Am I being investigated?

DANNY

Mr. Raven thinks you may be harboring a grudge.

MADDY

My whole life is a fucking grudge.

She turns and *shhhhhht!* puts the arrow dead center. Danny exhales with relief—

DANNY

Wow.

MADDY

Investigator. You go to some kind of school for that?

DANNY

No. I was working as a reporter, and—

MADDY

I hate reporters.

DANNY

I'm not one anymore.

MADDY

Fifteen years old, I'm pregnant, the fucking *Mountain Monitor* outs me. "Senator's Daughter in College Sex Scandal."

DANNY

That was before my time.

MADDY

What?

                              DANNY

          I wasn't working there yet. I was still in
          junior high.

Maddy gives him a suspicious look—

                              MADDY

          The thing's all set up, fly to Nevada, nice
          quiet operation, back in school within a
          week—

                              DANNY

          You could still have had—

                              MADDY

          A public abortion? With the Christian Cru-
          saders block-voting for my father?

                              DANNY

          So he advised you to keep the b—

                              MADDY

          I was a hopeful.

                              DANNY

          Hopeful—

                              MADDY

          An Olympic hopeful, figure skating. Nine
          months carrying Dewey Junior, another four
          to recover— but my body wasn't the same.
          Your center of gravity shifts, you can't do
          the jumps. That's what happened to Tonya
          Harding, you know. It wasn't Nancy Ker-
          rigan, it was her center of gravity. You
          mature, your perception changes— you never
          get it back.

She looks him over—

                              MADDY

          What's your name?

SILVER CITY and other Screenplays   101

                    DANNY
     Danny.

                    MADDY
     You're cute.

                    DANNY
     Thank you.

                    MADDY
     I'm gonna be investigated, I could do worse.

She nods to the tequila bottle—

                    MADDY
     You want a glass and some ice with that?

46   EXT. FEED LOT — DAY

COWSHIT is scraped around a water trough by one Mexican
worker on a tractor and another with a shovel—

                    YANEZ (O.S.)
     I'm too good to these guys.

WIDER

We TRACK with Tony Guerra and the feed lot boss, YANEZ,
as they walk among the pens—

                    YANEZ
     They take advantage of me.

                    TONY
     Sure—

                    YANEZ
     They borrow money, they come in all hung
     over—

                    TONY
     You work with the same bunch all the time?

                              YANEZ

More or less. (cautious) As far as I know
they're all citizens.

                              TONY

I wasn't askin that.

                              YANEZ

Mojados are a bit cheaper but they're not
worth the hassle. You need some hard huevos
to keep em in line. Not that I got anything
against em.

                              TONY

(chanting) *Chicano—Mexicano— luchamos mano a
mano—*

                              YANEZ

I wouldn't go that far. You should check into
the packing houses across town, they got a
lot of em in there, making chorizo—

                              TONY

Any of your own guys who haven't showed up
the last few days?

                              YANEZ

You're looking for this Lázaro, right?

Tony stops, surprised—

                              YANEZ

Cops were here this morning, asking the same
thing.

                              TONY

I'm not a cop.

                              YANEZ

No shit. But like I told them, I got no
Lázaros here.

                              TONY

So who brings them up? Here in Timberline
County—

Yanez looks around to be sure none of his workers are listening in—

                    YANEZ
You heard of Vince Esparza?

                    TONY
Heard the name—

                    YANEZ
He's the Saddam-fuckin-Hussein of labor contractors. They pay the *coyote* half up front to get them across the border, and when they're delivered here they owe Esparza the rest.

                    TONY
So they start in the hole—

                    YANEZ
And they stay in it. He keeps them moving around the county, keeps them isolated, keeps them scared—

                    TONY:
Where can I find him?

Yanez shakes his head—

                    YANEZ
You do not want to fuck with Vicente Esparza, my friend. I hired a few of his boys without knowing it once— they'd run off and were trying to work their way back home? Next thing I know I got a shotgun stuck in my face. *Un pistolero chingón, ¿no?*

47   EXT. MADDY'S BACKYARD — DAY

Danny and Maddy sit in half-busted furniture in the back yard, Dewey's BAND still PLAYING inside. They've killed much of the bottle of tequila—

                    MADDY

My first husband was a downhill racer. He won
a bronze at Innsbruck.

                    DANNY

Wow.

                    MADDY

He ditched me in— what— '85—

                    DANNY

My girlfriend just moved out.

                    MADDY

You poor baby—

                    DANNY

She took my couch.

                    MADDY

You can have this one if you want.

                    DANNY

I guess it was both of ours— she picked it
out, paid for half of it.

Maddy gets up and wanders over to the trampoline—

                    MADDY

Rodney— they called him Hot Rod— who won the
bronze? He runs a lodge in Aspen he got as a
settlement.

                    DANNY

He sued you for alimony?

Maddy starts to bounce on the trampoline—

                    MADDY

Daddy paid him off so he wouldn't file adultery
charges. Anything to avoid another public
scandal.

                    DANNY

You were adultering?

MADDY

Yeah, but so was he. But he was the one who hired
some fucking investigator to take pictures.

DANNY

We don't do much of that these days. Divorce
stuff—

MADDY

Transom-peeping.

DANNY

Nobody has transoms anymore.

MADDY

But you still peep.

DANNY

Mostly it's on— you know— computer records.
We have ways to access, we share information,
buy lists. Your credit balance, where you
travel, what videos you rent—

MADDY

That's an invasion of privacy.

Danny just smiles—

DANNY

So the skier ditched you—

Maddy stops bouncing, sits on the tramp for a moment—

MADDY

Then I tried living in California for a while
but there was nobody there to embarrass but
myself.

DANNY

So you <u>are</u> trying to emb—

MADDY

It's pointless. What could I do that they
haven't seen worse on some reality show?

                         DANNY
Well, senator's daughter, sister to the
future governor—

                         MADDY
They catch one president getting a BJ in the
Oval Office, the next one rigs the election
and gets away with it— people have lost the
ability to be scandalized.

                         DANNY
So now your ambition is—?

                         MADDY
Make sure my kid gets out of his twenties in
one piece, represent my country in 2004—

                         DANNY
Are you that good at it?

Maddy stands and stretches—

                         MADDY
You know the Amazon women amputated one of
their breasts— it got in the way of the
bowstring.

                         DANNY
I'd hate to see you go overboard. Sacrifice
a perfectly good breast—

Maddy smiles, faces him—

                         MADDY
Mine are still the originals, you know. 100
percent flesh and blood.

48   EXT. MELON FIELD — DAY

We FOLLOW Tony down a row of MELONS about to be picked,
several MEXICAN WORKERS stooped in the field in the

distance. He approaches a thick-set man who stands watching them, his back to us—

> TONY
>
> Excuse me?

The man doesn't turn—

> TONY
>
> *Con permiso, Señor— sabe usted dónde puedo encontrar a un tal Vicente Esparza?*

Vince Esparza, who stonewalled Danny back at El Rincón, turns and gives Tony a menacing look—

> VINCE ESPARZA
>
> And who wants to know?

49   INT. MADDY'S BEDROOM — DAY

Maddy's bedroom is also a bit of a rec room. Danny wanders looking at huge BLOW-UP PHOTOS of exotic animals mounted on the wall while Maddy sits on the edge of her bed cutting her toenails. Both are pretty drunk—

> DANNY
>
> I was doing this series— we used to call it investigative journalism—

> MADDY
>
> I'm older than you, honey, and I'm not that stoned. You don't have to explain everything.

> DANNY
>
> These were bad guys, they owned a lot of low-rent housing downtown, the building boom had just started, and they had a big offer to sell. But they couldn't legally evict their tenants. So they were doing strong-arm stuff, intimidating. There was some arson involved—

MADDY

The march of progress.

DANNY

Hey, with the profit they made they could have built these people a much nicer shithole some-where else in the city. The housing inspector who should have been on top of it all, this guy Skaggs, was taking payoffs. I had these two informants, very Deep Throat, meetings in parking garages, phone calls past midnight, the whole deal, and they give me the big lead. This is criminal activity they're exposing. I write the story and my editor Mitch, he trusts me enough to run with it—

MADDY

They were willing to testify in court?

DANNY

They said yes, if it came to that. But I didn't have them on tape—

MADDY

Uh-oh—

DANNY

And they were— it was a set-up. The landlords and the inspector sued the paper, one of my sources blows town and the other flat denies it. Big retraction, a settlement out of court and I'm seriously fired— worse, I'm the guy who fabricates. Every big story I'd covered before that, the assholes I'd exposed come back— "See, he made the whole thing up, this is the deal with these alternative rags."From that day on the *Monitor* concentrated on who bakes the best chocolate chip cookie in Denver. And me, I couldn't get a job deliv-ering a newspaper.

MADDY

The editor should have—

                    DANNY

He got fired too. He runs a whaddyoucallit—
Website.

                    MADDY

At least you did something.

Danny sits next to Maddy on the bed—

                    MADDY

I've just been taking up space and emptying
out my trust fund.

                    DANNY

You took all these pictures—

                    MADDY

(dismissive) That's a <u>hob</u>by.

                    DANNY

You raised a kid.

                    MADDY

(smiles) Isn't he gorgeous?

                    DANNY

His father— his biological father—

                    MADDY

Bugged out on the whole deal. I can't blame
him, with the publicity and what a little
tramp I was then. But Dewey Junior is— is
like a nice guy, you know? Despite me for a
mother.

                    DANNY

You raised a nice kid. Maybe that's what
you're good at.

Maddy shifts to sit behind Danny, putting her hand under
his shirt—

                    MADDY

One of the things I'm good at.

----

50   EXT. MELON FIELD — DAY

Vince Esparza is staring Tony down, staying between him
and the workers in the field. Tony is pointing at Vince's
ostrich-skin boots—

>   **TONY**
> It's the <u>shoes,</u> *ese*. Braceros don't be
> wearing their party boots on the job. Vince
> Esparza, man, you a <u>leg</u>end. People say you
> got crews workin all over the county.

>   **VINCE ESPARZA**
> People say a lot of shit isn't necessarily
> true.

>   **TONY**
> I'm looking for a guy name Lázaro Huerta.

Tony notes Esparza's reaction to the name—

>   **VINCE ESPARZA**
> I don't keep track of their names. I'm not
> running a summer camp here.

Tony points to the workers beyond Vince—

>   **TONY**
> Then would you mind if I was to ask your *jor-
> naleros* a few—

>   **VINCE ESPARZA**
> Yeah, I would mind. They here to work. They
> want to blow their nose, scratch their balls,
> talk about their girlfriends, they do it on
> their own time. This is a job here, this is
> private property.

>   **TONY**
> I just—

>   **VINCE ESPARZA**
> And if somebody who was not authorized to be

here was to get hurt, it would be my responsibility. *Entiendes?*

The threat is clear—

                    TONY
    Perfectamente.

Tony turns and we start away with him, muttering under his
breath—

                    TONY
    You hidin somethin, *pendejo*—

VINCE ESPARZA

Vince scowls as he watches Tony leave—

51   INT. AMERICAN LEGION HALL

Dickie stands before an audience of LEGIONNAIRES, giant
wall of STARS AND STRIPES behind him as he speaks. TV NEWS
CAMERAS capture it all—

                    DICKIE
        I therefore reject the naysayers— the prophets
        of gloom and doom— and look forward to pro-
        moting an expansive economy— to encouraging
        the private sector to create jobs for our
        hard-working citizens— and I do mean <u>cit</u>izens—

LAUGHTER from the audience—

                    DICKIE
        We need a security checkpoint at our national
        border, not a revolving door!

APPLAUSE and CHEERS—

----

52   EXT. ROADSIDE — LATE DAY

Tony watches from his car, parked by the melon fields, as two WORKERS cross to a CONVENIENCE STORE on the other side of the highway—

53   INT. CONVENIENCE STORE

RAFI searches the shelves nearby while FITO sticks a frozen burrito in the microwave and zaps it. Tony enters, strolls over by them—

> TONY
>
> *Burritos helados— como los preparaba mi madre.*
> (Frozen burritos— just like Mom used to make.)

They try to ignore him—

> TONY
>
> *¿Conocen a un tal Lázaro Huerta?* (Do you know someone named Lázaro Huerta?)

He sees fear in their faces as they exchange a look—

> TONY
>
> *No tengan miedo— no soy La Migra.* (Don't be afraid— I'm not Immigration.)

Fito gets up the courage to speak—

> FITO
>
> *Si no es de La Migra no tenemos que decirle nada.* (If you're not Immigration we don't have to say anything.)

> TONY
>
> *Pero pueden ayudar a un compatriota. O mejor dicho a su familia.* (You could help a fellow countryman. Or at least his family.)

He follows them toward the check-out counter, decides to try a wild shot—

> TONY
>
> *Han descubierto el cuerpo.* (They found the body.)

Tony knows he's struck paydirt from the men's reaction. The men look like they may make a run for it, throwing a panicked glance to the door as somebody else enters—

> TONY
>
> *Bueno, sí no se sienten seguro aquí, dígame dónde y cuándo.* (If it's not safe to talk here, tell me where and when.)

The CASHIER rings up their items and Rafi pays. He takes a look out across the highway, then quickly scribbles something on the back of his receipt, pushes it to Tony. They hurry out—

> TONY
>
> *Hasta luego, hermanos.*

He glances at the writing on the receipt, then up to the waiting cashier—

> TONY
>
> Gimme three of those lottery tickets. I'm feelin lucky all of a sudden.

54   EXT. HIGHWAY — TIRE

We start on the FLATTENED rear TIRE of Tony's car, then TILT to see him approaching as we hear his feet on the roadside gravel. He looks around at the now-empty field, then kicks the hubcap—

JOHN SAYLES

                              TONY
          Somebody fuckin with me.

55   EXT. HIGHWAY — TONY'S CAR — LATE DAY

It's almost sunset as Tony lifts the flattened tire off
the jacked-up car. He's got the RADIO on, singing along
with the SONG that's playing—

BOOTS

We FOLLOW a pair of ostrich-skin COWBOY BOOTS, approaching
the car—

TONY

Tony lays on his back to wiggle his spare tire onto the
bolts—

BOOT

The booted foot goes up, braces against the far bumper of
the car, then pushes— WHUMP! We hear TONY SCREAM—

56   INT. MADDY'S BEDROOM — EVENING

Maddy sits by the bed in a T-shirt, watching Danny sleep.
A KNOCK on the door. She crosses and it's Dewey Jr., who
doesn't seem fazed that his mom has a guy in her bed—
                            MADDY
          What's up, sugar?
                            DEWEY
          Can the guys stay over tonight?

MADDY

They don't have homes?

DEWEY

They don't have satellite, there's some stuff
we want to watch.

MADDY

You'll have to sort out where everybody
sleeps.

DEWEY

I can handle that.

MADDY

You sounded good today.

DEWEY

We were alright.

MADDY

You were kickin it. You should find a club to
play in.

DEWEY

(shrugs) We don't have any of our own
material.

MADDY

So write some. Write about what a mess your
mother is like Eminem does.

DEWEY

Yeah. See ya—

He leaves and she looks back to Danny on the bed. She
crosses, nudges him awake with her foot—

DANNY

Huh?

MADDY

Closing time at the zoo. Get your clothes on.

DANNY

Wow. I slept. I haven't slept for days.

She has her cell phone in hand and is dialing—

                    MADDY
    I don't sleep much unless I pass out.

Maddy waits for her party to answer—

57   INT. CHURCH ASSEMBLY HALL

The words "ONE GOD, ONE FAMILY, ONE NATION" are emblazoned
on a red, white and blue backdrop as Dickie speaks before
a large RELIGIOUS GROUP. There is APPLAUSE after each of
his buzzwords—

                    DICKIE
    This is a nation based on Christian princi-
    ples. What I'm promising to work for is a
    government that respects those principles— a
    government that supports traditional family
    values— that respects the sanctity of human
    life— a government strong enough, brave
    enough, to maintain the cultural equilibrium—

BACKSTAGE

Lloyd the campaign flunky stands next to Chuck Raven as
they watch from backstage—

                    LLOYD
    What's "cultural equilibrium" mean?
                  CHUCK RAVEN
    No handouts for homos.
                    LLOYD
    Oh.

                DICKIE (UP FRONT)
    I will work to make us truly one nation,
    under God—

Chuck frowns and pulls his BEEPING cell phone out—

CHUCK RAVEN

(annoyed) Who is this?

58   INT. MADDY'S BEDROOM

Maddy paces with the phone—

MADDY

Chuck? It's Maddy Pilager calling—

Danny turns to look at her, surprised—

MADDY

Never mind how I got your cell number you
little creep, I just fucked your messenger
boy— Danny— what's your last name again?

DANNY

Oh shit—

MADDY

Danny O'Shit— yeah, well you send anybody
else after me I swear I'll put an arrow
through his neck— I love you too.

She tosses the phone on the bed and heads for the bathroom—

MADDY

He says you should check in with your office
more often, Danny. You were fired this
morning.

59   INT. MADDY'S HOUSE — LIVING ROOM — NIGHT

Danny comes down into the living room, a little bewildered, shirt unbuttoned and holding his shoes in his
hand. He finds Dewey Jr. alone, poking at his computer
keyboard—

                    DANNY

(embarrassed) Hey—

                    DEWEY

You get the boot?

                    DANNY

I guess so.

                    DEWEY

Don't take it personally. She's kinda moody.

                    DANNY

Right.

Danny sits to slip his shoes on. Dewey watches him

                    DEWEY

So you're a detective?

                    DANNY

Investigator.

                    DEWEY

You look for missing people?

                    DANNY

That can be part of the job, yeah.

                    DEWEY

You usually find them?

                    DANNY

(shrugs) Depends on how long they've been
missing.

                    DEWEY

Twenty-three years.

Danny stands. The kid is serious—

                    DANNY

Who is it?

                    DEWEY

My father. Dewey Hamilton.

                              DANNY
          Right, you're Junior—

                              DEWEY
          How would I start, you know, like if he's
          moved out of state—?

                              DANNY
          Sometimes they're not too— sometimes people
          don't want to be found. And if you do, it can
          be pretty disappointing— birth parents—

                              DEWEY
          Things are messy you got to face them sooner
          or later.

Danny considers this, impressed. He crosses to sit next
to Dewey at the computer—

                              DANNY
          You're on the Web, right?

                              DEWEY
          Wired to the eyeballs.

                              DANNY
          Okay, there's a couple things you can try—

                                        FADE TO BLACK.

60   INT. HOSPITAL — MORNING

Danny rushes down a HOSPITAL CORRIDOR, checking room numbers. He passes one open door, puts on the brakes and goes
back to enter it—

61   INT. HOSPITAL ROOM

Danny comes into the four-bed HOSPITAL ROOM— two
PATIENTS sleeping, one empty bed, one bed curtained off.
Danny crosses and pulls a curtain back—

                              TONY
          Oye, jefe— glad you could make it.

Tony is propped up with his eyes open. He has a CAST on
his arm and BANDAGES on his head—

                              DANNY
          You're conscious—

                              TONY
          Painkillers, man. I'm flyin.

                              DANNY
          They said you had an accident.

                              TONY
          Wasn't no accident.

                              DANNY
          You were on the job for me— I'll make sure
          the agency pays for everything.

                              TONY
          If I gotta miss work—

                              DANNY
          They'll pay for that too.

                              TONY
          It was him. I saw the boots— you know the one
          that puts its head in the sand—

                              DANNY
          Ostrich—

                              TONY
          Ostrich-skin boots. Puts its head in the sand
          cause it don't wanna see when they cut its
          throat. It was vehicular <u>hom</u>icide, man. Dude
          tried to kill me with my own car.

Tony shifts his eyes toward the bedside table—

                              TONY
          That paper on the table—

Danny picks up the RECEIPT from the convenience store, reads it—

                    DANNY
Fito and Rafi— Carbonville—

                    TONY
They knew our dead man. They pretty spooked but you can try em. They got maybe three words of English—

                    DANNY
Spooked by—?

                    TONY
The same *hijo de puta* who pushed the car over on me. Vince Esparza—

                    DANNY
(the name connects) Vince—

                    TONY
Vicente Esparza. I give you odds he had something to do with this Lázaro kickin the bucket.

               SKAGGS (O.S.)
O'Brien.

Sheriff Skaggs steps into the room with Deputy Davis. The deputy hangs by the door while Skaggs comes to Tony's bedside. Danny stuffs the receipt in his pocket—

                    SKAGGS
I've been trying to track you down.

                    DANNY
This is Sheriff Skaggs. My friend Tony Guerra—

                    SKAGGS
(to Tony) Shaving accident?

                    TONY
If you make me laugh I break my ribs again.

SKAGGS

Haven't heard a peep out of you, Danny. That wasn't our agreement.

DANNY

I— I'm off the case.

Skaggs looks him over—

SKAGGS

Step on your own dick again? (to Tony) Used to be a reporter, this guy. Till his mouth got way ahead of his brains.

DANNY

Look, there's a lot more to this thing then just some illegal alien floating in a lake. The people who hired me—

SKAGGS

The people who hired you fired you. Which means you're out of the conversation.

DANNY

(grasping) This is a cover-up, isn't it? They just hired me to pretend they didn't know where the—

SKAGGS

That means make yourself scarce, son. I need to talk to your amigo here. Alone.

Danny considers standing up to Skaggs, then reluctantly steps out—

DANNY

Later, Tony.

We FOLLOW Danny out past the other patients—

62   INT. SEE-MORE DETECTIVE AGENCY

The other employees are trying to listen to Danny arguing with Grace in her office, despite Lupe running the vacuum cleaner—

> GRACE (O.S.)
> You sleep with the client's sister? That is so unprofessional—

63   INT. GRACE'S OFFICE

> DANNY
> That's not why Raven wanted me off the case, is it?

> GRACE
> No, but he—

> DANNY
> He wanted me off because I'm getting close to something they want to hush up!

> GRACE
> That's the whole point of the job, Danny! And he doesn't trust you to do it.

> DANNY
> I don't have all the pieces, but this dead guy, Lázaro—

> GRACE
> You don't have any of the pieces—

> DANNY
> He knew something, saw something that they were hiding—

> GRACE
> Danny—

> DANNY
> —and they set him up, had him killed, maybe by this—

> GRACE
> Danny, Raven fired you because he found out you used to be a reporter.

Danny pauses a moment, letting this sink in—

> DANNY

Danny
> That doesn't change anything.

> GRACE

> He called yesterday morning. If you'd check
> your cell phone once in a—

> DANNY

> That sheriff has been right on my tail. He
> must be in on it, too—

> GRACE

> Danny, I cannot deal with your paranoia! Take
> the rest of the week off, come in Monday, we'll
> sit down and see what we can salvage of your
> so-called career.

A brief silence, Danny willfully calming himself—

> DANNY

> My expenses so far— I could use some cash—

> GRACE

> (sighs) Fill out a voucher and Hilary will take
> care of you. Look, Danny, I'm sure you were doing
> a very good job—aside from banging Maddy
> Pilager—

> DANNY

> Hey, she got me stoned—

This is too much. Grace points to the door—

> GRACE

> Out.

64   INT. SEE-MORE DETECTIVE AGENCY — HILARY'S DESK

We see cash in new twenty-dollar bills being counted out
on the desktop—

                                    HILARY
        Two hundred-forty, two-hundred sixty. Just
        sign here—

We WIDEN as Danny signs for the money, then scoops it up—
                                    HILARY
        And next time I want all the receipts.
                                    DANNY
        Right—

Danny is distracted, seeing Lupe heading out with her
vacuum cleaner—
                                    DANNY
        Lupe! Let me help you with that—

We FOLLOW Danny as he hurries over and relieves her of the
equipment. They head for the door—
                                    LUPE
        Thank you.
                                    DANNY
        Listen, Lupe— how'd you like to make two hun-
        dred dollars?

She gives him a suspicious look—

65   EXT. CARBONVILLE STREET — WORKER HOUSING — DAY

Lupe stands in front of a barracks-like row of WORKER
HOUSING, speaking in Spanish with a couple MEN hanging
around outside. She comes back to Danny waiting by his car—
                                    LUPE
        They think these two men— Rafi and Fito— have
        gone to the church.

She points and we PAN to see a CATHOLIC CHURCH just down the street, lots of cars parked around it—

> DANNY
>
> It's not Sunday.

> LUPE
>
> It's *Todos Santos*— the Day of the Dead.

66 EXT. CHURCH

We hear SINGING from inside the church, and then the two men from the convenience store, Fito and Rafi step out, Rafi turning to cross himself in the open doorway. They head back toward the housing block, but Danny and Lupe are waiting for them—

> DANNY
>
> Pardoname— Señores—

> LUPE
>
> *Discùlpenme Señores, pero este hombre quisiera platicar con ustedes un momentico—*

The men stop, look stricken—

> DANNY
>
> Tell them I came instead of Tony.

> LUPE
>
> *Es el jefe del hombre que les habló ayer.*

> FITO
>
> *No podemos ayudarle.*

> LUPE
>
> They don't trust you.

> DANNY
>
> (improvising) Tell them— tell them I have their names and if they want to stay in this country—

> LUPE
>
> You wouldn't do that to them, would you?

> DANNY

No, but they don't know that, do they? Tell them we can go somewhere else to talk—

> LUPE

Les puede armar un lío con La Migra. Solamente quiere hablar con ustedes, en cualquier sitio—

Fito and Rafi exchange a look. Both are uncomfortable to be seen with a gringo by the exiting churchgoers—

> RAFI

Dígale que debe acompñarnos a las ruinas. A la Ciudad de Plata.

> LUPE

They say you have to come with them to the ruins. To Silver City.

Danny doesn't like it, but doesn't know what else to do—

> DANNY

Can I trust them?

> LUPE

Can they trust you?

67   EXT. ACCESS ROAD — OLD MINE SITE

Danny's car moves through a blasted landscape— terraced MINE TAILINGS with only the hardiest little bit of scrub growing on them—

68   INT. CAR

Lupe sits in front with Danny as he drives—

> DANNY

So when do we get to this joint?

                              FITO
          Aquí estamos.

                              LUPE
          This is it.

Danny looks around at the ruined landscape—
                              FITO
          Lo enterró la ciudad hace muchos años. Pare
          aquí—

                              LUPE
          They buried the city years ago. Stop here.

69   EXT. FOOTHILL

Danny stops and they get out at the foot of a mountain.
A DIRT TRAIL, mostly overgrown, angles up the side of it—
                              DANNY
          What now?

Rafi points up the mountain—
                              RAFI
          Subimos.

Rafi leads the way, then Lupe, Danny, and Fito. Danny
shoots a quick look back to Fito in the rear—

FITO

Fito adjusts something long and metallic tucked between
his shirt and his pants. A pistol?

DANNY

Danny notes this, frowning—

70   EXT. DRIFTMOUTH

Rafi stops on a small level patch and waits for the others
to catch up. Danny and Lupe are a bit out of breath—

>   RAFI
> *Aquí estamos.*

>   DANNY
> This is where Lázaro died?

The men exchange another look, then Rafi begins to speak—

>   RAFI
> *Lázaro se murió en el desolladero.*

>   LUPE
> He says Lázaro died in— where they take the
> meat from the bones—

>   DANNY
> Slaughterhouse.

>   FITO
> Benagra.

>   DANNY
> The BenAgra slaughterhouse.

>   FITO
> *Lázaro era un recién llegado, muy tímido,*
> *tenía miedo de todo aquí en el norte pero*
> *especialmente le tenía miedo al jefe.*

>   LUPE
> Lázaro was a newly arrived, a very shy
> person, very afraid of everything in the
> north, but especially afraid of the boss.

>   DANNY
> And the *jefe* was?

                              RAFI
Vicente Esparza. *El que anda siempre con
pistola.*

                             DANNY
Vince Esparza carries a gun?

                              LUPE
Is the law here, no? Everyone must carry
his gun.

                             DANNY
Pretty much, yeah—

                              FITO
A nosotros nos tocó limpiar—

                              LUPE
We were the cleanin crew—

71 INT. FACTORY — CATWALK

LAZARO HUERTA, in goggles and slicker-coveralls, stands on
a dripping wet METAL GRID high above us, stepping uncer-
tainly from foothold to foothold, no safety line rigged to
his belt. He is dragging a length of STEAM HOSE behind him.
A roiling FOG of CLEANING STEAM fills the air around us,
and the NOISE of blasting hoses and BELTS being shifted
comes up under the dialogue—

                          LUPE (V.O.)
After midnight, when they stop the line, we
come in to clean the metal with scaldin hot
water mix with *clorina*—

                          DANNY (V.O.)
Chlorine—

                          LUPE (V.O.)
Yes, from hoses. There is always so much
noise, and you can't see from the steam—

FEET

We FOLLOW Lázaro's FEET as he gingerly moves across the catwalk to get into position—

> LUPE (V.O.)
> We have told Don Vicente that the job up above— cleanin the machine that takes the skin off the cows— is not safe, that there has to be more scaffoldin or something to hold onto. But he says only little babies are cryin for their mamas—

LAZARO

Lázaro steadies himself, points the nozzle of the steam hose down at the machinery below—

> LUPE (V.O.)
> —and he sends whoever he doesn't like to do it. This day he sends Lázaro Huerta. We told him not to shoot the esteam— a todo presión?

> DANNY (V.O.)
> Full-pressure

> LUPE (V.O.)
> —at full pressure when he is turnin it on, but he has not done this work before—

Lázaro yanks the valve open full-bore, STEAM blasting out and the hose recoiling—

FEET, CATWALK

Lázaro's FEET slip off the wet catwalk and he falls past us, holding onto the HOSE which loops over a catwalk crossbar, playing out rapidly, snapping tight for a second, then swinging as Lázaro's hold breaks—

72 EXT. DRIFTMOUTH

They sit resting on the little flat area. Very peaceful compared to the hell of the killing floor—

> **RAFI**
> *Se cayó, se chocó contra una de las bandas y después contra el lado de la máquina, y luego contra el piso. Es de cemento.*

> **LUPE**
> He falls and he hits one of the belts, then the side of the machine, and then the floor, which is concrete.

A brief silence as Danny and Lupe contemplate this image—

> **FITO**
> *No había nadie más sólo Don Vicente, Rafi y yo en este área de la fábrica.*

73 INT. SLAUGHTERHOUSE — FLOOR

We see a HOSE trained on the concrete floor, blasting water to push dried and still-liquid BLOOD into a DRAIN—

> **FITO (V.O.)**
> *El nos mandó esconder el cuerpo de Lázaro en un barril de basura y limpiar su sangre junto con la de los animales.*

> **LUPE (V.O.)**
> There was nobody in that part of the factory but these two men and Vicente their boss. He told them to put the body in a garbage barrel and to clean his blood with the blood of the animals.

> **DANNY (V.O.)**
> And then?

74 EXT. DRIFTMOUTH — NIGHT

We see a FLASHLIGHT approaching from below in the dark—

>   LUPE (V.O.)
>   At the end of work we carried it out to his
>   truck and he drove us here. He said he knew
>   this place from years ago, when he was hired to
>   hide other things.

The LIGHT comes closer. We see Rafi and Fito, scared,
carrying Lázaro's battered body, lit by Vince Esparza
carrying a flashlight behind them—

>   DANNY (V.O.)
>   What other things?

>   LUPE (V.O.)
>   Some kind of garbage—

Vince steps around and the FLASHLIGHT BEAM FILLS THE
FRAME—

75 EXT. DRIFTMOUTH

They are on their feet now—

>   LUPE (V.O.)
>   And they felt bad, treatin a man they knew,
>   human being, like he was garbage, too.

>   DANNY
>   So you left the body up here?

Fito points—

>   FITO
>   *Al dentro.*

Rafi pulls a dust-covered slab of plywood away to reveal
a small MINE OPENING. Danny steps up to peer into it—

FITO

Lo dejamos al fondo del pozo. Don Vicente nos dijo que ahora tenemos parte en un crimen, y que si la policía da cuenta, vamos al cárcel.

LUPE

We left it at the back of the tunnel. Vicente told them now they are part of a crime, and if the police finds out they are goin to jail.

RAFI

Si él no nos mata antes.

LUPE

If he doesn't kill them first.

RAFI

Fue la última noche que trabajamos al desolladero— Don Vicente la debió contar todo a alguien más importante. El día siguiente nos llevó pa' trabajar al campo.

LUPE

That was the last night they work at the slaughterhouse. He thinks this Vicente told somebody higher up, cause the next day he took them to work in the fields.

Fito pulls the object Danny noted before out of his belt— it is a FLASHLIGHT. He offers it to Danny—

FITO

Nos dió tanta pena dejar Lázaro en este hoyo. Regresamos tres días después—para darle cristiana sepultura, pero—

LUPE

It made us feel bad to leave him in this hole, so we come back three days later to bury him like a Christian, but—

DANNY

He wasn't there?

                    FITO

Se fue. Quizá fue uh milagro.

                    LUPE

He was gone. Maybe it was a miracle.

                    RAFI

Donde lo dejamos había mucha agua en el piso.
Cuando volvimos llegaba hasta la cintura—

                    LUPE

They left him where there was water on the
floor. When they came back it was this high—
(indicates hip high)

                    RAFI

Casi un río.

Danny takes the flashlight—

                    DANNY

You'll show me where?

                    FITO

Hay fantasmas ahí dentro—

                    RAFI

Ni soñando.

                    DANNY

All right. Wait for me here.

Danny flicks the flashlight on, steps into the mineshaft.
Rafi and Fito look to Lupe—

                    RAFI

Cree que el nos denunciará a la policía? (You
think he'll tell the police about us?)

Rafi and Fito don't want any part of it—

76 INT. MINE SHAFT

The ceiling isn't too low as Danny makes his way deeper into the old mineshaft. We hear WATER SOUNDS up ahead. Danny turns a corner into a narrower passageway, slightly downhill. He stops and listens— WATER SOUNDS up ahead, and something else, a METALLIC CLUNKING. Danny starts ahead, turns a corner—

77 EXT. MOUNTAINSIDE

Fito and Rafi lead Lupe down to the car—

                    LUPE
     Dijo que debemos esperarle— (He said we
     should wait.)

                    FITO
     No me gusta estar aquí. (I don't like to be
     here.)

They step out by Danny's car. Immediately there is the *WHOOOP!* of a POLICE SIREN and they whirl to see a white INS PATROL CAR speeding toward them! Fito and Rafi panic, begin to run—

                    LUPE
     No huyan! No pueden escapar! (Don't run! You
     can't get away!)

Lupe flinches as the patrol car kicks up dirt blasting past her—

78 INT. MINE

Danny moves ahead slowly, the WATER SOUND louder until *THUMP! WHOOSH!* he falls through a hole in the floor down to the level below, disappearing from sight!

79 INT. MINE — LOWER LEVEL, WATER

Danny comes up sputtering, the FLASHLIGHT still ON and clutched in his hand— he is flailing to keep his head above WATER that is only a few feet from the tunnel ceiling, water on the move and full of bulky objects— *CLANG!* One bumps the wall and Danny swings his light— it is a huge, badly rusted BARREL, with a SKULL AND CROSSBONES stencilled near the top and the word TOXIC still legible— in fact the chamber is full of such barrels, bumping against each other and against the sides of the shaft and Danny has to push to keep from getting squished between them. There is a current and he feels himself being pulled—

> **DANNY**
> Hey! Out there! I'm in the water! Help me!
> Ayúdeme!

His VOICE ECHOES but there is no response from outside. He begins to fight the current, pushing back and searching the ceiling with the light till he sees another hole through the ceiling. He jockeys a barrel over beneath it, and with a huge effort hauls himself on top of the barrel, partially sinking it, then uses this purchase to push up into the hole—

80 INT. MINE — UPPER LEVEL

Danny strains to haul himself up, dragging himself onto the rocky floor. He rolls on his back, gasping for breath, shaking from the exertion, the flashlight resting on his chest. It FLICKERS, then goes OUT.

BLACKNESS.

> **DANNY**
> (in the dark) Terrific.

81 EXT. DRIFTMOUTH

Lupe waits anxiously at the opening, calling in—

                    LUPE
     Mr. O'Brien? Are you there? Mr. O'Brien?

Lupe gasps as Danny steps out of the driftmouth, dripping
water—

                    LUPE
     You got all wet.

Danny just looks at her, sits on a large rock—

                    DANNY
     Where are the guys?

                    LUPE
     They took them away.

                    DANNY
     Took them—?

                    LUPE
     La Migra come and chase those men and take
     them away.

Danny sighs. What next?

                    DANNY
     How come they didn't take you?

                    LUPE
     (proudly) I carry my citizen papers. Always.

82 EXT. CARBONVILLE STREET

Danny pulls his car over at the head of the MAIN STREET,
a small Day of the Dead PARADE in progress beyond the
wooden POLICE BARRIERS. Danny and Lupe get out—

                    DANNY
     Guess I'll have to leave you out here.

SILVER CITY and other Screenplays

                              LUPE
          Is okay—

                              DANNY
          (nods toward the parade) How come you didn't
          take the day off?

                              LUPE
          I belong to the *Iglesia Evangélico*. This—
          (indicates parade) this is the devil's work.

                              DANNY
          I'll keep that in mind. Thanks for your help—

                              LUPE
          You be careful, Mr. O'Brien.

Danny watches Lupe walk away. He sees—

MADDY

Maddy Pilager is a ways down the street, taking pictures
of the parade—

CLOSER, MADDY

She gets to one knee to line up a shot, PANS the camera— Danny
is standing in front of her lens. She stands—

                              DANNY
          Hey.

                              MADDY
          You again. Hey, I'm sorry about last night.
          I get disgusted with myself and take it out
          on other people.

                              DANNY
          Don't worry about it.

She looks him over—

                    MADDY

You been swimming?

                    DANNY

Cave diving.

PARADE — SHERIFF SKAGGS

Sheriff Skaggs, walking on the sidewalk parallel to the
parade with Deputy Davis to check out the crowd, is not
pleased when he sees Danny up ahead—

DANNY AND MADDY

It's extremely awkward between them—

                    MADDY

I'm sorry if I got you in trouble.

                    DANNY

The thing I was investigating— I'm in a
little over my head—

                    MADDY

Did you get fired?

                    DANNY

Probation—

                    MADDY

Sorry. (hopeful) Do you think you might call
me sometime?

                    DANNY

Look, Maddy—

                    MADDY

You're scared of me, aren't you?

                    DANNY

No. But I am scared of your family.

FIRECRACKERS POP, making them turn. Danny sees someone else—

POV — VINCE ESPARZA

Vince Esparza, a bit drunk, wanders alongside the costumed PARADERS, calling out—

> **VINCE ESPARZA**
> *Qué viva la Huesuda! Vivan los espíritus!*

He grabs a man in a SKELETON COSTUME and waltzes a few steps with him to the amusement of the SPECTATORS on the sidewalk—

DANNY

Danny looks down—

VINCE

We TILT with Danny's gaze to Vince's BOOTS—

DANNY AND MADDY

Danny makes the connection—

> **DANNY**
> Would you say those are ostrich skin?
> **MADDY**
> That guy's boots? Yeah. Tony Lamas—
> **DANNY**
> Excuse me.

He steps away, leaving Maddy a bit bewildered—

DANNY AND VINCE

Danny catches up and begins to walk parallel to Vince, who SINGS ALONG with the PARADERS' SONG. Vince notices Danny staring at him—

> **VINCE ESPARZA**
> You got a problem my friend?

> **DANNY**
> You're Vince Esparza, aren't you?

Vince stops and stares at Danny for a long moment, then smiles and steps out of the street, waving for Danny to follow him—

> **VINCE ESPARZA**
> Come on. We gotta talk, you and me.

SKAGGS

The Sheriff frowns as he sees Danny and Vince step behind a building—

83 EXT. ALLEYWAY

Vince leads Danny into an ALLEYWAY parallel to the street. The sound of a BRASS BAND playing a DIRGE comes from the parade—

> **VINCE ESPARZA**
> You the one been stirrin up all the shit, huh?
> Askin about tattoos, botherin my workers— now
> I hear the police are lookin for me—

> **DANNY**
> I've got nothing against you. It's the people
> above you— the ones who had you dump the bar-
> rels in the mine. They knew about Lázaro,
> didn't th—

WHAM! Vince turns suddenly and throws Danny against a building wall, getting nose to nose with him—

                    VINCE ESPARZA
          What the fuck is it to you? You don't come
          down here to where I live askin me fuckin
          questions!

                    DANNY
          I'm not after you! It's them—

                    VINCE ESPARZA
          Tha's right, you don't care about me, an I
          don't care about you! I don't care you live
          or you <u>die!</u>

Vince pulls a PISTOL out from under his shirt and sticks it up under Danny's chin. The dirge is almost deafening now, Vincent yelling to be heard over the MUSIC—

                    VINCE ESPARZA
          You see this? You know what this is, *cabrón?*
          You ask me one more fuckin question—

                    SKAGGS (O.S.)
          Vincent Esparza—

                    VINCE ESPARZA
          Qué mierda—?

Vince turns toward the voice, gun still in hand *BLAM! BLAM! BLAM!*

Vince is blasted backward, pistol flying from his hand! He spins around as he falls and grabs Danny around the neck to try to hold himself up. They are locked in the strange embrace for a long moment, Vince looking into Danny's eyes in bewilderment—

                    VINCE ESPARZA
          Qué mierda es esto?

His grip loosens and he slides to the ground, leaving
Danny shaken, his front smeared with BLOOD—

> **DEPUTY DAVIS (O.S.)**
> Don't move!

SHERIFF AND DEPUTY

Deputy Davis is in a three-point shooting stance, arms
trembling slightly, keeping a bead on Danny—

> **DEPUTY DAVIS**
> Just freeze right there.

Sheriff Skaggs lays his hand gently on the deputy's arm—

> **SKAGGS**
> Lower your gun, Dave.

> **DEPUTY DAVIS**
> He—

> **SKAGGS**
> One's deader'n a doornail and the other's
> unarmed. Put it <u>down.</u>

> **DEPUTY DAVIS**
> (scared now) He had his gun out, he could have—

> **SKAGGS**
> Put it in the holster and go keep that crowd
> from coming back here. <u>Go.</u>

Davis holsters his gun and heads for the street, looking
back uneasily. Skaggs walks up and squats beside Vince's
body, rolling him face up. Vince has a BULLET HOLE in the
face and two in the chest—

> **DANNY**
> Aw, Jesus—

> **SKAGGS**
> You said it.

                    DANNY
He wasn't going to shoot your deputy.

                    SKAGGS
Boy's a little overtrained. This is Esparza?

                    DANNY
Yeah.

Skaggs cocks his head as he gazes down at the body—

                    SKAGGS
He's got that wanted for questioning, killed-
while-resisting-arrest look about him.

84 INT. SHERIFF'S DEPARTMENT — INTERROGATION ROOM

In a very bare room, Sheriff Skaggs sits on a desk as
Danny paces the room, adrenaline out of control after the
shooting—

                    DANNY
They didn't clean up the cyanide waste,
they just dumped it into an old mine.
Esparza was working for Bentel then, my
guys said he told them he'd dumped something there before. Only it's flooded now,
flooding more every day, and somehow
Huerta's body got swept away by it, pushed
out through the mountain into one of the
streams that feeds the lake— this is
sounding crazy, isn't it?

                    SKAGGS
Throw a dead body into a cave, and three days
later it comes back out in the world, all on
its own— sure, a lot of people'll buy that.

                    DANNY
The water pressure—

SKAGGS

(calm) Their names? These Mexicans you say you talked to—

DANNY

Oh come on, you followed us and had the Immigration people pick them up!

SKAGGS

Did I?

DANNY

Half this town is illegal and Immigration is going to bother to drive out into the middle of nowhere and just happen to run into my witnesses?

Skaggs is enjoying this—

SKAGGS

Mr. Quiñones and Mr. López have been debriefed by the INS. According to them they were working at BenAgra Packing with a certain Lázaro Huerta, also an undocumented alien, until one day he chose not to show up for work. That's the last they saw of him.

DANNY

Of course they're going to say that, they're—

SKAGGS

They're back on a plane to see their families within twenty-four hours, courtesy of the United States government. Unless, of course, you decide to include that crock of shit you just told me in your official statement. In which case they'd be accessories to wrongful death at the least, possibly murder.

DANNY

They'd be fucked.

SKAGGS

Bien jodido is the phrase, I believe.

DANNY

(grasping) But the slaughterhouse—

SKAGGS

The slaughterhouse operates within the guide-
lines that have been set by law. All we've
got is failure to report an accident and
illegal burial, which begins and ends with
Vince Esparza. (warning) Doesn't it?

Sheriff Skaggs starts out—

SKAGGS

I'll give you a few minutes to think about it.

DANNY

You called his name.

Skaggs stops by the door—

DANNY

You were trying to find him— you called his
name out—

SKAGGS

Your buddy in the hospital had us on the
lookout. "Vehicular homicide."

Skaggs steps out. Danny is left to decide what to do—

85 INT. *DENVER DEFENDER* HALLWAY, OFFICE

Nora follows a harried manager, LEO, down the HALLWAY—

NORA

Do I absolutely have to go to this one
tomorrow morning? It's the same speech every—

LEO

I don't have time now, Nora—

                              NORA
        If I spent a few hours checking up on some
        of his statistics instead of—

They turn into the NEWSROOM with its dozens of little
hutches. She doesn't notice at first that most of her fellow
EMPLOYEES are standing together sharing a troublesome rumor—

                               LEO
        Later—

He hurries away from her. Nora realizes everybody is up
and watching Leo for a cue—

                              NORA
        What's the deal?

                             MARCY
        Where have you been?

                              Nora
        Out reporting the news. I know it's easier
        just to watch it on cable, but—

Leo calls from in front of his office—

                               LEO
        Staff meeting in fifteen minutes, people!
        That means everybody!

                             MARCY
        (watching Leo disappear) Then it's true.
        They'll say nobody will be let go, but when
        they bought the *Sentinel* they cut thirty jobs
        in the first month.

                              NORA
        (concerned now) They who? What are you
        talking about?

                             MARCY
        We've been sold to Gold Mine Publishing. That
        Bentel owns?

---

86 INT. BAR — EVENING

Danny sits nursing a beer at a nearly empty neighborhood bar, the BARTENDER regarding him suspiciously. Danny is still wearing the same clothes, the BLOOD on his shirt now dry and crusty. A snide ATTACK AD paid for by "Citizens for Frontier Values" runs on the TV behind the bar—

> **CHUCK RAVEN (O.S.)**
> Don't even think about it.

Danny swivels to see Chuck Raven standing behind him—

> **CHUCK RAVEN**
> Whatever pathetic publicity stunt you're hatching in that drug-addled brain of yours—

> **DANNY**
> I don't work for you.

> **CHUCK RAVEN**
> Right, you were dismissed when we discovered an incident of substance abuse on the job. Anything you say—

> **DANNY**
> Don't threaten me—

> **CHUCK RAVEN**
> You're the boy who cried wolf, O'Brien. It was in all the papers.

> **DANNY**
> A murder was com—

> **CHUCK RAVEN**
> What, murder by deregulation? That kind of thinking went out in the last century.

> **DANNY**
> That's not the point—

> **CHUCK RAVEN**
> The point is that without a smoking gun all

you've got is an opportunity to fuck up your
sorry excuse of a life even more than—

Danny is up in his face now, angry—

DANNY

People like you think you got everything covered, you think nobody cares enough to fight
back— but some day your shit's gonna catch up
with you! And when it does—

CHUCK RAVEN

You're a <u>loser,</u> Danny! This has been estab-
lished beyond doubt. Just try to be a good
one, okay?

Chuck pivots and marches out. Danny sees Grace, looking a
bit sheepish, waiting a few feet away—

GRACE

Don't you think you should change your shirt?

DANNY

How'd you find me?

GRACE

I'm a detective.

DANNY

You said we were investigators—

She sits by him—

GRACE

<u>I'm</u> a detective. You're an investigator. And
the first rule is, don't go finding more than
you're looking for.

This isn't easy for Grace—

GRACE

If it wasn't for Mort— all his plans. Every

scheme he's ever had has had a jinx on it,
his wife has to support him— he thinks he's
a failure. If this Silver City thing were to
fall through—

                    DANNY
And he's in with the Pilagers.

                    GRACE
Up to his neck.

Grace lays a bulging envelope on the counter—

                    DANNY
Hush money?

                    GRACE
Severance pay.

Danny nods. He didn't expect anything else—

                    GRACE
Don't make trouble, Danny. It won't do any
good.

Danny studies Grace for a moment, finding it impossible
to be mad at her—

                    DANNY
How'd you ever hire a basket case like me?

                    GRACE
Look who I married.

Danny smiles, picks up the envelope, half pulls the wad
of new bills out—

                    DANNY
(musing) Travel expenses.

                              FADE TO BLACK.

87 EXT. DOWNTOWN — PARKING LOT — MORNING

We see the CAPITOL DOME in the BG as we watch a wooden
SHIPPING CONTAINER that holds a COFFIN being loaded into
the bed of an official state PICKUP TRUCK. We're in the
lot behind a GOVERNMENT BUILDING—

REVERSE

Danny, cleaned up from yesterday, stands watching sadly.
Nora appears and stands to one side, waiting a moment
before announcing herself—

> **NORA**
>
> Danny?

Danny looks over, surprised to see her but too addled from
sleeplessness to show that he's pleased—

> **DANNY**
>
> I hear you've been bought. I mean, not you
> personally, but—

> **NORA**
>
> (shrugs) Part of the happy Bentel family.

> **DANNY**
>
> (nods toward container) That's a man named
> Lázaro Huerta in the box. On his way home—
> what's left of him.

> **NORA**
>
> This is your case?

> **DANNY**
>
> (shakes his head) I'm out of the snoop
> racket.

> **CONTRERAS (O.S.)**
>
> Mr. O'Brien, yes?

They turn to see CONTRERAS, a well-dressed bureaucrat. He
offers his hand to Danny—

> **CONTRERAS**
>
> Ramón Contreras from the Mexican Consulate.
> On behalf of the aggrieved family, I offer
> you my sincere gratitude for your generosity.

> **DANNY**
>
> I'd like to wire some money on top of the
> casket and shipping— you think they'd—?

> **CONTRERAS**
>
> Anything you can send will be appreciated,
> (nods toward container) There are several
> children— If you'll excuse me? The paperwork—

> **DANNY**
>
> Nice to meet you.

Contreras continues past to confer with the DRIVER. The
WORKMEN are tying the container down. Danny rubs his eyes—

> **NORA**
>
> You haven't been sleeping.

> **DANNY**
>
> Not lately, no.

> **NORA**
>
> I split up with Chandler.

This wakes Danny up a bit—

> **DANNY**
>
> Really?

> **NORA**
>
> I was grousing about communications monopo-
> lies and he gave me his usual line and we got
> into a fight and one thing led to another.
> (shrugs) Conflict of interests.

> **DANNY**
>
> Many a promising merger has failed due to
> conflict of interests.

                              NORA

How does that make you feel? Us splitting up?

                             DANNY

Euphoric.

                              NORA

(smiles) That's how I felt all night. I
should be suicidal— my paper's been co-
opted, I've got all these people to call and
tell they're not invited to Aspen for the
wedding—

                             DANNY

Were you going do one of those ski-lift cer-
emonies?

                              NORA

It would have been a very tasteful, very Cau-
casian event—

                             DANNY

I know a great caterer if you change your
mind.

She looks him over for a long moment—

                              NORA

Maybe we could— could see each other some
time—

                             DANNY

That would be great.

A long look between them—

                              NORA

So you quit your job?

                             DANNY

Grace fired me.

                              NORA

What do you do now?

DANNY
(thinks) Well— first I have to repaint the
living room—

Nora smiles—

88 EXT. OFFICE BUILDING — EARLY MORNING

Karen steps down to the basement door of the website
office, yakking with a COWORKER—

KAREN
It's like he's a bad actor who doesn't really
believe himself in the part, you know? But
you read these polls— I think the questions
must be like "Would you rather have Dickie
Pilager as the next governor—"

She turns the key and opens the door—

KAREN
—"or have your pancreas pulled out through
your nose with a rusty coat hanger?" And <u>still</u>
thirty-three percent of the people prefer the
coat hanger— (sees) What's this?

She bends to pick up a folded piece of PAPER slipped under
the door. She unfolds it— a schematic DRAWING and some
writing under it—

KAREN
(reading) "Silver City." Weird. Somebody left
us a treasure map.

89 EXT. SPEAKING PLATFORM — ARAPAHO LAKE

Dickie stands on a PLATFORM with the sparkling lake and

the majestic Rocky Mountains rising behind him. We have returned to the scene of the discovery, as if nothing has happened. The NEWS CAMERAS are rolling and a throng of UNIFORMED PERSONNEL— police cadets, park rangers, Eagle Scouts- surround him, artfully seated on a tight semi-circle of BLEACHERS—

> **DICKIE**
> I promise to respect and support our American traditions— our right to bear arms— our right to the freedoms of religious worship and expression— so fundamental to our liberty.

CHUCK RAVEN

Chuck paces behind the bleachers, talking on one cell phone while holding a second in his hand, Leslie and Lloyd dogging his heels—

> **DICKIE (O.S.)**
> I promise to support a smaller, more effi-cient government— No longer must the Big Brother of the social welfare system—

DISSOLVE TO:

90 INT. RADIO STATION — LOUNGE — TV SET

Dickie appears live on the TV SET in the radio station LOUNGE where Cliff Castleton works—

> **DICKIE (TV)**
> —dictate our daily lives— intruding, impeding, regulating the very air that we breathe—

Cliff scowls, takes a gulp of antacid—

DISSOLVE TO:

91 EXT. TAILINGS — SILVER CITY

Mort happily drives a SIGN for his development company into the barren ground as a SURVEYOR CREW stakes out lots behind him—

> DICKIE (V.O.)
> What I'm talking about, my fellow citizens, comes down to that precious word— "freedom."

DISSOLVE TO:

92 INT. TROPHY ROOM

A glass case full of TROPHIES and division-title FLAGS behind them, Wes Benteen and his new COACH shake hands and pose with a ceremonial FOOTBALL as SPORTSWRITERS and NEWS CREWS crowd around capturing the moment—

> DICKIE (V.O.)
> The freedom enjoyed by those bold individuals who came to a wild frontier and built the West that we love so dearly—

DISSOLVE TO:

93 EXT. DRIFTMOUTH

Mitch and Karen, who is carrying a VIDEO CAMERA, SUN-GUN, and BATTERY PACK, stand in front of the Silver City drift-mouth. Mitch is in serious respiratory trouble. He reaches out and touches the CEMENT PATCH poured overnight to block access to the mine. Karen, puzzled, takes another look at the map Danny drew—

> DICKIE (V.O.)
> —those steadfast men and women whose spirit of daring and conquest inspires us to this day—

DISSOLVE TO:

94 EXT. MADDY'S BACK YARD

Maddy Pilager draws and holds, zen-like—

> ### DICKIE (V.O.)
> —the freedom from fear of those who envy
> our good fortune, who scorn our democratic
> institutions—

—till the arrow releases itself and becomes one with the
bullseye at the center of a "PILAGER FOR GOV." POSTER—

                                          DISSOLVE TO:

95 EXT. EXHIBITION MINE 95

Casey Lyle shows a half-dozen TOURISTS how to pan for
gold. He smiles as a shiny residue of metal separates—

> ### DICKIE (V.O.)
> —freedom from the cultural tyranny of the
> special interest groups and New Age dema-
> gogues who would who seek to deny us the har-
> vest of our God-given bounty under the false
> banner of environmental correctness—

                                          DISSOLVE TO:

96 EXT. VAIL STREET

FOREIGN WORKERS line up for the bus back down to Carbonville—

> ### DICKIE (V.O.)
> —the freedom to seek health, happiness, and
> yes, fortune in this glorious mountain state
> of ours—

                                          DISSOLVE TO:

97 EXT. ARAPAHO LAKE

We TRACK IN tight as Dickie wraps up his heartfelt speech—

> **DICKIE**
>
> That is the freedom I promise you my fellow
> citizens. But let not a man be judged by the
> promises he makes—

We ZOOM past him to gaze at the lake at the base of the
mountains—

> **DICKIE (O.S.)**
>
> —but by the works he leaves behind. May God
> bless you all!

We hear APPLAUSE and CHEERING as we CONTINUE ZOOMING in
at the crystal water. The CROWD SOUNDS begin to FADE—

WATER SURFACE — CLOSER

The surface is calm, mirrorlike. Suddenly a DEAD FISH
floats up in front of us. Then ANOTHER and ANOTHER and
ANOTHER and ANOTHER—

CREDITS ROLL

SUNSHINE STATE

BY

JOHN SAYLES

Introduction

I HAD ORIGINALLY THOUGHT TO adapt a short story of mine, "Treasure," about two families whose fortunes crisscross while dredging for buried pirate treasure on Florida's gulf coast. But when I went down in the late 1990s to scout locations and get shooting ideas, the place that I had remembered from only ten or fifteen years earlier no longer existed. Development of a particularly homogenous corporate flavor had transformed the coast, other forays to Panama City Beach and Apalachicola were equally fruitless, and I couldn't see spending the money (and the time to find it) to do a period film. Stymied, I remembered friends who had told me about American Beach, an all-black enclave on Amelia Island, near Jacksonville on the east coast of the state. I took another trip down, drove onto Amelia, and started to feel like I had something. It was a place with some rich racial history, and on the verge of massive development. Florida is a state that advertising and tourism built, and identity—what exactly does your history mean to you if you exaggerate and distort it to sell tickets to outsiders?—can shift rapidly. Tourism is one thing on a mom-and-pop level, of local businesspeople and their roadside attractions. Corporate tourism, which is usually headquartered far away and makes almost everyone in town an employee, is something very different.

To provide a little outside perspective I used a device similar to the clairvoyant indigenous woman in *Men with Guns*, a trio of "Olympian golfers" who at first seem to be flesh-and-blood real estate types, but with each appearance prove to be playing on a much higher level. It also has two main parallel stories as in *Lone Star*, with Marly, who will probably have to leave town to save her life, and Desiree, who realizes she may have to come back for a while to get hers together, sharing all kinds of emotional space (Marly's mother being Desiree's theatrical mentor, among other things), but only ten seconds of screen time together. Besides providing guides into the white and black communities, they also help embody our love/hate relationship with the small town—either the bedrock of American common sense and human values or a vicious nest of vipers who know way too much about your business. The character of Francine represents yet another connection to place, that of the booster who understands "how hard it is to invent a tradition." Some serious whitewashing must be done to turn murdering, pillaging, slave-running pirates into campy-cute theme park icons, but given the bloody and ignoble nature of much of our past, we can't very easily celebrate the thing itself.

Sunshine State is another mosaic of a movie, with some of the characters completing a more satisfying arc than others. There is a central event, Old Buccaneer Days, to structure chronological time, and the past, in the form of the Indian bones, reveals itself to ironically bail out the present (for the moment). My favorite bit of writing is the goodbye scene between Marly and Jack—for what isn't said (and in the playing by Edie Falco and Tim Hutton, for how they don't say it). The constant tourist-town pressure to be in a "sunshine state" of bliss provides the running tension that Asteroid did in *City of Hope*, a reminder that if you're not happy and don't have material things you must be a godawful un-American loser. If you've seen the movie you'll notice that I ended up dropping the alligator-loose-in-the-mall scene, which was fun to shoot and cut together okay but broke the tone somehow. Though it would have looked snappy in the coming attractions.

SUNSHINE STATE

1 EXT. PARK — NIGHT — SKY

We look into a dark NIGHT SKY. Peaceful, then something looms over us— a SHIP. A wooden sailing ship of the seventeenth century, sails hanging limp, becalmed—

CLOSER — FLAG

The Jolly Roger, skull and crossbones on a black background, hangs from a mast—

PIRATE

We see a figure in SILHOUETTE. Suddenly his features are ILLUMINATED as something FLAMING goes sailing overhead and *THUMP!* lands on board the ship—

SHORE — TERRELL

We begin to make out the features of a thirteen-year-old boy, TERRELL, lit by FLAME several yards away. He is watching something, transfixed. He holds a forgotten CIGARETTE LIGHTER in his hand, flicked on—

BURNING SHIP

The ship is BURNING on deck. The SAILS CATCH FIRE—

DETAIL — FLAG

The Jolly Roger catches FIRE—

DETAIL — PIRATE

The figure is a WOODEN PIRATE with a parrot on his shoulder and a cutlass raised in his hand, paint blistering off as the FLAMES lick around him—

TERRELL

Terrell watches, seemingly unaware of the POLICE SIREN getting louder and louder, LIGHT STROBING behind him —

DISSOLVE TO:

MURRAY (O.S.)
  In the beginning there was nothing.

2 EXT. GOLF COURSE — MORNING — SKY 2

Fleecy clouds in a BLUE SKY. The TITLE appears —

SUNSHINE STATE

We FOLLOW as a GOLF BALL is set on a WOODEN TEE

FOURSOME

MURRAY SILVER, a real estate developer in his early sixties, steps up to address the ball with his driver. Behind him are the other members of the usual foursome—JEFFERSON CASH, BUSTER BIDWELL and SILENT SAM. Cash is the youngest, still in his forties. We're on a beautifully landscaped GOLF COURSE set in Florida palmetto and pine—

CASH
  Wilderness.

                    BIDWELL

Worse than wilderness.

                    MURRAY

Endless, raw acreage, all of it infested with
crocodiles—

                  SILENT SAM

Alligators.

                    MURRAY

Crocodiles, alligators— if you're talking
retirement bungalows it's not a selling
point. Mosquitos that would strip you to the
bone.

                     CASH

It was swamp land—

                    MURRAY

Swamp land they were asking ten cents an acre,
this was worse. The old name, in Seminole,
means "You shouldn't go there."

                    BIDWELL

But we bought it.

                    MURRAY

We bought it because we knew— <u>knew</u>— that you
don't sell land. I mean what is land— a patch
of dirt, a tree maybe— who cares?

                  SILENT SAM

Farmers care.

Murray hits his drive. They watch it down the fairway—

                    MURRAY

Farmers are only in the TV ads. People with
tractors, amber waves of grain— they shoot it
all in Canada. No, this is certified, public
accountants from Toledo with a fixed pension
and a little nest egg who don't want to spend
the golden years trekking through slush. A
<u>dream</u> is what you sell, a <u>con</u>cept. You sell

sunshine, you sell orange groves, you sell
gentle breezes wafting through the palm trees—

Sam steps up to tee his ball—

                         CASH
    There were palm trees?

                       BIDWELL
    In the brochures there were palm trees.

                      SILENT SAM
    Stately ones.

                         CASH
    And when they came down and saw it?

                        MURRAY
    As long as the dredge stayed three lots ahead
    of the buyers, we were in like Flynn.

Sam hits his drive—

                        MURRAY
    Remember, this was the end of the earth, this
    was a land populated by white people who ate
    <u>cat</u>fish, and almost overnight, out of the
    muck and the mangroves we created—
    (he indicates their surroundings)
    —<u>this</u>.

                         CASH
    Golf courses.

                        MURRAY
    Nature on a leash.

We TILT off his face, SKY filling the frame—

3 EXT. SEA-VUE DINER — MORNING — OVERHEAD VIEW

We CONTINUE the TILT through SKY till we look down on a strip of BUILDINGS set along an Atlantic BEACHFRONT —

GROUND LEVEL

The SEA-VUE RESTAURANT sits across from a MOTEL of the same name, right on the BEACH in an area with a mixture of business and residential buildings. The strip has a bit of a fifties feel to it. A SOUND TRUCK passes, LOUDSPEAKER blaring—

> **LOUDSPEAKER**
> "Ahoy there! It's that time of year again—the Delrona Beach Chamber of Commerce invites you to join us for the annual Buccaneer Days festivities! Attend our inaugural gala tonight at the Plantation Island Marina— live music and plenty of free booty for the little ones! Maps for the Buccaneer Days Treasure Hunt can be obtained at the—"

CLOSER — PARKING LOT

DESIREE and REGINALD PERRY step out of their rental car, stretching. Reggie checks out the restaurant, a bit hesitant—

> **REGGIE**
> You sure this place is okay?

> **DESIREE**
> What do you mean "okay"?

> **REGGIE**
> Black people go in here?

> **DESIREE**
> If they're desperate to pee they do. Stay out here if you want.

> **REGGIE**
> Your mother—

                    DESIREE
        I need to go before we get there, Reggie.

Desiree is already heading for the diner—
                    REGGIE
        Hey, relax—

4 INT. RESTAURANT — TREASURE CHEST

Gold-foil-wrapped CHOCOLATE DOUBLOONS tumble into a
TREASURE CHEST—

WIDER

MARLY TEMPLE, an unhappy woman in her late thirties, dumps
out a mesh sack of chocolate coins by the cash register.
The diner is decorated with a pirate motif—
                    MARLY
        Krissy— you want to take the register? I got
        to get back to the motel.
                    KRISSY
        (calling) Your husband called.
                    MARLY
        Ex.
                    KRISSY
        He called. Says he needs to see you.
                    MARLY
        He calls again you tell him to take a long
        walk off a short pier.

She turns as the Perrys come in—
                    MARLY
        You folks like a table or a booth?

                    DESIREE
        Could I use your bathroom?

                    MARLY
        (points) Back there and to the right—

                    DESIREE
        Thank you.

Desiree hurries back toward the rest rooms. Marly watches
her for a moment, curious, then sees something out the
window—

                    MARLY
        Buzzards—

POV — MEN

A group of MEN, mostly in sports jacket sets and ties,
stand at the edge of the road, one of them pointing at
the motel—

MARLY, REGGIE

                    MARLY
        Excuse me—

We HOLD on Reggie, still a bit uncomfortable as he checks
out the diner. KRISSY, a waitress, approaches to take over
at the cashier desk—

                    KRISSY
        Hey there. You been taken care of?

5 EXT. MOTEL

The men break up and head for their cars. Only JACK

SILVER CITY and other Screenplays

MEADOWS, dressed more casually, stays behind. He stares
at the motel—

                    MARLY (O.S.)
Need a room?

He is surprised to find Marly standing beside him —
                    JACK
Pardon?

                    MARLY
You been gawpin at the motel. We got a few
vacancies but it's gonna fill up with this
Buccaneer business.

                    JACK
Oh— no, I was just— looking the property over.

                    MARLY
The property.

                    JACK
The whole strip here, actually.

                    MARLY
If you're from the county, I had our sign
moved back—

                    JACK
Actually I was trying to imagine what this
area would look like without any buildings.

                    MARLY
Kind of mentally undressing it.

                    JACK
You could say that.

                    MARLY
You work for that Plantation outfit?

                    JACK
(hesitant) Actually, yes— I'm supervising the
expansion over at—

                    MARLY
They don't have enough of this coast already?

                    JACK
This is just a feasibility study— a what-if
kind of thing.

                    MARLY
What if I told you my daddy wouldn't sell to
Plantation Estates if they had his nuts in a
trash compacter?

                    JACK
(grins) I'd be happy to pass the message on
to Acquisitions.

He offers his hand—

                    JACK
I'm Jack Meadows—

Marly doesn't take it—

                    MARLY
You're a developer.

                    JACK
Just a landscape architect. Help them decide
what they want, move the dirt around.

                    MARLY
Uh-huh—

                    JACK
They wanted my opinion on the—this whole
shoreline here—

                    MARLY
So— how's it look?

                    JACK
What?

                    MARLY
(indicates motel and diner) Without anything
on it?

Jack is not sure if Marly is flirting or making fun of him. He holds her eyes for a moment—

> **JACK**
> Looks terrific

6 EXT. DELRONA BEACH STRIP — MORNING — BINOCULAR POV

We PAN from Marly and Jack to the Sea-Vue SIGN, looking THROUGH BINOCULARS—

> **LESTER (O.S.)**
> HQ says that's where we establish our beach-head, then spread out and take the rest of it.

CU MAP

A MAP of the triangular island with sectors marked and arrows sweeping in from the ocean. It looks like the plan for the Normandy invasion. A PENCIL appears to indicate various routes of attack —

> **LESTER (O.S.)**
> The other side have this whole end of the island locked up, and they're infiltrating into Lincoln Beach over here—

> **GREG (O.S.)**
> We're not opposing?

> **LESTER (O.S.)**
> Zoned residential, hostile native population—it's a minefield. Whereas right here—
>   (indicates beach strip with pencil)
> —is the soft underbelly of the island.

WIDER — AGENTS

A pair of real estate agents, LESTER and GREG, stand out on

a PIER, their backs to the ocean, Greg looking at the Sea-
Vue Motel through binoculars while Lester wields the map.
Greg is much younger—

> **GREG**
>
> A key property.

> **LESTER**
>
> Point of weakest defense. You make the
> frontal assault, I go behind the lines.

> **GREG**
>
> Somebody on the inside?

> **LESTER**
>
> I'm working on it

7 INT. PARK — JOGGING TRAIL — MORNING

EARL PINKNEY, a bank clerk in his fifties, jogs slowly on
a beautiful PARK TRAIL. He looks back over his shoulder,
sees that he is alone, slows to a halt at a spot he's
checked out before. He pulls a length of rope from the
pouch of his hooded sweatshirt, tosses it up—

ROPE

We FOLLOW the rope up and over a tree branch. As it swings
down we see that the end has been tied in a NOOSE—

EARL

Earl ties the free end to another tree, leaving the
noose dangling three feet over his head. He steps on a
fallen log, reaches and grabs the noose, tightens it
around his neck. He takes a deep breath, closes his
eyes—

FEET

Earl's feet as he jumps off the log, swinging for a moment, then *CRACK! FLUMP!* Earl falls into the frame, the broken branch falling on top of him—

> **EARL**
> Shit.

> **YORDAN (V.O.)**
> Shock and outrage this morning—

8 EXT. PARK — MORNING

DICK YORDAN, a TV reporter, stands facing a CAMERAMAN, the blackened remains of the PIRATE SHIP FLOAT scuttled on its flatbed behind him—

> **YORDAN**
> —as Delrona Beach residents woke to discover
> an act of senseless vandalism—

CLOSER — SHIP

In daylight we can see its proportions — no more than fifteen feet long—

> **FRANCINE (O.S.)**
> This is a disaster. It's always the lead
> float in the parade.

REVERSE

FRANCINE PINCKNEY, the Delrona Beach Chamber of Commerce resident sparkplug, stands with OFFICER BRYCE of the Wakahatchee County Sheriff's Department while a bored PARK EMPLOYEE waits by a pickup truck. We can see Yordan and the Cameraman on the other side of the float—

OFFICER BRYCE

Same kid set another fire a couple years
back. Abandoned crab shack in Lincoln Beach—

FRANCINE

(very upset) This is so not in the spirit of
the celebration.

PARK EMPLOYEE

Where you want me to haul it?

9 EXT. HOUSE — LINCOLN BEACH NEIGHBORHOOD — DR. LLOYD

DR. LLOYD, an African-American man in his late sixties,
stands knocking on the door of a house in a pleasant-
looking but somewhat deserted BEACH NEIGHBORHOOD. In the
BG we can see a POLICE CAR parked in front of another
beachfront house. MRS. PIERCE answers the door in her
bathrobe—

MRS. PIERCE

Dr. Lloyd—

DR. LLOYD

Good morning, Mrs. Pierce, sorry to bother
you—

MRS. PIERCE

Oh, you're always welcome.

DR. LLOYD

I'm trying to round up some folks for this
County Commission meeting tonight? I know
it's very short notice, but they—

MRS. PIERCE

I'd like to help, but I've been feeling
poorly— oh, my, will you look at that?

Two POLICE OFFICERS step out from the house in the BG and
get into their patrol car—

MRS. PIERCE

It's that boy poor Mrs. Stokes took in.

DR. LLOYD

He's in trouble again?

MRS. PIERCE

First her girl went wild and run off to God
knows where and now this. Some people—

She shakes her head as the patrol car pulls away. Desiree
and Reggie's rental car passes in the opposite direction—

DR. LLOYD

What I'm worried about is them sneaking this
public domain business through without us
making a showing. If we could field even a
dozen residents—

MRS. PIERCE

I thought all that was settled when they took
the cemetery.

DR. LLOYD

I'm afraid it won't stop there—

Mrs. Pierce sees the rental car stop in front of the same
house—

MRS. PIERCE

Now who's this coming to call?

EUNICE'S HOUSE

Reggie and Desiree walk from their car toward the house—

REGGIE

Seems kind of deserted.

DESIREE

(distracted) More people come on the week-
ends.

They reach the door of a well-kept HOUSE. Desiree braces herself—

> **DESIREE**
> Do I look okay?

> **REGGIE**
> Relax. This is gonna be fine.

> **DESIREE**
> You don't know her.

Desiree knocks on the door. They wait. Finally the door opens and there stands Terrell, looking very bummed out—

> **DESIREE**
> Hi—

Terrell just looks at them—

> **DESIREE**
> Is uhm— Mrs. Stokes here?

Terrell turns and goes back inside. Reggie looks to Desiree, who shakes her head. Who was that?

> **DESIREE**
> I have no idea.

They wait another moment, and then EUNICE STOKES, in her sixties, appears at the door. She is smiling tightly, wiping tears from her eyes with a handkerchief—

> **EUNICE**
> Well, well— Desiree. Never thought I'd live
> to see you back here.

> **DESIREE**
> (reserved) Hello, Mama.

Eunice gives Reggie a once-over—

> ### EUNICE
> My Lord, you did get a handsome one, didn't
> you?

10 INT. TEMPLE HOUSE — DAY

A CU of FURMAN TEMPLE, eyes sightless from advanced diabetes—

> ### FURMAN
> My days, life was simpler. You knew where you
> stood. A man was left to make his own way in
> the world— you didn't have none of these
> pressure groups and advocate groups and spe-
> cial innerest groups handicappin the race.

We SLOWLY PULL BACK —

> ### FURMAN
> It went to the swiftest and the smartest and
> the strongest. So if you could carve yourself
> out a little piece of something you known that
> you _earned_ it. The hoopin crane, the spotted
> owl, the Florida gator, the colored man, the
> white man, the Spanish— they all started from
> scratch and if you couldn't survive the course
> that was just tough titty. Nowdays, what they
> got, it's not natural. We been zoned and reg-
> ulated and politically corrected and vironmen-
> tally sensitized to the point where it's only
> your multi-internationals with a dozen lawyers
> sittin round waitin like buzzards for something
> to _liti_gate that can afford to put one brick
> on top of another. The little man, no matter
> how much grit or imagination he brings to it,
> they got him so tied down he can't nearly
> breathe. You smoke a damn cigarette they make
> you feel like a baby strangler. Where it's all

JOHN SAYLES

headed I don't want to know, but if they expect
my cooperation they just shit outa luck. Only
reason I hang on to this poor wreck of a body
is to spite the sonsabitches. They made me put
in to that Social Security mess for some fifty
years and I'm not givin up the ghost till I use
up every damn penny of it.

He tilts his head and we WIDEN further to see a young
NURSE prepping a SYRINGE for an injection. A pair of GREY-
HOUNDS nap near his feet—

                    FURMAN
          Which one are you?

                    GWEN
          Gwendolyn.

                    FURMAN
          You think I'm full of crap, don't you?

                    GWEN
          It's time for your insulin, Mr. Temple.

11 EXT. BUILDING SITE — DAY — STAKE

A wooden STAKE is pounded into hard ground—

WIDER

We're in a flat, scrubby wasteland. DUB, the site foreman,
pounds the stake in with some effort as nearby a pair of
earth-movers, LYLE SHIFLETT and BILLY TRUCKS (commonly
known as "Chief"), prep a SCRAPER and a FRONT-LOADER for
action. Shiflett chews tobacco. We see Jack and a couple
of SUITS in the BG, looking at landscaping PLANS—

                    DUB
          Good luck moving this shit. There's three
          inches of soil then it's solid limestone.

SHIFLETT

More work, more pay.

(sees)

What you think you're doing?

We PAN to see another worker, QUARLES, wrapping a strip of red cloth around the bole of a TREE—

QUARLES

They want this one saved.

SHIFLETT

Zat right?

(to Billy)

Whatta you think, Chief? That thing gonna make it?

QUARLES

Mr. Meadows say it's part of the design concept.

SHIFLETT

Chief's concept of design is he gets up on his machine an everything that didn't flat gets that way. Fast.

QUARLES

(serious) Plantation already sold this lot with a tree on it. When they pack your cracker asses back to Georgia there better goddam still be one.

SHIFLETT

No point savin any of this scrub—

QUARLES

Used to be this was all Exley family. Sea-isle cotton.

BILLY

(looking around) Hasn't nothin been planted here for a hundred years.

TODD NORTHRUP, a nervous PR man in his forties, leads a trio of prospective BUYERS past with Jack bringing up the rear —

>   NORTHRUP
> It doesn't look like much now, but when Jack gets finished—

>   BUYER
> What goes here?

>   JACK
> Where you're standing? That's our main drainage basin—

>   NORTHRUP
> (quickly) A lake.

>   BUYER
> A lake?

>   JACK
> It will go down fourteen feet at its deepest. And what we dig out will form a hill over here—

>   NORTHRUP
> With one of our deluxe homes on top of it.

>   BUYER
> Deluxe?

>   NORTHRUP
> With the maximum amenities. The lake, an ocean view—

>   JACK
> The elevation—

One of the buyers swats a mosquito—

>   BUYER 2
> These bugs gonna be here, too?

12 INT. EUNICE HOME — DINING ROOM — NIGHT

Reggie and Desiree sit with Terrell and Mrs. Stokes at
the dinner table. Everybody is a bit uncomfortable—

> **DESIREE**
> Anesthesiologist.

> **REGGIE**
> It's a specialty. If there's a surgical pro-
> cedure, I'm the one who renders the patient
> unconscious—

> **EUNICE**
> You knock people out with gas.

> **REGGIE**
> That's pretty much it.

> **EUNICE**
> I'd be afraid not to wake up.

> **REGGIE**
> A lot of people feel that way.

> **DESIREE**
> Reggie's the head of his department.

> **EUNICE**
> Is that right? And at such a prestigious hos-
> pital. I'll have to tell that to Dr. Lloyd.

> **DESIREE**
> Dr. Lloyd still coming down?

> **EUNICE**
> He lives here now. His Etta Mae passed some
> years ago—

> **DESIREE**
> Awww—

> **EUNICE**
> You wouldn't have heard that, would you?

She turns to Reggie as if for support—

> **EUNICE**
> She doesn't write, she doesn't call—

                         DESIREE

Mama—

                         EUNICE

Girl caught the first thing smokin and never
looked back.

                         DESIREE

I took the bus, Mama, not the train.

                         EUNICE

It's an expression. Terrell, go run this gravy
through the microwave again. It's gone cold.

Terrell takes the gravy boat and exits. Desiree mouths the
question almost silently—

                         DESIREE

Who is that?

                         EUNICE

Your cousin Sidney Wilkins' son. Sidney that
married Athena Hines?

                         DESIREE

Why isn't he with them?

Eunice just shakes her head—

                         EUNICE

She doesn't write, she doesn't call. I'm surprised she even let on she'd got married. Her
own mother doesn't get invited to the wedding—

                         DESIREE

We had a civil service, Mama. It wasn't in a
church.

Eunice is stopped in her tracks by this—

                         EUNICE

But it's legal—

                         DESIREE

It's legal, official, all that. Don't worry.

SILVER CITY and other Screenplays   185

                         EUNICE
Something they do up there, what is it—?

                         REGGIE
Boston.

                         EUNICE
Somehow I've never been north of Washington D.C.

                         REGGIE
Well, you'll have to come visit us.

Desiree doesn't seem thrilled by the idea—

                         EUNICE
When Terrell's out of school maybe we'll do
that.

Terrell comes back in with the reheated gravy—

                         EUNICE
How bout that, Terrell? You like to see
Boston?

13 INT. AUDITORIUM — NIGHT

CITIZENS have gathered for a meeting, seven COUNTY COM-
MISSIONERS facing them, seated at a table. A huge MAP
of the island with various land tracts marked in red
is mounted behind them. Dick Yordan is there, bored,
with an equally- bored CAMERAMAN. Earl Pinkney, very
much alive, stands indicating on the map with a
pointer—

                         EARL
The proposed boundary for Delrona Beach is
indicated by the red dotted line—with the
inclusion of Lincoln Beach all the way up to
the Exley Plantation tract—

                         DR. LLOYD
Excuse me—

Dr. Lloyd is standing. He has only mustered a half-dozen supporters—

> CHAIRWOMAN
>
> If you'd like to make a motion, Dr. Lloyd, you'll have to wait till Commissioner Pinkney is finished.

> DR. LLOYD
>
> I'd like to register a protest.

> CHAIRWOMAN
>
> (sighs) In regard to what?

> DR. LLOYD
>
> The notice for this meeting was not properly advertised—

> CHAIRWOMAN
>
> We met all the legal requirements—

> DR. LLOYD
>
> You purposely chose a date when the majority of our people would be unable—

> CHAIRWOMAN
>
> By 'our' people you mean residents of Lincoln Beach?

> DR. LLOYD
>
> As you know very well, many of us only come up on the weekends—

> EARL
>
> And many are only summer people—

> DR. LLOYD
>
> I don't believe that denies us a right to object to this expropriation—

> CHAIRWOMAN
>
> Incorporation—

> DR. LLOYD
>
> Whatever you want to call it. You've already conspired to take away a third of our original tract—

CHAIRWOMAN

That was a private transaction between Exley Plantation Estates planned community and individual property owners. The county commission only became involved when Plantation submitted their development plan.

DR. LLOYD

(getting hot) If you folks hadn't already approved it under the table they wouldn't have gone ahead—

Todd Northrup wearily raises his hand—

NORTHRUP

As spokesman for the Exley Corporation, I have to object to your implication that—

DR. LLOYD

Your people are all set to start digging up land with an important historical significance to our community—

NORTHRUP

We've made several offers to mitigate—

DR. LLOYD

—a history that has been consistently ignored by this commission!

Dr. Lloyd points at Northrup, addressing the commissioners—

DR. LLOYD (getting hot)

You let them take our cemetery—

EARL

We're talking about very old business, Dr. Lloyd. If you have a problem with the current agenda—

DR. LLOYD

We don't want to be part of the town of Delrona Beach, and they've made it very

clear over the years they don't want anything to do with us! If the beachfront
prices hadn't skyrocketed, they wouldn't be
so interested in—

                    EARL
The concept of eminent domain is—

                  DR. LLOYD
Is a weapon you people use to—

                  CHAIRWOMAN
Gentlemen, gentlemen— if we're going to have a
debate I have to ask you to follow procedure—

14 EXT. MOTEL — LATE EVENING

The LIGHT in the Sea-Vue SIGN comes on. TRAFFIC passes the
motel. A converted FLATBED TRUCK, crudely-painted hype about
a man-eating alligator on its sides, pulls into the lot—

15 INT. MOTEL ROOM

Marly is putting her clothes back on. SCOTTY DUVAL, good-
looking, late twenties, still lies under the bed sheets,
lost in thought

                    SCOTTY
I'm thinking of going out there again.

                    MARLY
Out where?

                    SCOTTY
The Tour.

                    MARLY
Golfing.

                    SCOTTY
There's a kind of syndicate— couple dentists,
fella who owns the Buick dealership— they want
to sponsor me. For a percentage of my winnings.

                    MARLY

How much can you make?

                    SCOTTY

First you have to qualify, then it depends on
where you stand at the end of each tournament.

                    MARLY

You did this before?

                    SCOTTY

I tried a couple years back. I was fine till
I got on the green. Then—
(he shrugs)
Little case of the yips.

Marly looks at him—

                    SCOTTY

It's an adrenaline thing. You're in the back-
swing of your putt and you like tighten and—

                    MARLY

Yip!

                    SCOTTY

Something like that.

                    MARLY

You had them bad?

                    SCOTTY

Your margin of error is so small, anything can—

                    MARLY

So this is like choking— like the baseball
guy who suddenly couldn't throw from second
to first—

                    SCOTTY

Killer drive, beautiful approach shot, and then
I couldn't get the damn thing in the hole.

                    MARLY

That would seriously cut into your winnings,
wouldn't it?

Scotty doesn't answer—

> MARLY
>
> And it's better now?

> SCOTTY
>
> I won't know till I get out there.
> (shrugs)
> I could always sink them in practice.

A silence. Marly sits on the edge of the bed, thinking—

> MARLY
>
> You'll be travelling a lot.

> SCOTTY
>
> That's the life.

> MARLY
>
> Are there like— groupies?

> SCOTTY
>
> I suppose. If you win.

Marly crosses to the window, peeks out. She's waiting for him to ask her to come along. He doesn't—

> MARLY
>
> I never could understand wanting to watch it.
> It's like those fishing shows on TV—

> SCOTTY
>
> Yeah.

> MARLY
>
> Does that make you feel bad?

> SCOTTY
>
> Hey— I don't go watch people wait on tables
> or run the check-in desk.

Marly is stung but tries not to show it—

> MARLY
>
> (quiet) Right, you don't.

Another silence. They don't really have much more to say to each other—

MARLY
(softly) Yip.

16 INT. AUDITORIUM — NIGHT

The county commission meeting is breaking up. Northrup has buttonholed Yordan as his Cameraman packs up. We can see Dr. Lloyd and Earl Pinkney in a heated exchange in the BG—

YORDAN
If they picket the ground-breaking that's news and I've got to cover it.

NORTHRUP
It's only news if you bring that TV camera. You just ignore these people and they'll go away.

YORDAN
What am I supposed to do?

NORTHRUP
It's not an official ceremony, there's no ribbon-cutting or anything— It'll be totally boring, I promise.

YORDAN
I still have to show up.

NORTHRUP
How about this— if he's got less than twenty people you don't turn the camera on.

YORDAN
Less than ten.

Northrup shakes his hand—

NORTHRUP
Deal.

They shake—

YORDAN

Unless somebody gets arrested.

17 BEDROOM — NIGHT

Reggie and Desiree unpack their bags in a small bedroom. The walls are covered with POSTERS of macho-posing male rap stars and muscle-bound cartoon superheroes—

DESIREE

This is too weird.

REGGIE

Is it what you remember?

DESIREE

It's my room, yeah. But that boy's been living in here.

Reggie nods, looks around at the posters. A little intimidating—

REGGIE

Yeah, we got some serious testosterone working here. He's what exactly—?

DESIREE

His father was a cousin of mine. Grew up kind of wild.

REGGIE

And he's living here cause—?

DESIREE

She wants me to drive them downtown for some kind of hearing tomorrow—

REGGIE

He's in trouble?

DESIREE

(frustrated) She's not gonna give up any information. Punish me a bit.

Reggie

For being gone so long.

DESIREE

For everything.

REGGIE

Hey, she's the one who asked you to come down. Made the first move—

DESIREE

(shakes her head) It's too weird.

Reggie listens for a moment —

REGGIE

You can hear the ocean.

DESIRES

Yeah. I always loved that.

18 EXT. PORCH — NIGHT

Terrell sits watching the sea. He absently lights a MATCH from a book of matches. He looks at the FLAME for a moment, then lights the whole BOOK, shifting it in his fingers so as not to burn himself—

FADE OUT:

19 EXT. DOWNTOWN STREET — MORNING

Earl Pinkney stands in front of the BANK as the SECURITY GUARD unlocks the door. He watches—

EARL'S POV

A crew of VOLUNTEERS wearing matching T-SHIRTS with a picture of a snarling PIRATE printed on the front and "BUCCANEER DAYS — Delrona Beach" on the back set up scaffolding for a platform while others stretch a huge banner advertising the event over the street. The Perry's RENTAL CAR crawls past the workers—

20 INT. CAR

Desiree drives, her mother in the passenger seat and Terrell in the back—

>   **DESIREE**
>   They fixed up all the facades—

>   **EUNICE**
>   Nobody but tourists shop here now.

>   **DESIREE**
>   Where do the regular people go?

>   **EUNICE**
>   There's a shuttle bus comes by, leaves you at
>   the mall.
>   (points)
>   It's just up ahead here.

21 EXT. STREET — MORNING

Desiree pulls to the curb. Eunice and Terrell get out of the car.

>   **EUNICE**
>   This won't take but an hour or so.

>   **DESIREE**
>   You hope.

REVERSE

Eunice is heading into the County Courthouse—

>   **EUNICE**
>   Terrell just needs to talk with somebody.
>   We'll call you back home when it's over—

22 EXT. BEACH — MORNING

Reggie crosses from Eunice's yard to the beach, his shoes
still on, and begins to walk parallel to the shore—

> **DR. LLOYD (O.S.)**
> Prettiest beach on the Atlantic Coast.

Reggie turns to see Dr. Lloyd gaining on him, a wad of
flyers in hand—

> **REGGIE**
> Yeah, it is pretty.

Dr. Lloyd hands him a flyer—

> **DR. LLOYD**
> If you'd like to help save it, we're having
> a protest rally Monday, over at the ground-
> breaking.

Reggie glances at the information—

> **REGGIE**
> I'm just visiting—

> **DR. LLOYD**
> Believe me, they won't know the difference.

> **REGGIE**
> This is like an ecological thing?

> **DR. LLOYD**
> We're trying to save an endangered species. Us.

> **REGGIE**
> I heard about this place when I was a kid,
> but I never— I guess it used to be something.

> **DR. LLOYD**
> The forties and fifties, Lincoln Beach was
> it— the only oceanfront in three counties we
> were allowed to step onto. Black folks— I'm

talking about the pillars of the community—got together, bought this land, built the houses. Then it grew on its own. You'd drive through a couple hundred miles of redneck sheriffs, park your ride on the boardwalk, step out, and just <u>breathe</u>.

He points to a cement slab with no building left on it—

                    DR. LLOYD
          Right there was Henry's Lounge. That place
          used to <u>jump</u>.

They turn up a residential street. Pretty quiet these days—

                    REGGIE
          So what happened?
                    DR. LLOYD
          Civil rights happened. Progress. Used to be
          if you were black, you'd <u>buy</u> black. Jim Crow
          days, if you wanted your shoes shined or your
          laundry done or a taxi ride to the train sta-
          tion, you went to your <u>own</u>. You wanted some
          ribs, chicken, fish sandwich— chances are a
          black man owned the place you got it in. Now
          the drive-throughs will serve anybody, but
          who owns them? Not us— our people just
          wearing paper hats and dippin them fries out.
          All we got left now are funeral parlors and
          barber-shops.

                    REGGIE
          But now we can do anything.
                    DR. LLOYD
          Them than can get over do fine. Them that
          can't are in a world of trouble—

23 INT. FAMILY COURT HEARING ROOM — DAY

Terrell sits facing a family court JUDGE, a county PROS-
ECUTOR and a SOCIAL WORKER, Eunice at his side—

EUNICE

Tell the judge what you told me.

TERRELL

(hesitant) I said I'm sorry for what I did.
I wasn't thinking right.

JUDGE

You know that sorry isn't going to cut it in
this case, don't you, Terrell?

TERRELL

Yes, M'am.

JUDGE

You're still on probation for a previous
offense and you deliberately commit this act
of vandalism—

TERRELL

Yes, M'am.

JUDGE

Do you have any explanation for your actions?

TERRELL

No, M'am.

JUDGE

You know that when somebody destroys something that stands as a symbol for a group of
people, that's called "desecration"—

SOCIAL WORKER

It's a wooden pirate, your Honor.

JUDGE

An icon of this community, nonetheless.
You're almost old enough, given your record
and the nature of the crime, to be tried as
an adult—

SOCIAL WORKER

Your Honor—

                        JUDGE
    You've got two strikes against you. A third,
    and—

                     PROSECUTOR
    Your Honor, Mrs. Stokes has assured us that
    she will be able to— maintain control of the
    situation. We'd be satisfied, barring further
    incidents, with an order for some sort of
    counseling, possibly some restitution or com-
    munity service—

                        JUDGE
    That's very generous of you.

The Judge focuses on Terrell—

                        JUDGE
    So, young man— what's it going to be?

24 EXT. LORETTA'S HOUSE — DELRONA BEACH — DAY

Desiree approaches a house in the poorer section of Delrona. She slows as she sees LORETTA, a woman her own age,
hanging wash at the side of the house—

                       DESIREE
    Loretta?

Loretta looks over her wash. It takes her a moment to
register—

                       LORETTA
    Well. Look at you.

Loretta comes around in front of the clothesline, wiping
her hands, but doesn't come any further—

                       DESIREE
    Mama said you were still in Delrona.

LORETTA

Haven't moved an inch.

They are clearly uncomfortable with each other—

LORETTA

I saw you on a TV commercial. Told my kids I went to school with you but they didn't believe me.

DESIREE

You've got kids.

LORETTA

Three of em. Gettin big. So this is the first you been back since—?

DESIREE

I came for the service when my father passed but I only stayed a day.

LORETTA

That was a good while ago, your father. Pretty slow for you, down here.

DESIREE

(shrugs) You get busy— Look, I— I kind of wanted to apologize.

LORETTA

For what?

DESIREE

For Carter.

LORETTA

Girl, that's another life you're talking about. Twenty-five years.

DESIREE

We were best friends. I shouldn't have gone after him when—

LORETTA

But you <u>did</u>. You always did pretty much what you wanted.

                    DESIREE

I didn't do it to hurt you. I just—

                    LORETTA

Ancient history.

An awkward pause—

                    DESIREE

Carter still in town?

                    LORETTA

He's inside sleeping. Works nights at the box
factory.

                    DESIREE

(smiles) You got married.

                    LORETTA

After awhile, yeah. You know, when you left—

                    DESIREE.

When I was sent away—

                    LORETTA

—everybody thought it was Carter got you
pregnant.

                    DESIREE

It wasn't.

                    LORETTA

That's what he says too, nowadays.

                    DESIREE

It wasn't him. I guess I didn't worry too
much about the rumors—

                    LORETTA

Made your big exit and never looked back.

                    DESIREE

Some drama, huh?

                    LORETTA

We ate that shit up. Course I had to listen
to everybody run you down, being the tragic

---

ex-girlfriend. Like that was gonna make me
feel better.

                    DESIREE
And Carter—

                    LORETTA
Carter went around actin the daddy.

                    DESIREE
Really?

                    LORETTA
Better you knock your girl up than have
people think someone <u>else</u> did it behind your
back.

Desiree nods. She tries to sound cheerful—

                    DESIREE
But it all turned out fine, didn't it?

Loretta looks around at her surroundings—

                    LORETTA
I suppose I could've done worse.

25 EXT. LINCOLN BEACH

                    DR. LLOYD
So you're the one finally snagged Desiree Stokes.

                    REGGIE
I'm the one—

                    DR. LLOYD
(smiles) That girl drew men like <u>flies</u>.

                    REGGIE
I can imagine.

Dr. Lloyd offers his hand—

          DR. LLOYD (offers his hand)
I'm Elton Lloyd.

                        REGGIE
Reginald Perry. We're staying at her mother's
for a few days.

                       DR. LLOYD
Wonderful woman, Eunice. A true Christian.

                        REGGIE
Her— nephew is it—?

                       DR. LLOYD
Her nephew's son. Young Terrell.

Dr. Lloyd shakes his head, mood growing somber—

                       DR. LLOYD
I blame it on the drugs. It's a pestilence.

                        REGGIE
Something happened with his—?

                       DR. LLOYD
Eunice didn't tell you?

                        REGGIE
She and Desiree haven't been—

                       DR. LLOYD
(smiles) If you need to ask you don't deserve
to know.

                        REGGIE
That seems to be the attitude.

                       DR. LLOYD
Terrell's father was going through a rough
stretch, he'd separated from his wife— He
came over one day, high on who knows what,
they had a screaming argument— and he had a
weapon.

They stop walking, look out over the ocean. Reggie knows
what's coming next—

                       DR. LLOYD
Shot that woman dead and then turned the gun

SILVER CITY and other Screenplays   203

on himself. Horrible thing to witness. Terrell
must've been six, maybe seven.

> **REGGIE**
> He saw it?

> **DR. LLOYD**
> He sat with the bodies two days before some-
> body came over and found him. A pestilence.

A shiny new CONVERTIBLE cruises up alongside them, LEOTIS
"FLASH" PHILLIPS leaning out of it—

> **FLASH**
> Afternoon, gentlemen. Y'all know where
> Buster's Place is?

> **DR. LLOYD**
> Buster's Place is long gone, brother. Nothing
> left there.

Flash stops the car, looks around, seeming disoriented.
Dr. Lloyd stops as well, recognizing—

> **FLASH**
> You sure?

> **DR. LLOYD**
> I know you.

> **FLASH**
> I don't think so—

> **DR. LLOYD**
> (smiles) Sure I do. You used to be the Florida
> Flash.

26 INT. MOTEL OFFICE

Greg dogs Marly as she goes through some paperwork at the
registration desk—

GREG

What I'm trying to say is there's an opening
here that might close up pretty quick—

MARLY

My father's the owner.

GREG

I understand he's currently— indisposed.

MARLY

He's legally blind if that's what you mean.

GREG

You know, some of the black folks down in
Lincoln Beach have contacted the historical
register people—

MARLY

That's their business.

GREG

What happens, you draw that kind of attention, the environmentalists come right on
their heels.

MARLY

Yeah, they're pesky little buggers.

GREG

Once they target an area— well, you certainly
won't be able to sell your property for what
it's worth.

Marly looks up from her ledgers —

MARLY

What's it worth?

GREG

Not a great deal at the moment. And since the
Exley Plantation and all these resort condos
have come in, your taxes have jumped thirty
percent. You small business folks are being
squeezed—

Marly stands to exit—

> MARLY

Tell me about it.

27 EXT. MOTEL GROUNDS

Greg follows Marly past the various units—

> GREG

We realize this is a big decision for you. One of the oldest businesses left on the beach, family goes back generations in the area—

> MARLY

So you're not from the Plantation? There were some men here yesterday—

> GREG

(alarmed to hear this) Did they make you an offer?

> MARLY

—Just sniffing around, I think.

> GREG

Those people are relentless.

> MARLY

And you're not?

> GREG

Well— Exley Plantation is only for the elite. Whereas what we have in mind is a much more— democratic kind of development. Something for everybody.

> MARLY

Convenience stores, burger chains, T-shirts—

> GREG

Retail outlets, yes, that would be a part of it—

The day manager, ROSELLEN, passes—

                    MARLY

   103 empty?

                  ROSELLEN

   Should be. Your husband called. Needs to talk
   to you.

                    MARLY

   I don't need to talk to him.

She opens the door to a unit with her master key—

                    MARLY

   You want to develop anything on this island
   you can forget about it without the county
   commission in your pocket.

                    GREG

   (quiet smile) Oh— I'm sure we can work something out.

28 INT. BANK — DAY

Earl Pinkney crosses the LOBBY of a BANK, walking a bit
stiffly, beads of sweat on his forehead. STEVE TREGASKIS,
a bearded man in his mid-thirties, enters, waves to him—

                    STEVE

   Earl—

For some reason Steve is dressed as a PIRATE—

                    EARL

   Hey, Steve. I'll be right with you.

                    STEVE

   I got those signatures—

                    EARL

   Just give me a minute.

29 INT. BATHROOM

Earl shuts himself in a TOILET STALL, immediately peels off his jacket and hangs it on the door hook. He unbuttons his shirt—an Ace BANDAGE is wrapped around his middle, a couple thick BUNDLES of new hundred-dollar BILLS starting to slip out. He tucks them back in, tightens the bandage. We hear an AMPLIFIED VOICE from outside —

> **FRANCINE (O.S., microphone)**
> Testing—testing—

30 EXT. DOWNTOWN STREET

Francine stands on the platform-in-progress testing the PA system —

> **FRANCINE (microphone)**
> Testing one, two, three— Good afternoon and welcome— to Delrona Beach's annual Buccaneer Days!

The Volunteer workers don't look up from their tasks—

31 EXT. THEATER — PARKING LOT — DAY

Desiree, Eunice and Terrell stand by the rental car staring at the exterior of a little COMMUNITY THEATER BUILDING. Desiree looks anxious, Terrell looks catatonic—

> **EUNICE**
> She'll be happy to see you.
> **DESIREE**
> No she won't.
> **EUNICE**
> Well you can ask anyway.

Desiree looks at Terrell, then back to her mother—

DESIREE

Wait for me here.

32 INT. THEATER — STAGE — MISS DELIA

DELIA TEMPLE, in her sixties, orates in front of a wooden
WAGON. She is precise and passionate—

MISS DELIA

"In the afternoon when school was out and the
last one had left with his little dirty snuf-
fling nose, instead of going home I would go
down the hill to the spring where I could be
quiet and hate them. It would be quiet there
then, with the water bubbling up and away and
the sun slanting quiet in the trees and the
quiet smelling of damp and rotting leaves and
new earth—"

DESIREE

Desiree enters the tiny theater from the back, sits,
smiling as she watches Miss Delia act—

MISS DELIA (O.S.)

"—especially in the early spring, for it was
worst then. I could just remember my father used
to say—"

STAGE

Four adolescent and teenage BOYS and one GIRL of various
shapes, sizes and races stand in a frozen tableau around
the wagon behind Miss Delia—

MISS DELIA

"—that the reason for living was to get ready
to stay dead a good long time."

Miss Delia walks among the frozen figures, regarding them with distant sadness—

> **MISS DELIA**
> "And when I would have to look at them day after day, each with his and her secret and selfish thought, and blood strange to each other and strange to mine, and to think that this seemed the only way I could get ready to stay dead, I would hate my father for planting me."

She BREAKS CHARACTER and the others UNFREEZE—

> **MISS DELIA**
> And then I go on from there. Now the important thing is to freeze yourself in an interesting but reasonably comfortable position. Jaime, you were about to fall over.

She turns and sees Desiree—

> **MISS DELIA**
> We will resume with the first act tomorrow. Kim Li, you should be off book by then. Thank you all very much for your work today.

The young actors say goodbye and drift off, happy to be released. Desiree comes up to meet Miss Delia on the edge of the stage—

> **MISS DELIA**
> It _is_ you, isn't it?

> **DESIREE**
> Hello, Miss Delia.

They hug. Miss Delia is very Southern, very emotional—

                              MISS DELIA
           Desiree. It is so wonderful to see you!

                               DESIREE
           My mama told me you were still running this.

                              MISS DELIA
           They'll have to drag me off the stage. Several
           members of the local press have suggested that
           very thing.

           She indicates the departing kids—

                              MISS DELIA
           This is my special group— young people who
           are having some difficulties? The school
           sends them over.

                               DESIREE
           What's the play?

                              MISS DELTA
           As I Lay Dying? Rather loosely adapted, but
           I don't believe Mr. Faulkner would object.

                               DESIREE
           Must blow their minds in town.

                              MISS DELIA
           Most of the year we feed them your standard
           comedies. They forgive me my pretensions.

           Miss Delia indicates the stage—

                              MISS DELIA
           Scene of your many triumphs.

                               DESIREE
           I let you down.

                              MISS DELIA
           Whatever do you mean?

                               DESIREE
           When I left. I was the lead—

MISS DELIA

Oh— we did have to make a few adjustments, but the show must go on.

DESIREE

You played it?

MISS DELIA

Having a Queen of Egypt so considerably older than her Anthony was very— pro_voc_ative.

DESIREE

I got to do it once when I got to New York. In the park. I played the handmaiden who gives her the asp— Charmian—

MISS DELIA

I'm sure you were wonderful. And now—I trust you're still sharing your talent with the public?

DESIREE

I— I do industrials. Representing things—

Desiree is embarrassed—

DESIREE

I do lots of auto shows.

MISS DELIA

A temporary engagement in the world of commerce. You're still so young—

DESIREE

(shakes her head) I had my chance, Miss Delia. It just didn't happen.

MISS DELIA

Well— I must say that my youthful aspirations had nothing to do with becoming the Sarah Bernhardt of Delrona Beach. We— ad_just_, don't we?

DESIREE

Yeah.

                    MISS DELIA
You would have been stunning as Cleopatra.

                     DESIREE
I was starting to show.

Miss Delia smiles at a memory—

                    MISS DELIA
I played Juliet when I was pregnant with my
twins.

(sees)

Why hello, there. Come on in—

We PAN to see Eunice and Terrell standing uncomfortably
at the back of the house—

                     DESIREE
I uhm— you remember my mother?

                     EUNICE
Mrs. Temple—

                    MISS DELIA
So nice to see you.

                     DESIREE
And this is my— this is Terrell. Terrell is
uhm— it's sort of a favor

                    MISS DELIA
Whatever I can do.

                     DESIREE
The social worker over at the courthouse
recommended you as a— since you've got this
special program—

                     EUNICE
For community service—

                    MISS DELIA
(bales them out) I can always use another
volunteer. Do you have any acting experience,
Terrell?

                              TERRELL
No, M'am.

                              EUNICE
He knows how to use tools. Anything you can
think of, Terrell can put it together.

                            MISS DELIA
(smiles) Well then— you could do me a great
service, Terrell. My character, Addie Bun-
dren, is deceased? In the second act I arise
from the dead to deliver my soliloquy, but
the local funeral parlor doesn't have anything suitably— rustic.

Terrell has no idea what she's talking about—

                            MISS DELIA
Do you think you could build me a coffin?

33 EXT. DOWNTOWN — CEREMONY — DAY

A CROWD has gathered to watch a Buccaneer Days ceremony
focussed on a PLATFORM built to resemble the deck of a
ship—

                         OFFICER BRYCE
We hereby claim sovereignty over this island
of Playa de Sueños—

CLOSER

Officer Bryce, dressed as a Spanish SEA CAPTAIN, stands
reading a proclamation as his SAILORS guard Steve Tregaskis, dressed as the pirate CALAVERA, hands bound before
him, balanced on the edge of the prow—

                         OFFICER BRYCE
—in the name of His Majesty Felipe el Segundo
of Spain!

EARL

Earl watches morosely from the doorway of the bank.
Todd Northrup looks on, grinning, several yards
away—

> **OFFICER BRYCE (O.S.)**
> Furthermore— this tribunal declares the
> mulatto Calavera—

PLATFORM

Francine waves to Earl from her spot on the platform—

> **OFFICER BRYCE**
> —otherwise known as Captain Skull, guilty of
> piracy on the high seas, a crime against God
> and Nature—

EARL

Earl waves back halfheartedly—

> **OFFICER BRYCE (O.S.)**
> —and sentence him to be cast into the sea—

PLATFORM

> **OFFICER BRYCE**
> —therefore to perish by drowning. Does the
> condemned wish to make a final statement?

> **STEVE**
> A curse on the lot of you! Up the Jolly Roger!

With that the sailor closest to Steve pokes him in the
back with a cutlass— a SCREAM from the crowd as he leaps
off the prow and SPLASH! lands in a portable swimming pool

below. APPLAUSE. Francine steps forward with a microphone, reading from a sheet of paper—

> FRANC1NE
>
> Thus was the black flag of the buccaneer replaced by that of imperial Spain, one of many reversals of fortune that mark the colorful history of our community. We'd like to thank Presto Pools for the loan of their equipment, and want to remind you—

STEVE

Helped dripping from the pool—

> FRANCINE (O.S.)
>
> —that the annual Buccaneer Days Treasure Hunt will begin tomorrow morning in the Delrona Mall. Entrants should meet at the Piercing Pagoda at ten o'clock—

34 EXT. EUNICE STOKES' HOUSE

Reggie is helping bring in groceries from the rental car—

> REGGIE
>
> Guess who I met while you were gone?

> DESIREE
>
> You're not going around telling everybody I'm back, are you?

> REGGIE
>
> I didn't recognize him without his helmet and pads on. You remember a football player named Flash Phillips?

We HOLD on Desiree's face, not thrilled to hear the name—

35 EXT. LINCOLN BEACH — ABANDONED HOUSE

Flash is poking around outside a boarded-up house that
looks like it's been abandoned for several years. He peeks
through a crack in one of the boards. He makes a mark on
a STREET MAP of Lincoln Beach—

36 EXT. MARINA — STREET FAIR — EVENING

LOCALS and TOURISTS stroll through a gantlet of FOOD
STANDS and GAME BOOTHS, most with some sort of pirate or
Florida theme. Competing MUSIC Plays from many of the
venues—

NORTHRUP AND FRANCINE

Northrup and Francine Pinkney walk through the scene, com-
miserating—

> **NORTHRUP**
> It's like every step we take is on someone
> else's toes—

> **FRANCINE**
> The town expects me to work miracles with a
> handful of volunteers—

> **NORTHRUP**
> Now there's a bunch from Lincoln Beach say
> they're going to picket our ground-breaking
> on the expansion next week—

> **FRANCINE**
> They burn the ship, they complain about
> parking—

> **NORTHRUP**
> The whole point of the Plantation is to be
> away from that sort of thing.

> **FRANCINE**
>
> And this afternoon— it was embarrassing.

Northrup finally falls into synch with Francine's line of thought—

> **NORTHRUP**
>
> Hey, no— I thought it went fine. For a— you know— chamber of commerce sort of thing.

> **FRANCINE**
>
> Nobody came.

> **NORTHRUP**
>
> It was a terrific turnout.

> **FRANCINE**
>
> Something isn't clicking—

> **NORTHRUP**
>
> I worked this one place, every year we had the blessing of the fleet. The bishop in his hat, the boats all dolled up— what a draw.

> **FRANCINE**
>
> I can't do religious here.

> **NORTHRUP**
>
> True—

> **FRANCINE**
>
> And what's our fleet? A bunch of charter boats and day-sailors—

> **NORTHRUP**
>
> But you've got history to burn.

> **FRANCINE**
>
> People hate history.

> **NORTHRUP**
>
> Indians, pirates, Spanish gold, the plantation thing—

> **FRANCINE**
>
> Mass murder, rape, slavery—

NORTHRUP

Hey— Disnify it a little and they'll come back for more. You just need a hook. One place I worked in Wisconsin, the whole thing was built on wurst.

FRANCINE

Wurst—

NORTHRUP

Weisswurst, bratwurst, knockwurst— Bavarian people. Lots of strudel shops, service people in leather shorts and dirndls—

FRANCINE

And this worked?

NORTHRUP

The beer tasting helped people get in the mood.

FRANCINE

Free liquor.

NORTHRUP

(musing) I like a woman in a dirndl—

FRANCINE

I've hired this guy to be a special attraction, used to be a big Seminole—

NORTHRUP

An Indian?

FRANCINE

No, not the Seminoles, the Seminoles—

NORTHRUP

The football team?

FRANCINE

Of course, the football team. What would I want with a real Indian? This guy used to be a big deal. Hung out at Lincoln Beach, drove around town in a red Mustang.

NORTHRUP

Local hero— that's good—

FRANCINE

I just hope he shows up.

We HOLD at one of the BOOTHS as they continue past. A handful of small BOYS stare at a very large ALLIGATOR lying in an enclosure with crudely-painted hype surrounding him. The owner, SMOOT, leans on the fence looking bored—

BOY

What's his favorite thing to eat?

SMOOT

Small children.

BOY

Is he alive?

Smoot regards the alligator for a long moment. It is absolutely motionless, eyes closed—

SMOOT

Hard to say.

BOY

What you showing a dead alligator for?

SMOOT

You pay anything to look at it?

BOY

No.

SMOOT

Then don't complain.

We PAN and FOLLOW as Shiflett and Dub wander in the opposite direction, brews in hand—

DUB

He was the last of the Mohicans.

                    SHIFLETT
Bullshit—

                      DUB
All right, the next to the last.

                    SHIFLETT
They were already extinct by that time. He
was like a Shawnee, Pawnee— Here's Billy,
he'll know—
(calling)
Yo Chief! Chief!

Trucks is intensely playing one of the carnival games. He
doesn't look up as his co-workers join him—

                     BILLY
Yo Asshole.

                    SHIFLETT
Settle a bet for us— what kind of Indian was
the guy on *Daniel Boone*?

                     BILLY
He was Jewish.

                    SHIFLETT
I don't mean the <u>ac</u>tor, I mean the character.

                     BILLY
How the fuck should I know?

                    SHIFLETT
Aren't you like a full-blooded whatever it is—?

                     BILLY
Creek.

                      DUB
Regular Creek or Shit Creek?

The guys laugh. Billy just keeps playing—

                    SHIFLETT
So where was Daniel Boone supposed to be?

SILVER CITY and other Screenplays

                        BILLY

Somewhere in the woods.

                      SHIFLETT

More specific that that. Can't you tell by
Indian lore—

                        BILLY

"Lore"?

                      SHIFLETT

Like from the trees or something?

                        BILLY

What the fuck do I know about trees?

                      SHIFLETT

So your ancestors didn't—

                        BILLY

My parents sell lawn ornaments to stupid
white people outside of Waycross.

                         DUB

You're shittin me.

                        BILLY

Get you a great deal on a set of ceramic
ducks.

We PAN and FOLLOW Lester and Greg as they pass, cutting
out of the fair and heading toward downtown—

                        GREG

Kept saying it was her father's decision.

                       LESTER

The last thing we want to deal with is some
old Gomer with a chip on his shoulder.

                        GREG

Maybe the mother—

                       LESTER

A flake. Runs a little theater group,
finds homes for retired greyhounds. The
story is she hasn't stuck her nose inside

----

that restaurant since the day the old man built it.

> GREG

Not a businesswoman.

> LESTER

She won't be any help, but she won't get in the way.

> GREG

So we're back to the daughter.

> LESTER

The old man used to be there twenty-four-seven, running the show, but the daughter—she's paying four employees to handle the same load.

> GREG

She wants a life.

> LESTER

Their rack rate is too low for her to have a life.

> GREG

The restaurant—

> LESTER

The restaurant's a wash.

They turn to enter a—

37 INT. WATERFRONT BAR

—waterfront BAR. Nautical wall paintings, mostly LOCALS scattered around the place —

> LESTER

You know the money even a moderately suc-cessful franchise could generate in that spot? I'm sorry, all she's doing there is taking up space.

Greg puts a hand up to shield his face —

                              GREG

      Right now she's taking up space at the end of
      the bar.

                            LESTER

      See?

BAR COUNTER

Marly sits alone, drinking shots at the bar —

                       LESTER (O.S.)

      This is not a dedicated professional.

APRIL, the bartender, comes over as Marly signals —

                             APRIL

      You're not having another of those—

Marly just looks at her and pushes her glass forward.
April fills it with a shot of tequila —

                             APRIL

      Saw Steve at the pirate thing today.

                             MARLY

      They hang him?

                             APRIL

      Walked the plank. He said he really needed to
      talk to you.

                             MARLY

      Why doesn't he just come by the motel?

                             APRIL

      I don't know— could it have something to do
      with there's a restraining order and the last
      time you had him arrested in the parking lot?

                             MARLY

      He was drunk as a skunk.

> APRIL
>
> Lately he's been club soda with lime.

> MARLY
>
> How come you're always defending him?

> APRIL
>
> I'm not de<u>fen</u>ding him, I'm just saying he's
> on the wagon.

April acknowledges a signal from a customer and draws a
couple beers—

> APRIL
>
> Your golf pro was in the other night.

> MARLY
>
> He's not <u>my</u> golf pro.

> APRIL
>
> I thought you—

> MARLY
>
> (touchy) He's nearly ten years younger than
> me. Besides, he's going on tour.

> APRIL
>
> Like with Tiger Woods? On TV?

> MARLY
>
> I don't think he'll get as much air time as
> Tiger.

> APRIL
>
> He ask you to go with him?

> MARLY
>
> It didn't come up.

> APRIL
>
> You want to?

Marly just gives her a look. April looks past Marly to
the floor—

                    APRIL

So there's a guy over there been checking
you out.

                    MARLY

Be still my beating heart.

She waits a beat for appearance sake —

                    MARLY

What's he look like?

                    APRIL

Not bad.

                    MARLY

Tattoos?

                    APRIL

None visible.

                    MARLY

Does his shirt say "Go Gators" or "Stomp 'Em
Seminoles"?

                    APRIL

It doesn't say anything.

                    MARLY

Obviously not my type.

                    APRIL

He's cute.

                    MARLY

Okay, I'm gonna turn around and look at this
guy, but only to see what falls under your
definition of cute.

                    APRIL

If you're at twelve o'clock he's about
seven-thirty.

Marly casually swivels in her chair, leans back against
the bar, searches—

POV — JACK

Jack is with some of the same men he was with the other
morning. He sits slightly apart from them, checking out
the room—

CU JACK

Lost in thought—

                    MARLY (O.S.)
        Trying to imagine what'd it'd be like without
        all us crackers here?

He looks up. Marly sits at the empty table next to him—
                        JACK
        You're everywhere.

                       MARLY
        It's a small island.

                        JACK
        Listen, I didn't mean to be— intrusive the
        other morning. I thought they'd already con-
        tacted you.

                       MARLY
        Don't worry about it. There's days I imagine
        the whole thing blowing away in a hurricane.

                        JACK
        Must be a lot of work. Being a hotelier.

                       MARLY
        Motelier. And we got the restaurant too.
        Lord, I hated working there when I was a kid.

                        JACK
        And now?

                       MARLY
        Oh, now I got three girls working for me hate
        it as much as I do.

SILVER CITY and other Screenplays   227

                              JACK

So why—?

                              MARLY

Poetic justice. What are you drinking?

                              JACK

Draft. How about you?

                              MARLY

Shots. Tequila.

                              JACK

Whoah.

                              MARLY

I figure you're gonna drink, why fuck around?

She signals across to April for another—

                              MARLY

You're from up north?

                              JACK

(shrugs) They tell me everybody on this coast
came from somewhere else.

                              MARLY

Not me. Six generations on this sandpile. At
least.

                              JACK

That's impressive.

                              MARLY

You go back that far, your people were either
planters, slaves, or fugitives.

                              JACK

And yours were—?

                              MARLY

I'm not sure what they were running from, but
this is where they stopped.

                              JACK

I'm from Newport. In Rhode Island?

                              MARLY
      Like with the yachts and the big estates—
                              JACK
      That's the place. My Dad took care of their
      lawns.

A slightly awkward pause —
                              JACK
      So— you never left—?
                              MARLY
      Oh I left, all right. You're looking at a
      former Weeki Wachee Girl.
                              JACK
      What's that?
                              MARLY
      Over near Homosassa, there's this show, been
      running since the late forties—
                              JACK
      And you acted in it?
                              MARLY
      Performed. You do it underwater.
                              JACK
      Oh.
                              MARLY
      Here— we'll have a contest—

She claps her hand over his mouth, pinches his nose shut—
                              MARLY
      Now you do it to me.

He puts his hands on her face, cutting off her air. They
look at each other for a long moment. April comes with
fresh drinks for them, clears the old ones. She leans down
close to Marly's ear—

APRIL

This isn't the guy I meant.

Marly follows her with her eyes, sees Greg yakking with Lester at a table. Marly shrugs. April leaves. Jack taps her wrist so that she takes her hands away—

JACK

Ahhh! You win.

Marly holds for several seconds more, then signals and Jack takes his hands away. She has a big phony smile plastered on her face—

MARLY

I can hold it twice as long if I haven't been drinking.

JACK

I'm impressed.

MARLY

The important thing is to keep that <u>smile</u> on your face. Even if you snort some water down your nose.

JACK

How long did you work there?

MARLY

Three years. Then I met my ex. He had this band Skeeter Meter?

JACK

Like a rock band—

MARLY

They were big around Tampa. Ever listen to the Allman Brothers?

JACK

Sure.

MARLY

Lynyrd Skynrd?

JACK

Uh- huh—

MARLY

Then you've heard Skeeter Meter. He was good-looking, Greek— his daddy was a sponge diver before all the sponges died out.

JACK

What'd they die of?

MARLY

Boredom.

Jack starts to laugh—

MARLY

Clinging on to some rock, soaking up whatever rolls over you—

Marly looks around the room—

MARLY

—almost as bad as Delrona Beach.

JACK

Lots of changes happening. Things might pick up.

MARLY

Don't hold your breath.

38 INT. BEDROOM — NIGHT

Desiree and Reggie get into bed together—

DESIREE

They used to say there were only three people folks around here worshipped—the Father, the Son and the Florida Flash.

REGGIE

I was watching the day he got hurt. Must of run the replay a hundred times.

DESIREE

Yeah. He stopped coming up here, left school.

REGGIE

So you were one of the adoring masses?

DESIREE

(a bit defensive) I was in high school, he was on national TV. What do you think?

Desiree slides in. They hold each other—

REGGIE

That's some heavy story about Terrell—

DESIREE

Yeah.

REGGIE

Big responsibility she's taken on, a kid like that.

DESIREE

Can you help him?

REGGIE

Me? What am I, a shrink?

DESIREE

I mean help him build this thing—

REGGIE

Carpentry and adolescent psychology— two things I know nothing about.

DESIREE

Try, okay? For me?

She kisses him—

REGGIE

I'll do what I can.

DESIREE

(musing) Maybe we'll head back on Monday.

REGGIE

(surprised) We just got here.

> **DESIREE**
>
> I don't want to get sucked into any of this.
> I don't like who I am down here. And I don't
> trust my mother.

39 EXT. EUNICE STOKES' HOUSE — FRONT PORCH — NIGHT

Eunice sits on the porch listening to the waves. She calls
out as Dr. Lloyd passes by on foot—

> **EUNICE**
>
> That you, Elton?

Dr. Lloyd steps into the porch light. They are very close
friends but still a bit formal with each other—

> **DR. LLOYD**
>
> It amazes me how little sleep I need these days.

> **EUNICE**
>
> You've got restless feet. Always have.

He comes up to the screen—

> **EUNICE**
>
> I'm sorry I couldn't be there for you at the
> meeting—

> **DR. LLOYD**
>
> You had your emergency. How did the hearing go?

> **EUNICE**
>
> He's still on probation. He has to do commu-
> nity service—

> **DR. LLOYD**
>
> It could have been much worse.

They listen to the waves for a moment—

> **EUNICE**
>
> We can fall so quickly—

SILVER CITY and other Screenplays

> DR. LLOYD
> Just a stumble, not a fall.

> EUNICE
> If you could just go and get it and hand it
> to them—

> DR. LLOYD
> Nobody handed us anything.

> EUNICE
> Of course they did. People fought their
> whole lives just to keep their heads above
> water. We got to start on dry land.

They are silent again—

> DR. LLOYD
> So Desiree's back.

> EUNICE
> Visiting. She's not back.

> DR. LLOYD
> Hurricane Desiree.

Eunice shakes her head—

> EUNICE
> The nights I sat here wondering where that
> girl could be.

40 EXT. GOLF COURSE — NIGHT

Marly and Jack wander across a deserted golf course, SECU-
RITY LIGHTS throwing long SHADOWS. Marly sits abruptly on
the edge of a sand bunker. Jack eases down beside her.
Both have had a lot to drink—

> MARLY
> We used to come out here and neck when I was
> in high school. Didn't have these lights
> then.

Jack looks over at the lights—

                    JACK

    Security.

                    MARLY

    More like birth control. You do golf courses?

                    JACK

    Design them? No— that's kind of a specialty.

                    MARLY

    You play it?

                    JACK

    Golf? No.

She looks at him. They are both pretty drunk—

                    MARLY

    I gotta tell you— sex with me when I'm this
    drunk? It's like being at the dentist—

                    JACK

    The dentist.

                    MARLY

    When they shoot you up with Novocain? You can
    tell something's going on in there, but
    you're not sure exactly what it is.

                    JACK

    I understand.

                    MARLY

    So forget it.

                    JACK

    It wouldn't cross my mind.

She kisses him—

                    MARLY

    Like tomorrow I won't even remember I kissed
    you.

                    JACK

    I'll come by and remind you.

She smiles—

> **MARLY**
>
> Do that.

She pokes him lightly with a finger, as if to test that he's real—

> **MARLY**
>
> You honestly don't golf?

> **JACK**
>
> Never took it up.

> **MARLY**
>
> Good.

She lies back on the grass, looks up at the sky—

> **MARLY**
>
> The important thing— is to keep that smile on your face. Even if you're drowning.

FADE OUT:

41 EXT. GOLF COURSE — MORNING

Buster Bidwell is stuck in the rough, surveying his lie as the others move up the fairway beyond him—

> **CASH**
>
> The polar ice cap is melting.

> **MURRAY**
>
> This is news?

> **CASH**
>
> What they say, with this global warming? The ice cap, all that Arctica, Antarctica, could melt. And the ocean, all over the world, gets twenty feet higher.

> **SILENT SAM**
>
> It's good we live on the second floor.

CASH

They say that here it'll be a wading pool, all the way up to Orlando.

BIDWELL

Whole problem started with the invention of the internal combustion engine. That and air conditioners.

Bidwell tries to hit out of the rough. The ball dribbles off to the right—

BIDWELL

Damn it.

CASH

They say every day another species goes extinct.

MURRAY

So?

CASH

It's tragic.

MURRAY

We still need a lizard the size of a twelve-passenger van? Most of these things, if they came back, people would not be thrilled.

WHACK! Bidwell knocks the ball out of the trap but over the green and into the woods—

BIDWELL

What are we betting?

SILENT SAM

Five dollars a side, fifty on the match, throw out your worst hole.

BIDWELL

I think it'll be this one.

We move toward the green with the men—

MURRAY

My grandparents were peasants in a country where they used Jews for target practice. When they didn't eat beets, they ate turnips. When they didn't eat turnips, they ate beets. We got my Tateh over here, she wouldn't go to the park. "The next time I look at grass," she'd say, "it should be growing over my body."

CASH

I like to watch the whaddayoucallit— Jungle Channel.

MURRAY

Animals eating animals.

CASH

It's educational.

MURRAY

If you're a wolverine, possibly. How to hibernate in three easy lessons. For human beings, what are we going to do with this information? When is the last time you were stalking a creature in the wild?

BIDWELL

I go duck hunting with my son.

MURRAY

That's right, I forgot. You people shoot birds.

BIDWELL

The shooting isn't the point. You're out there when the sun comes up, surrounded by nature—

MURRAY

Nature is overrated.

Silent Sam chips onto the green—

SILENT SAM

But we'll miss it when it's gone.

42 EXT. SAND TRAP — SCOTTY DUVAL

Scotty Duval has lined up a dozen balls in a SAND TRAP
and is blasting them one by one onto a practice green —

                    MARLY
    Scotty—

We SHIFT to include Marly, standing watching him—

                    SCOTTY
    Hey.

                    MARLY
    Sorry to distract you—

                    SCOTTY
    No, I need it. Come closer— come on, down
    into the pit—

Marly hesitantly climbs down and approaches him—

                    SCOTTY
    Where I'm heading you don't play in a vacuum.
    TV cameras, gallery right on top of you—

Marly flinches as Scotty blasts a ball just past her nose—

                    SCOTTY
    Try to keep that distance.
    (glances at her)
    You okay?

                    MARLY
    I thought we should— like— make it official.

                    SCOTTY
    What?

                    MARLY
    Breaking up.

                    SCOTTY
    Oh.

> MARLY

You're going off on your Tour and all—

> SCOTT

Yeah.

He hits another shot. Marly backs up—

> MARLY

I suppose if you win just one tournament you
make more than a whole year working here.

> SCOTTY

It's not the money.

> MARLY

It's not?

> SCOTTY

My game is getting stale. I've been shooting
low seventies, but it doesn't mean anything.

He pauses, looks at her—

> SCOTTY

It's this thing that I do, better than almost
anybody else on earth. If I let it down, if
I don't take another whack at the highest
level, the purest—

(he shrugs)

Pretty stupid, huh? I'm talking about golf
like it's important.

> MARLY

It's not stupid at all. You really love it.

He nods, a bit embarrassed. He knocks a ball onto the
green, running it very close to the hole —

CU MARLY

MARLY

(quietly) You just don't love me.

43 EXT. LINCOLN BEACH, ABANDONED FISH SHACK — MORNING

Reggie and Terrell pull boards from the shell of a fallen-down
FISH SHACK. A giant papier maché CRAB, patches of chicken-wire
frame exposed, lies in pieces on a slab in front of it—

REGGIE

Buster's Place.

TERRELL

Uh-huh.

REGGIE

How long has it been like this?

TERRELL

All messed up?

REGGIE

Yeah—

TERRELL

Couple years. There was a fire.

Reggie shoots a look at him, then looks back to the
wrecked building—

REGGIE

And nobody's fixed it up or taken it down?

TERRELL

(shrugs) People it belong to didn't come
back.

They pull some boards—

REGGIE

So do you have, like, a crew?

TERRELL

On a boat?

> REGGIE

Guys you hang with.

> TERRELL

No.

> REGGIE

What are you into? Interested in?

> TERRELL

(shrugs) Stuff.

> REGGIE

Like— sports? Music?

> TERRELL

I guess.

They work for a moment in silence. Reggie looks at the pile of scrap wood they've accumulated—

> REGGIE

Think this is enough?

> TERRELL

Never built a coffin before.

44 EXT. MALL PARKING LOT — DAY

Flash sits in the back of the parking lot in his convertible, head in his hands for a long moment. Not a happy camper. He looks up and across the lot—

POV — MALL

A CROWD already gathering under a banner that reads—

DELRONA BEACH MALL WELCOMES PIRATE QUEEN PAGEANT

MEET SEMINOLE LEGEND "FLASH" PHILLIPS

FLASH

Flash sighs, gets out of the car—

FURMAN (V.O.)

It used to be five yards and a cloud of dust.

45 INT. TEMPLE HOUSE — BACK BALCONY — CU FURMAN — DAY

FURMAN

No mouthguards, no faceguards, helmet just a
scrap of leather to keep your brains in if
they cracked your skull. What it is now, is
just technology and hormones. Colored boys
flippin the ball all over the field, women in
the locker room— that aint gridiron.

MISS DELIA (O.S.)

What are they doing?

WIDER

Miss Delia works in her little backyard as Furman sits
above, a glass of iced tea in hand, greyhounds around
his feet. A little TV on a stand in front of him plays
a college FOOTBALL GAME, extension cord running back
into the house—

FURMAN

You say something?

MISS DELIA

What are these women doing in the locker room?

FURMAN

Talking to the players.

MISS DELIA

They must find it very distracting.

FURMAN

They're too damn busy worryin about their
stock portfolios to notice. It's a wonder
they can tell a hand-off from a hole in the
ground.

MISS DELIA

And how do you know they're colored?

FURMAN

(testy) Who?

MISS DELIA

The young men flipping the ball. When you can't see the television.

FURMAN

When you ever hear of a white boy name Deeshon?

Miss Delia works in silence for a moment—

MISS DELIA

Carlota will be here for your dinner tonight. I've got rehearsal and then an Audubon meeting.

FURMAN

You and your birds.

MISS DELIA

They start clearing on the Plantation Estates expansion next week. The old Exley property?

FURMAN

Lincoln Beach.

MISS DELIA

Not anymore. There's a colony of wood ibis we're very concerned about—

FURMAN

Colored folks say there's a curse on that land.

MISS DELIA

I'm sure it's seen its share of misery.

Marly comes out through the back of the house—

MARLY

Hey Mama— Daddy—

JOHN SAYLES

She kisses her father—

FURMAN

Something wrong at the motel?

MARLY

Everything's fine, Daddy.

FURMAN

Then why aren't you there?

MARLY

I got a day manager, remember? Rosellen?

FURMAN

People will steal you blind, you don't
watch em.

MARLY

She's got it under control.

Marly indicates the greyhounds, greeting her excitedly, to
Miss Delia—

MARLY

Are these new ones?

MISS DELIA

I can't remember when you were here last—

MARLY

They all look alike to me.

FURMAN

We full up?

MARLY

Yes Daddy. The celebration—

FURMAN

How bout the restaurant?

MARLY

They keeping us hoppin.

FURMAN

Got to make it while it's there—

                    MARLY

I know, Daddy.

                  MISS DELIA

Steven has been calling for you.

                    MARLY

He knows I don't live here.

                  MISS DELIA

It was nice talking with him—

                   FURMAN

Got a screw loose. That deep-sea diving—

                    MARLY

That was his father—

                   FURMAN

It puts pressure on the brain—

                    MARLY

Steve done plenty of things put pressure
on his brain, but diving isn't one of
them.

                  MISS DELIA

He says he's turning over a new leaf. I certainly hope so. He had such promise—

                    MARLY

When did Steve ever have promise?

                  MISS DELIA

When he had his musical group and you were
with the circus—

                    MARLY

It wasn't the circus, Mama, we stayed in one
place.

                  MISS DELIA

When you were performing in the aquarium— you
were both so hopeful.

                    MARLY

Well, we grew up. Daddy? There was a fella
from a development company over this morning—

FURMAN
You give him the boot?

MARLY
I was thinking this might be a good time, if you ever wanted to sell—

FURMAN
And watch them turn the beach into a damn strip mall?

MISS DELIA
It's not exactly in pristine condition at the moment, is it?

FURMAN
You lifted one little finger to keep that business runnin?

MISS DELIA
I have not.

FURMAN
Then hold your peace.

(to Marly)

She worries about the birds.

MISS DELIA
It's a severely compromised habitat. The sandhill cranes have absolutely forsaken us—

FURMAN
Good for them! They don't have the sense to fly off somewheres that's more accomodatin to em, they get what they deserve. Now your seagulls, they're just like people, willin to scrap each other for every little bit they get—

MISS DELIA
Your father is a strict Darwinian—

FURMAN
She likes to throw her education at me—

> **MARLY (defeated)**
> Anyway, this developer— I told him you probly
> weren't interested.

Miss Delia looks sympathetically at her daughter—
> **FURMAN**
> You can bet your last dollar on that one.

46 EXT. DOG TRACK — DAY

A MECHANICAL RABBIT whizzes by us on a rail. A pack of
GREYHOUNDS appear, racing after it. BETTORS SHOUT—

EARL, BETTORS

BETTORS shout encouragement as the RACE ENDS. Only a few are
happy with the outcome. Earl is not one of them—

TICKET WINDOW

Earl is at the LINES for the TICKET WINDOWS. There are
three people in front of him for the twenty dollars
window. He cracks open his wallet— not too many bills
left. He decides to take the big plunge, and switches over
to the one hundred dollar window—

47 EXT. EUNICE STOKES' HOUSE — FRONT YARD — DAY

Reggie watches as Terrell lays boards out on the ground—
> **REGGIE**
> They give you specs for this thing? Like
> dimensions—
> **TERRELL**
> There's a picture in the book.

Terrell picks up a paperback copy of *As I Lay Dying* and flips to the right page—

                    REGGIE
        If she's going to get into it—

                    TERRELL
        (shows him) Here—

Reggie looks—

                    REGGIE
        This doesn't give us a measurement.

                    TERRELL
        You taller than her—

                    REGGIE
        Right.

Reggie lies on the ground while Terrell selects the longest boards to lay beside him and mark with a pencil—

                    REGGIE
        We'd better cut some holes so she can breathe

48 INT. MALL — DAY

                    SMOOT (O.S.)
        A hide like iron and jaws of steel—

Desiree is strolling through the main floor of the Delrona Beach MALL, presently taken over by the Jolly Roger celebration and various offshoots. She slows to look at Smoot's alligator, listlessly stretched out in a plastic pool in the middle of the main floor, surrounded by staring SHOPPERS. Some toss COINS into the pool—

                    SMOOT
        —this animal hasn't changed a whisker since
        the age of the dinosaurs. Formerly endan-
        gered by rednecks like me, the American
        alligator has made a big comeback in the

----

last twenty years, spreading out through
the swamplands and waste canals of southern
Florida—

Desiree passes on to a historical EXHIBIT consisting of
a plaster TOPOGRAPHICAL MAP of the island and a few
ARTIFACTS in a glass case. UNDERHILL, a fairly dry aca-
demic, gives his presentation to a handful of bewildered
shoppers—

UNDERHILL
We don't know much about the Timucuas till the
arrival of the Spanish, when they were involved
in blood conflicts with Pánfilo de Narvaez and
Ponce de Leon, among others. The British
report that they massacred a large group of
Christianized Indians in a Franciscan mission
on this island in the late 1600's, but as to
date no evidence has been found to support
this. For the next two hundred years, pirates
and privateers used this coast as a base of
operations, raiding Spanish galleons laden
with gold and silver—

Desiree passes on by Francine, talking with eight or nine
teenage GIRLS dressed in prom-type outfits, waiting to
promenade in the Pirate Queen fashion segment—

FRANCINE
Now I asked them if you could keep your outfits and they said that wouldn't be possible—

The girls MOAN

FRANCINE
However— however— they have agreed to a one-
time-only twelve percent discount coupon to
all contestants—

Desiree passes on further to where the JUDGES and AUDI-ENCE (mostly parents and friends of the girls) mill around. Something she sees makes her stop—

POV — FLASH

Flash Phillips is greeting FANS as he stands with other JUDGES waiting for the competition to start—

CU DESIREE

Desiree hangs back—

FLASH, CLOSER

Flash, looking and feeling conspicuous, is approached by OLNEY, a shopper in his fifties—

> **OLNEY**
> Flash Phillips!

> **FLASH**
> Hey—

Olney pumps his hand—

> **OLNEY**
> Man, I used to watch your narrow ass leave them tacklers grabbing the wind. How you doin?

> **FLASH**
> Not bad—

Olney turns to his wife—

> **OLNEY**
> Yo, baby, this is Flash Phillips! The Heisman guy—

                    FLASH

I didn't win the—

                    OLNEY

Well you <u>would</u> have, they didn't pop your
knee out.

                    FLASH

That's nice of you to say.

                    OLNEY

Would've made a decent pro, too, you put on
some muscle.

                    FLASH

Are you— uhm— local, or—

                    OLNEY

We live down Lincoln Beach.

                    FLASH

Cause I'm having a barbecue tomorrow, over
where Buster's used to be? You should drop by—

                    OLNEY

More of this Pirate Days hustle?

                    FLASH

No, it's uhm— I'm going to be your neighbor—

Olney calls to his wife again —

                    OLNEY

Baby! The Florida Flash is moving <u>in</u>!

Flash sees Desiree, smiles automatically, offering his hand—

                    FLASH

Hi. I'm Flash Phillips—

                    DESIREE

I know.

                    FLASH

And you're—?

                    DESIREE

Desiree.

This stops him. He looks at her more carefully—

                    FLASH

Damn.

                    DESIREE

Yeah.

                    FLASH

Wow. You still living here?

                    DESIREE

Visiting my mother.

                    FLASH

Stokes, right? She's got a house on Carver
Street, facing the beach—

                    DESIREE

That's her. You running for office?

                    FLASH

Naw, I— I just like to know who my neighbors are.
Desiree.

                    DESIREE

Flash-from-the-past.

                    FLASH

That was some crazy shit, back then.

                    DESIREE

It sure was. How've you been doing?

                    FLASH

Great, lately, yeah— There were some—when I
got hurt I kind of— lost it a little bit, you
know? I left—

                    DESIREE

I remember.

                    FLASH

You look terrific. Have I—seen you on TV or
something? You look familiar—

DESIREE
I ought to look familiar, we were—

FLASH
I mean the adult you. The way you look now.

DESIREE
I do instructional videos, infomercials—

FLASH
Right. Damn. You were just a little bitty
girl—

She nods toward the Pirate Queen contestants, climbing
onto the stage—

DESIREE
I was their age.

FLASH
Not <u>that</u> little. I would of been in jail—

DESIREE
I won this contest when I was fifteen years
old. We got together right after that.

An awkward pause, Flash starting to remember some details,
wondering how guilty he should feel—

FLASH
Yeah. Well, I was pretty young myself—

FRANCINE
(on stage, with microphone) Good afternoon,
ladies and gentlemen— We'll be starting the
evening wear segment of the competition in
just a moment—

FLASH
Listen, I'm having this barbecue tomorrow—

DESIREE
Where Buster's place used to be.

FLASH
Right—

Desiree gives him a little wave, smiles enigmatically, and walks away, leaving Flash off balance—

> **FRANCINE** (microphone)
> —and I'd like to take this opportunity to thank our participating retailers here at the mall—

CU DESIREE

Fighting emotion as she hurries through the gathering crowd—

> **FRANCINE** (microphone)
> —Sixteen Candles, Belissima, Cynthia's Closet, the Prom Palace—

49 EXT. FORT — DAY

We're in a Civil War masonry FORT. A squad of UNION SOL-DIERS are drilling—

STAIRS — MARLY

Marly climbs the stone stairs up to the wall overlooking the water.

A bearded SENTRY stands with rifle shouldered by a huge cannon. It is Steve Tregaskis—

> **STEVE**
> Who goes there?

Marly throws up her hands—

> **MARLY**
> Don't shoot. It's your ex-wife.

Steve is not thrilled to see Marly in this context—

                         STEVE

        I'm on guard duty—

                         MARLY

        April said you needed to see me.

He looks down to the parade ground nervously—

                         STEVE

        Pretend you're just a tourist checking out
        the artillery—

                         MARLY

        Oh come on—

                         STEVE

        I'm serious. We've got an inspector coming by
        to review the unit.

Marly shakes her head, then pretends to look at the cannon—

                         MARLY

        Nice uniform.

                         STEVE

        I hate playing a Yankee.

                         MARLY

        You're Greek, for chrissake, what difference does
        it make.

                         STEVE

        I was born down here. It's a matter of cul-
        tural affinity.

                         MARLY

        So what's the latest crisis?

                         STEVE

        No crisis, I just was wondering how you were
        making out.

                         MARLY

        Right.

                         STEVE

        Seriously.

MARLY

I've found inner peace. Now what's the angle?

STEVE

I heard about something and thought it would be nice to cut you in on—

MARLY

Not interested—

STEVE

It's a once-in-a-lifetime kind of thing—

MARLY

So was our marriage, and once was enough.

STEVE

Just hear me out on this. Then, if you're not ready to become a co-investor, maybe we could figure out a reasonable rate of interest and—

MARLY

(incredulous) You want to borrow money from me?

STEVE

There's a chance here to get in on the ground floor of something very big. Tell me— what do we not have on this island?

MARLY

Let's see— an opera house, a ski resort, a good Thai restaurant—

STEVE

Are you familiar with water slides?

MARLY

Big plastic chute thing—

STEVE

That's the flume—

MARLY

Water flows and you slide down in your bathing suit.

> **STEVE**
>
> We don't have one.

> **MARLY**
>
> Always knew I was culturally disadvantaged.

> **STEVE**
>
> Any idea how much money those things pull in?

> **MARLY**
>
> A: You'll never get a zoning permit—

> **STEVE**
>
> Don't be so sure—

> **MARLY**
>
> B: I don't have any extra money lying around
> to throw at half-assed business propositions—

> **STEVE**
>
> I hear you're about to come into some.

> **MARLY**
>
> Is that so?

> **STEVE**
>
> My sources inform me that you've been
> approached by some big developers from Tal-
> lahassee.

> **MARLY**
>
> Your sources don't know diddly. Besides, C: Even
> if I did have some extra money, which I don't,
> I'd run it through the leaf shredder and use it
> for mulch before I'd give a nickel of it to you.

Steve scowls, shifts the rifle to his other shoulder—

> **STEVE**
>
> I hear your golfer's taking a walk.

> **MARLY**
>
> They don't walk anymore. They use carts.

> **STEVE**
>
> He didn't ask you to come along on the Tour,
> did he?

                    MARLY

(hurt) You got any other business with me,
Steve? I am seriously hung over and I got to
get back to the motel—

                    STEVE

This is the real deal, and you just—

                    MARLY

It's only another scam, Steve, like your
band, like the mail-order iguana business,
like the treasure hunting—

                    STEVE

Skeeter Meter rocked—

                    MARLY

But you didn't care about the music, did you?
You just wanted to be rich and famous and get
laid a lot—

                    STEVE

You know why you're stuck running that flop-
house? You've got no vision.

                    MARLY

I can't believe you think I'd loan you money—
after all you put me through—

                    STEVE

Hey, that's over and done with, Marly.

A BUGLER calls ASSEMBLY below. SOLDIERS scurry to form
their ranks—

                    STEVE

You can't live in the past.

50 EXT. ROADSIDE — PHONE BOOTH — DAY

Earl Pinkney is in a phone booth at a combination gas
station/Indian River fruit stand. Earl is not happy—

SILVER CITY and other Screenplays   259

EARL

It's me— Earl— yeah, we should talk again— I
explained what I can do and what I can't—
Okay, eight o'clock. Same place?

51 INT. SHOPPING MALL — DAY

Beauty CONTESTANTS and SHOPPERS scatter in all directions
amid lots of SQUEALS and EXCLAMATIONS—

CLOSER

The huge alligator has climbed out of its pool and is
making its way toward a leather goods outlet as Smoot
tags alongside, dangling a noose on a pole—

SMOOT

C'mon, buddy, keep your trap shut.

He tries unsuccessfully to snare the creature around the
snout—

SMOOT

Don't worry, folks, he's not hungry, he's just
bored.

They bring us to Francine, smiling desperately as she
talks to Yordan, eating it up as his cameraman moves in
to get video footage—

FRANCINE

I think we're under control here—

YORDAN

This is terrific!

FRANCINE

I hope— when you report this— you'll be able
to put sort of a humorous spin on it—

SMOOT

Come on, you sumbitch, sit still for me!

52 EXT. PORCH — EUNICE'S HOUSE — DAY

Eunice sits on the porch showing Reggie photo albums. We hear HAMMERING and SAWING outside—

EUNICE

We had quite a little society in Jacksonville at the time. Young ladies were presented when they were sixteen. Often there'd be a piano recital, then a formal dance—

(points)

This is my sister at her cotillion.

REGGIE

Are there pictures of yours?

EUNICE

Oh, by the time my turn came along, it was— My father had suffered a financial reversal, as did many of the other important people in the community.

She doesn't want to linger on it—

EUNICE

Here we are at the beach.

PHOTOS

We PAN slowly over several PHOTOS of happy people posing at a crowded, lively beach scene—

EUNICE (O.S.)

In so many other ways we were on the outside looking in. But this was ours.

----

53 EXT. MOTEL PARKING LOT — LATE EVENING

The NO VACANCIES sign is ON. Earl Pinkney gets out of his car, parked next to Smoot's gator truck. Earl watches as Smoot pulls a couple RAW CHICKENS from a plastic garbage bag, climbs onto the tailgate and tosses them into the bed—

                         SMOOT
          Here you go, buddy.

EARL peeks over the side of the pickup bed as we hear LOUD THRASHING from within—

                         SMOOT
          He had a tough day out there.

                         EARL
          I can sympathize.

54 EXT. SEA-VUE RESTAURANT — NIGHT

Marly crosses the road to the restaurant. She sees—

POV — JACK

—Jack through the window, sitting alone in a booth—

MARLY

                         MARLY
          What the hell—

55 INT. DINER — JACK

Jack is reading the menu—

                         MARLY (O.S.)
          Seafood's a good bet.

We WIDEN to include Marly, standing over him—

MARLY

We guarantee it's only been thawed-out once.

JACK

Hi.

Marly sits across from him—

MARLY

How'd you end up here?

JACK

Oh— I'm ducking out on dinner with a couple potential buyers. I'm not much of a salesman.

MARLY

You just move the dirt around.

JACK

There's a lot of drainage issues, too—

MARLY

Now I'm really impressed. Somebody told me you're like a big name in this land architecture deal.

JACK

I guess.

MARLY

You go to school for it?

JACK

I went to business school. Came out, made a lot of money buying and selling companies— nice while it lasted.

MARLY

You didn't like it?

JACK

My boss went to jail.

MARLY

Oops.

JACK

It was a musical chairs kind of thing. The music stopped and he was— in a compromising position.

MARLY

So you went back to lawns.

JACK

There was this guy—Frederick Law Olmstead—

MARLY

The one who designed Central Park in New York.

JACK

(surprised) Right.

MARLY

It was an answer on *Jeopardy*. Famous Parks and Monuments.

JACK

Right. He's kind of the grandaddy of what I do. You take land that's wild and inaccessible and you— refine it some— showcase its natural beauty— accentuate the topography a little— and create a place that everybody, rich, poor and in-between, can come together and appreciate.

Marly considers this—

MARLY

So we're all invited over to Exley Plantation for a fish fry?

JACK

Well— the populist part of it has kind of fallen away. He designed some pretty grand estates, too.

MARLY

Working for rich people.

JACK

You're gonna put in the effort, you might as well be paid well.

                    MARLY

Not so loud, the staff'll hear you.

                    JACK

(smiles) You know what I mean, though.

                    MARLY

I do.

                    JACK

Do you uhm— remember on the golf course—?

                    MARLY

Something about being out there with some
guy I hardly knew—

                    JACK

Did he look like me?

Marly leans back, looking him over—

                    MARLY

You get Sundays off?

56 INT. MOTEL ROOM

Earl Pinkney sits nervously on the bed, facing Lester,
comfortable in the only upholstered chair—

                    LESTER

You sure you can pull this off?

                    EARL

They'll listen to me.

                    LESTER

The old college try isn't gonna do it for us.
We need results.

                    EARL

With my vote and two more I swing it's done.

                    LESTER

It can't be too obvious.

                          EARL

     It won't be. But you're on your own with
     Water Management—

                         LESTER

     That's just technical stuff. It's the anti-
     growth people— we can't have a lot of noise
     from them when the re-zoning comes up—

                          EARL

     There's always going to be a few die-hards.

Lester nods—

                         LESTER

     The usual format for this is to open an
     account for you offshore—

                          EARL

     (uncomfortable) It needs to be cash.

                         LESTER

     Cash?

                          EARL

     Hundred-dollar bills. New ones—

                         LESTER

     (grins) We have been a naughty boy, haven't
     we?

57 INT. HOTEL ROOM — TV SCREEN

We see Desiree on TV, hosting an infomercial—

                      DESIREE (TV)

     Hi. I'm here to tell you about an exciting
     new grilling system that will revolutionize
     the way you feed your family. This is not
     just another kitchen gadget, but a scientific
     breakthrough pioneered by certified health
     professionals—

FLASH

Flash sits back on the bed, watching, remote control in hand—

                    DESIREE (TV, O.S.)
        Now I don't know about you, but the mess and
        bother of conventional grilling—
                        FLASH
        (to himself) Desiree.

                                        FADE OUT:

58 EXT. BEACH NEIGHBORHOOD — MORNING

We hear a RELIGIOUS HYMN sung by a CHOIR as we see various ANGLES of the old Beach neighborhood— most houses well-kept, a few abandoned or only empty foundations. The last ANGLE is of a little CHURCH, cars parked around it during the Sunday service. The MUSIC is emanating from inside—

59 INT. CHURCH

Reggie stands between Eunice and Desiree, both SINGING with the rest of the CONGREGATION. Terrell just stands. Reggie has a hymnal out, trying to keep up, while the others know the song by heart—

60 EXT. PARK — MORNING

Earl strolls between several FLOATS getting their final touch-ups before the big parade. A VOLUNTEER secures a side panel onto one float with a NAIL GUN, then lays it down on the float, and moves to find some decoration. Earl picks up the nail gun, examines it—

FRANCINE (O.S.)
Honey—

Earl turns, startled, to see Francine hurrying past him—

FRANCINE
I'm gonna be riding with the fire department.
Can you drop the car at the high school and
have Jim give you a ride downtown? You're an
angel.

She hands him car keys and is gone. Earl considers the
nail gun—

61 EXT. PLANTATION ESTATES — FRONT GATE — DAY

Marly stops her beat-up Civic at the gate of the Plantation Estates. The SECURITY GUARD leans out with his
clipboard—

MARLY
Name Is Temple— Marly Temple? I'm visiting
Jack Meadows?

62 EXT. PLANTATION GROUNDS — DAY

Jack stands in front of a HOUSE built among the pines and
Sabal palms of the Plantation grounds, staring at it as if
communing. Marly pulls up beside him. Her muffler needs
replacing—

MARLY
This where they're putting you up?

JACK
No. It's one of the few units that hasn't
sold yet. I was just trying to figure out
why.

MARLY

I've haven't been in here since your outfit
made it over. It's pretty.

JACK

Thanks.

MARLY

Before, unless you were hunting armadillos—

She looks around—

MARLY

So you decide what trees live and what ones die.

JACK

That's part of it.

MARLY

Kind of like being God.

JACK

You remember the last big hurricane?

MARLY

Elmo. Picked a catamaran out of the marina
and run it through the window of Ernie's
Hardware on Third Street.

JACK

That's God. I'm just a hired hand.

63 INT. CHURCH

REVEREND SUTCLIFF addresses his flock from the pulpit—

REVEREND SUTCLIFF

A member of our community has asked to have
a word with us today. I hope you'll listen to
him with your hearts as well as your minds.
Dr. Lloyd?

REGGIE

Reggie watches as Dr. Lloyd takes the podium—

DR. LLOYD

                    DR. LLOYD
    Good morning. The matter I've come to discuss
    is not exactly religious— but it is a matter
    of the <u>spirit</u>.

64 EXT. CAUSEWAY BRIDGE — DAY

Marly's CAR is parked at the center of the CAUSEWAY
BRIDGE, no traffic behind her. Marly and Jack stand
looking over the side—

CLOSER

Marly indicates —

                    MARLY
    They were bombing around town in a car they'd
    kind of borrowed without asking? And there
    was this officer went after em— he was new on
    the force or he would have just called my
    daddy and let him take it out of their hides
    the next day.
                    JACK
    They tried to get away?
                    MARLY
    Hit the causeway doing ninety—
    (points)
    —saw a couple patrol cars waiting down there
    at the other end, and they tried to do one of
    those 180's out of a Burt Reynolds movie.
                    JACK
    (looking over the side) And they flipped—

                    MARLY

    The divers who pulled em out couldn't
    remember which was in the driver's seat. They
    were identical— Dickie and Danny.

She is quiet for a moment—

                    JACK

    They were younger or older than you?

                    MARLY

    Three years older. Played sports, honor roll,
    the whole deal.

                    JACK

    Tough on your parents.

                    MARLY

    My daddy never expected much from me. But the
    twins—
    (Shakes her head)
    Bet they were laughing till the minute they
    hit the water.

65 EXT. CHURCH

Dressed-up CHURCHGOERS exit, compliment Reverend Sutcliff—

CLOSER

Eunice is proudly showing Reggie off to her FRIENDS as
Desiree stands by, a bit tense, and Terrell tries to disappear without moving—

                    EUNICE

    This is my son-in-law, Reginald Perry, from
    Massachusetts— Reginald is an anesthesiologist.

She says it perfectly—

> REGGIE

A pleasure to meet you—

> CHURCH WOMAN

That's wonderful to have a doctor in the
family.

> REGGIE

It's a specialty

66 EXT. DESERTED AREA — MERMAID CAR

A sedan with a MERMAID FIGUREHEAD mounted on the roof
pulls off the road in a DESERTED AREA of the island—

EARL

Earl gets out of the car, nail gun in hand—

67 EXT. BUILDING SITE

Earl walks out past the parked EARTH MOVING VEHICLES on the
site where Billy and Shiflett were working—

CLOSER

Earl shields himself from the road behind a scraper, holds
the nail gun in both hands, pointing it at his forehead—

> TOURIST MAN (O.S.)

Excuse me?

Earl drops the nail gun, startled. He looks around the
side of the machine— a TOURIST COUPLE, both with Buccaneer Days TREASURE MAPS in hand, are smiling at him
eagerly—

TOURIST WOMAN
We saw your mermaid.

TOURIST MAN
This is it, isn't it? I mean if you're not done burying the treasure—

TOURIST WOMAN
We could come back—

TOURIST MAN
We gonna need a shovel, or is it just out on the ground somewhere?

68 EXT. RIVER — DAY

Marly and Jack paddle a CANOE down a tree-lined, grassy RIVER, Jack a bit out of synch—

MARLY
Daddy's people come out of the turpentine camps and pulp mills— just hired hands, mostly couldn't read or write. So having his own business— well. Thing is, it's _his_ dream, not mine. And it sure isn't my mother's.

JACK
She doesn't work there?

MARLY
She'll drive six blocks out of her way so's not to have to _look_ at it. Her own daddy was a minister up in Valdosta so she feels like she was raised for a higher calling.

JACK
Community theater.

MARLY
Last year she starred in _Mother Courage_. The year before it was _Electra_—

JACK
Whoah.

MARLY

I think people come out to see what the crazy lady's gonna do next.

JACK

And you wanted to be an actress—

MARLY

Hell, no. Oceanographer.

JACK

Yeah?

MARLY

Friends used to call me Jacqueline Cousteau.

JACK

But you didn't—?

MARLY

Shit happens, you know? And a lot of it happened to _me_.

Marly looks Jack over from the stern—

MARLY

You like what you do, don't you?

JACK

The actual work, yeah- but the politics-

MARLY

People fighting over land.

JACK

I tend to come in after the dust has settled.

MARLY

And home is—?

JACK

The head office is in La Jolla—

MARLY

California—

JACK

Yeah, but I go from job to job these days.

                              MARLY

No family.

                              JACK

An ex and a couple of kids. They live in Con-
necticut, with their— she's remarried.

                              MARLY

This guy I know is going out on that PGA
tour? Different town every week, maid makes
your bed, hang in the hotel bar and check out
the local talent.

                              JACK

Living the dream.

Marly rows silently for a bit, looking around—

                              MARLY

I saw a manatee in here once.

                              JACK

Yeah?

                              MARLY

They're naked-looking things— like old fat
ladies in a bathhouse. I felt guilty for
watching it.

(indicates)

They were planning to build all along here,
one of those assisted-living deals? Would
have done it, too, if the Feds hadn't snapped
it up first.

Jack is feeling a bit defensive—

                              JACK

That wasn't my company.

                              MARLY

I didn't say it was.

                              JACK

There's a lot of misconceptions— I mean, sure,

SILVER CITY and other Screenplays

most outfits it's just scorched earth and then
they throw up some high-rise piece of shit—

MARLY

Yeah, and people hear motel, they assume I'm
running some sort of hot-sheets operation.

JACK

For trysts.

MARLY

(smiles) Yeah. Trysts.

She nods at his paddle as he turns back to look at her—

MARLY

Don't put so much muscle in it. We're not in
a hurry.

69 EXT. CEMETERY — DAY

We TRACK around Reggie and Desiree as they stand contem-
plating a HEADSTONE in a small CEMETERY enclosed by a
metal fence—

DESIREE

I wish you'd gotten to know him.

REGGIE

Yeah—

DESIREE

He was strong— he didn't talk about it much
but you could tell he'd been through a lot of
things.

REGGIE

And all these other people?

DESIREE

Oh— this goes back to when the island was a
cotton plantation. They'd bury the slaves
here when they wore them out.

We've shifted so that Eunice is visible in the BG, picking
things off the ground—

                    DESIREE
          Leave off with that, Mama.
                    EUNICE
          They don't belong in here.

CLOSER, EUNICE

We see that she's gathered a half-dozen GOLF BALLS—
                    EUNICE
          It's bad enough we've got to pass through all
          their security to visit our dead, they got to
          throw this trash in here.

She starts tossing the balls back over onto the fairway
of the adjoining GOLF COURSE, visible through the fence—
                    DESIREE
          I don't think they mean to.
                    EUNICE
          It's a resting place, not a playpen.

70 EXT. DOWNTOWN — CEREMONY

Francine stands next to the newly chosen PIRATE QUEEN on
the ceremonial platform. The queen holds a large KEY and
faces a TREASURE CHEST on a stand, the lucky WINNERS, a
DIFFERENT TOURIST COUPLE in their sixties, standing by—
                    FRANCINE
          First of all we'd like to congratulate the folks
          who got to our treasure first— Mr. and Mrs.
          Morley Crandall of Eau Claire, Wisconsin—

Scattered APPLAUSE—

                    FRANCINE
          And now our newly-crowned Pirate Queen, Donna-
          jean Stamper, will do the honors—

A DRUMROLL. Donnajean unlocks the chest with the key—
inside is a layer of COSTUME JEWELRY laid on a pile of
GIFT CERTIFICATES—

                    FRANCINE
          Oh, my Lord, look at that! This is a genuine
          diamonique necklace, courtesy of Kweskin Jew-
          elers at the Citrus Highway Shopping Center—

71 EXT. LINCOLN BEACH — AFTERNOON

A BARBECUE in progress, a couple dozen Lincoln Beach RESI-
DENTS chatting and eating around a large portable grill—

FLASH

We start on a complicated KNEE BRACE, lots of straps
and buckles, then TILT UP to see Flash, playing host at
the grill, shifting pork ribs around with tongs and
entertaining a group of MEN. Reggie hangs on the
periphery. Some LOCAL BOYS throw a football around in
the BG—

                    FLASH
          We used to come down here Saturday nights
          after the game. Wild times.

                    OLNEY
          Get them local girls up in the dunes—

                    FLASH
          (cautiously)Yeah. Those were the days.

Reggie changes the subject—

I still remember that run you tore off against Georgia Tech—

FLASH

Orange Bowl. My freshman year—

REGGIE

Reversed field three times and just flattened that safety—

FLASH

You go to State?

REGGIE

No, I was up North. In high school.

FLASH

Uh-huh.

REGGIE

I played the same position, had the same number—

OLNEY

Number twenty-three—

REGGIE

Even used to leave my chinstrap hanging like you did. Drove Coach crazy.

FLASH

Where'd you play college?

REGGIE

Oh— my grades dipped some, so my parents had me sit out senior year, hit the books. Then in college—

He shrugs—

FLASH

My high school grades were too low to do to any dipping.

Olney and a few of the other men LAUGH knowingly—

> **REGGIE**

So you're moving in?

> **FLASH**

Well, Buster's Place here—the folks who owned it haven't been paying their county taxes, so I took over the payments. Then I've picked up a few more lots, kind of scattered around—

> **OLNEY**

Speculation.

> **FLASH**

More like preservation. This place was part of my— you know— growing up. Don't want it to fall to pieces. We got enough neighborhoods full of empty buildings— ho!

Flash snatches a wayward pass out of the air, tosses it back to the players—

> **OLNEY**

Still got them hands.

> **FLASH**

Yeah. These ribs looking done to you?

DUNE — DESIREE AND DR. LLOYD

Desiree sits with Dr. Lloyd on a dune, moodily looking down onto the scene on the beach—

> **DR. LLOYD**

Don't get to church much anymore. Sundays when I'm down here I go visit Etta Mae.

> **DESIREE**

We saw Daddy today.

> **DR. LLOYD**

He was one of a kind, your father. The old breed. Businessman, race man—

                      DESIREE

We'd go into Jacksonville and people would
say "Oh, you're Mr. <u>Stokes</u>'s daughter" and
then they'd all fuss over me.

                    DR. LLOYD

Those days we didn't have politicians, we had
men like your father. Carried some <u>weight</u> in
that city.

                      DESIREE

It got to where I could hardly breathe when
I was near him.

Dr. Lloyd gives her a look—

                    DR. LLOYD

That man loved you to death.

                      DESIREE

I only felt his eyes on me— judging me—

Dr. Lloyd looks back toward the beach—

                    DR. LLOYD

It's hard to live up to what come before us.

THEIR POV — TERRELL

Terrell stands aside from the other boys, watching them
play with the football—

                 DR. LLOYD (O.S.)

One way or the other—

DESIREE, DR. LLOYD

                    DR. LLOYD

Don't suppose I could get you out for this
protest tomorrow?

SILVER CITY and other Screenplays

                    DESIREE
         (shakes her head) I burned my bridges here a
         long time ago.

                    DR. LLOYD
         Eunice wants you to have her place when she's
         gone—

                    DESIREE
         That's too far ahead for me to think about.

                    DR. LLOYD
         Maybe.

Dr. Lloyd is suddenly silent. Desiree senses something,
studies his face—

72 EXT. EUNICE HOME — DAY

Eunice steps down from her porch, heading out. She slows
as she sees the completed COFFIN, a rough wooden box
propped up against a tree trunk. She frowns, touches it
warily—

73 EXT. WEEKI WACHEE — LATE AFTERNOON — UNDERWATER

A WOMAN drifts down into the frame, at first appearing to
be a dead body, then turning with the flick of her MER-
MAID TAIL, smiling, beckoning gracefully with her arms.
She is replaced by ANOTHER MERMAID, then ANOTHER—

VIEWING AREA

Marly and Jack stand with several other AUDIENCE MEMBERS
watching the WEEKI WACHEE GIRLS perform. Jack is stunned—

                    JACK
         Which one did you play?

                    MARLY
I had a solo number. "Siren of the Deep."

                    JACK
You must have been something.

                    MARLY
I hated to come up. It was like I was meant
to live down there. You're soaring, you know?
Weightless—

She watches, transfixed, nostalgic—

                    MARLY
I still do the routine in my dreams.

                    JACK
It's good you live by the ocean.

                    MARLY
(with finality) I don't swim any more.

                    JACK
No?

                    MARLY
When you leave the job they make you hand in your
tailfin. I haven't been in the water for years.

74 EXT. LINCOLN BEACH — LATE AFTERNOON

Reggie is flipping burgers on the grill now, watching
uneasily as Desiree and Flash walk and talk apart from the
others —

                    DESIREE
You married, Lee?

                    FLASH
I was.

                    DESIREE
Kids?

                    FLASH
Two. Don't see enough of them. Their mother

moved down to Miami, married some Cuban guy. Listen, I'm really glad I found you again—

                    DESIREE

Yeah?

                    FLASH

There's something I've been thinking about for a while— something I need to talk to you about.

                    DESIREE

Here we are.

                    FLASH

It's— it's about your mother's property.

Desiree is stunned—

                    FLASH

You don't want to wait too long before—making plans.

                    DESIREE

For my mother—

                    FLASH

What I worry about is that you'll try to hold on to the house there till it's too late—

                    DESIREE

Too late for what?

                    FLASH

All these new resorts and time-sharing outfits over in Delrona have sent their taxes through the roof.

                    DESIREE

What's that got to do with us?

                    FLASH

Lincoln Beach is the only unincorporated parcel left on the island. They see us up here sitting on a beautiful stretch of sand, driving over their causeway, using their town services, not pulling our weight—

                    DESIREE

They never wanted a thing to do with this—

                    FLASH

Well they do now. Wouldn't be the first little community to be dragged kicking and screaming into the bigger town next door.

                    DESIREE

They can do that?

                    FLASH

All they need is one judge who sees it their way. So what we're offering is a chance for people here to sell before they get taxed out of their homes.

                    DESIREE

We—?

                    FLASH

I'm putting together a small group of investors. Now if your mother was willing to set a precedent, the terms might even be a little more favorable.

                    DESIREE

You'd pay her more?

                    FLASH

It's the spirit of the thing. Since she's been here from the beginning—

They walk in silence for a bit, Desiree not happy with the news—

                    FLASH

No big pressure. Just think about it.

                    DESIREE

Sure.

                         FLASH

So— you and the straight-arrow there—

                        DESIREE

Reggie.

                         FLASH

You're—?

                        DESIREE

Just married.

                         FLASH

Seems like a real nice guy.

                        DESIREE

Yeah. He is.

75 EXT. TRAILER PARK — EVENING

Billy paces outside his TRAILER, talking on a cell phone
while an ELDERLY WOMAN painstakingly paints a plaster LAWN
FLAMINGO in front of the trailer next door. It is the
newest in a menagerie of similar hand-painted ornaments
arranged in a permanent garden—

                         BILLY
        No, they all went to check out the titty
        bars down in Jacksonville— They're all
        right, they're just— guys, right?— We start
        clearing Monday— yeah— yeah— doesn't the
        teacher make allowances for that? Well,
        tell her I flunked it too. No, don't tell
        her that. Tell her I'll work with her on
        it when I get home— No, we go to Alabama
        after this, then there's a break— I miss
        you too— Think about me, all right?

Billy punches his phone off. He is lonely and restless.
He looks over to where the woman is staring at the
flamingo's beak, puzzled—

                    BILLY
          It's yellow with a black tip.
                 STEVE (O.S.)
          Skeeter Meter.

Billy turns to see Steve watching him from the doorway of
the trailer across the row—
                    BILLY
          Huh?
                    STEVE
          (points) Your T-shirt.

Billy is, in fact, wearing an old Skeeter Meter T-shirt—
                    BILLY
          Oh, yeah— you remember them?

Steve crosses and offers his hand—
                    STEVE
          Brother, I <u>was</u> them. Lead guitar and vocals.
                    BILLY
          (shakes) Right. You dressed in all that
          lizard skin—
                    STEVE
          Iguana. You're with the construction guys.
                    BILLY
          We're clearing a site.
                    STEVE
          Listen, have you ever built a water slide?

76 INT. PORCH — EUNICE'S HOUSE — NIGHT

Desiree sits watching as Reggie puts a coat of PAINT on
the interior of the screened porch—

                            REGGIE
You said it was a guy named Lee.

                            DESIREE
Leotis—

                            REGGIE
(realizing) Leotis "Flash" Phillips. Shit.

                            DESIREE
I'm sorry—

                            REGGIE
You got nothing to be sorry about, baby.

                            DESIREE
I should have told you more.

                            REGGIE
What? That he was a celebrity? Used-to-be
famous kind of thing—

                            DESIREE
You're not jealous—

                            REGGIE
I didn't know you then. And if I had— you
would have completely ignored me.

                            DESIREE
Reggie—

                            REGGIE
I couldn't compete with the <u>high</u> school
jocks, much less Mr. Heisman Trophy.

                            DESIREE
Come on—

                            REGGIE
And now you're with a guy who puts people to
sleep for a living—

                            DESIREE
Stop.

Reggie stops, loads his brush up again—

                    REGGIE
Does he even know?

                    DESIREE
I don't think so.

                    REGGIE
You gonna tell him?

                    DESIREE
Is there any point?

                    REGGIE
I don't know. If the baby had—

                    DESIREE
If the baby had lived everything would be
different.

                    REGGIE
Yeah.

                    DESIREE
But it's not.

                    REGGIE
And if he'd cut left instead of right on that
draw play—

They are quiet for a long time, thinking. Desiree notices
something in the NEWSPAPER spread on the floor to catch
paint—

                    DESIREE
How you doing with Terrell?

                    REGGIE
Kid's pretty good with a claw hammer and a
hand saw. This was 1925 he'd have a <u>future</u>.

Desiree, frowning, tears a square off from the newspaper—

77 INT. FRANCINE AND EARL'S BEDROOM — NIGHT

Earl sits on the bed with Francine, giving her a foot rub—

FRANCINE

Totally clueless.

EARL

I know.

FRANCINE

People think that it's just <u>there</u>, like Christmas or Thanksgiving. They don't appreciate how difficult it is to invent a tradition.

EARL

You do it so well, baby.

FRANCINE

And at the end of the day, is there acknowledgement? Is there so much as a thank you?

EARL

I know—

FRANCINE

Not a peep. I might as well be their mother.

EARL

It's an important role. If you weren't there—

FRANCINE

The time involved— the way I neglect you—

EARL

Naw—

FRANCINE

What have you been up to? I've hardly seen you.

EARL

Oh— the usual.

FRANCINE

You're my rock, you know that, don't you?

EARL

Sure—

FRANCINE

Even during all that bad stretch, when you

had your gambling problem? I knew it wasn't
gonna last forever cause you're my rock, and
I count on you.

                    EARL
I thought the parade went awful well this year.

                  FRANCINE
Did you really?

78 INT. HOTEL BEDROOM — NIGHT

Marly wakes in bed in an upscale hotel. She looks at Jack,
asleep next to her, frowns—

                    MARLY
     Shit.

79 INT. BATHROOM

Marly looks at herself in the bathroom mirror, rumpled,
her mouth dry—

                    MARLY
     Idiot.

80 INT. LIVING ROOM — MINIBAR

The mini-bar door opens. Marly's hand appears, pulling out
all the miniature bottles of liquor—

81 EXT. BALCONY — DAWN

Marly sits on the balcony overlooking the ocean. She has
miniature bottles of liquor lined up on the railing, ice
bucket beside her, drink in hand. The sun is coming up.
Marly squints, seeing something far down the beach—

POV — MAN AND DOGS

A MAN stands a water's edge down the beach, DOGS scampering all around him—

82 EXT. BEACH — SUNUP

The man is Furman, standing with his bare feet in the surf, greyhounds playing around him—

> **FURMAN**
> Come on dogs.

He turns and heads back toward the house, cautiously crossing the sand—

> **MARLY**
> Daddy?

> **FURMAN**
> That you, Marly?

Marly waits by the back of the house—

> **MARLY**
> You need any help?

> **FURMAN**
> Naw. I can still see light— shapes— You on your way to work?

> **MARLY**
> Sort of.

> **FURMAN**
> I used to see the sun come up every day. Only the shrimpers got up earlier. You remember Clarence Green, worked in the kitchen for me, he'd be there at the back— "Mornin, Clarence." "Mornin, Mr. Furman." They don't call you like that no more.

MARLY

Not for a long time, Daddy.

FURMAN

I said how if the integration came I was gonna close up. Morning come when there was four of em, polite young people, settin in a booth waitin for one of my girls to serve em. Clarence, he was back there tremblin like a leaf. Didn't know how I was gonna react. I said "What you think about this, Clarence?" "Oh," he says, "I reckon if you feed em once they won't none of em come back." "And why not?" I ask. "Scuse me for saying, Mr. Furman, but the food's a lot better down to Buster's Place."

Marly smiles. She has heard the story before—

FURMAN

Sometimes you spend a long time worrying about a day, aint so bad when it finally comes.

MARLY

I can't do it anymore, Daddy.

FURMAN

Developers been after you again.

MARLY

It's not them—

FURMAN

They make all this noise about that damn swamp buzzard—

MARLY

(familiar with this song) Snail kite—

FURMAN

I'll tell you who the endangered species is— it's the small bidnessman!

I know, Daddy. But it's me. I hate going in there—

Furman is quiet for a long moment—

FURMAN

People used to come to Plantation Island, ask
where can I stay the night? Where can I get
a good meal? Furman Temple's place, they'd
tell em. Right on the beach. You go see
Furman, he'll take care of you.

MARLY

I know, Daddy. But what should I do?

FURMAN

I left it in your hands, darlin. You're a
sensible girl, you always have been, if you
don't count marrying that musician. You'll
figure it out.

MARLY

I'm sorry.

FURMAN

I already been out in the world and done my
damage. Now it's your turn.

A silence—

FURMAN

Come on you dogs! Y'all are retired, you not
supposed to be running anymore.

83 EXT. BANK — DOWNTOWN — MORNING

VOLUNTEERS are taking the Buccaneer Days decorations down—

84 INT. BANK — CASH ROOM — MORNING

We hear other BANK EMPLOYEES chatting in the next room as Earl tops a metal CASHBOX off with wads of hundred-dollar bills, pulling them rapidly from the bottom of his shirt. He fills the box, slides it back into its compartment, locks it, and tucks in his shirt. He takes a deep breath, heads out to the bank lobby—

85 EXT. CAR LOT — DAY

Flash leans against a car in a city CAR LOT. He moves to approach as a rental car pulls in—

DESIREE

Desiree steps out of the rental car, looking grim. Flash slows as he sees it's her.

> **FLASH**
> Hi—

She holds up the paint-splattered section she ripped from the NEWSPAPER. An AD for the car lot, with the salesmen, including Flash, all standing in front of the stock—

> **DESIREE**
> "Score Big Savings with our All-American Sales Team."

> **FLASH**
> Yeah—

> **DESIREE**
> You work here.

Flash looks back to the office, takes Desiree's arm, steering her toward a row of cars—

> **FLASH**
> Some of the time, sure. What's the problem?

Desiree sees the convertible Flash rode into town in. It has a price sticker on the windshield—

> **DESIREE**
> Who are you buying property for?

> **FLASH**
> It's mine. It's in my name.

> **DESIREE**
> But who is it <u>for</u>? Whose money you use to buy it?

Flash is busted and he knows it. He considers making up a story, decides not to—

> **FLASH**
> These people—

He indicates the office—

> **FLASH**
> They own lots of things. Businesses, real estate—

> **DESIREE**
> They own Exley Plantation?

> **FLASH**
> Technically, yeah, but it wouldn't be called that if they— if things came to the point where they took it over. There'd be a different style, different name, more modest-income units—

> **DESIREE**
> Which you would get to sell.

Flash stops to face her—

> **FLASH**
> That's part of the deal, yeah.

> **DESIREE**
> What you get for tricking people into—

FLASH

I'm not <u>trick</u>ing anybody. They don't want to
sell, they don't have to. They do want to
sell, they get a decent price.

Desiree glares at Flash—

FLASH

Hey, who do <u>you</u> do work for?

DESIREE

That's different—

FLASH

Life moves on, shit gets bought and sold.
There's a handful of people who run the whole
deal and there's the rest of us who do what
they say and get paid for it.

Desiree doesn't know what to say to this—

FLASH

That neighborhood was <u>over</u> years ago. Hell,
you got out as soon as you could.

DESIREE

I left cause I was fifteen and I was pregnant.

Flash realizes what Desire's intensity is really about—

FLASH

Oh.

DESIREE

That's right.

FLASH

You never let me know.

DESIREE

What would you have done?

FLASH

Back then?

He thinks—

                              FLASH
My life was kind of falling apart on me. I
guess I wouldn't have been much help.

                              DESIREE
And you had other girls—

                              FLASH
Yeah.

Desiree softens slightly—

                              DESIREE
When I started to show Mama and Daddy sent me
to my Aunt Thelma in Macon. Then I lost the
baby, and I just kept going.

                              FLASH
Lost the baby.

                              DESIREE
Little boy. I was gonna name it Lee.

Flash takes a moment to absorb this—

                              FLASH
How'd you get by on your own?

                              DESIREE
I lied a lot. Lied about my age, lied about
my experience, hooked up with whoever was
likely to do me some good—

                              FLASH
Lying is a kind of acting, I suppose.

                              DESIREE
When you act, when you act on stage, you're
supposed to be after some kind of <u>truth</u>. When
you lie you're just out for yourself.

                              FLASH
You never had kids— after—?

                    DESIREE
I can't, there were some complications— I was
so young.

                     FLASH
You must be pretty mad at me.

                    DESIREE
There's a nineteen-year-old football player,
thinks he's got the world in his pocket— I'd
like to smack his oversized head.

Flash nods—

                     FLASH
Not much of him left to smack.

                    DESIREE
It wasn't your fault. I was who I was too.
But if we'd put somebody in the world—

She doesn't need to go on—

                    DESIREE
My Mama's not gonna sell her house.

Desiree turns and heads back to her car—

86 EXT. BUILDING SITE — DAY

A couple dozen CREW MEMBERS and BYSTANDERS, including the
local TV NEWS CREW have gathered for the ground-breaking
of the new site, standing around Billy on his front-
loader—

Dr. LLOYD

Dr. Lloyd looks at his watch. He's mustered only eight or
nine potential protesters, who are CHANTING—

                      PROTESTERS
        Stop Plantation Estates! No more expansion!
        Stop the digging now!

NORTHRUP

Northrup is standing by a construction TRAILER, talking
with Yordan. Jack stands nearby—
                      NORTHRUP
        What did I tell you? Just the same handful of
        malcontents.
                      YORDAN
        We'll frame them out. Won't hurt to get some
        footage of the machinery.
                      NORTHRUP
        The chanting—
                      YORDAN
        We won't run the sound. Keep your shirt on.

Northrup signals and we PAN to—

Dub, who signals and we PAN to—

Billy and Shiflett who shift their IDLING MACHINERY into
action—

DR. LLOYD — PROTESTERS

The PROTESTERS are CHANTING LOUDER—

BILLY

Billy lowers the blade and scoops up several yards of
ground. He rises up to see what he's done, frowning—

PROTESTERS

Suddenly silent. They move closer to see—

TV CAMERAMAN

Pressing forward, camera running—

JACK

Reacting—

NORTHRUP

Northrup's jaw drops as he sees—

POV — EXCAVATION

The hole Billy left is full of tangled, brownish HUMAN BONES!

NORTHRUP

The bystanders are abuzz all around him as he moves forward. Shiflett and Billy hop down, stepping close to see—

> **SHIFLETT**
> We got bones, Boss.

> **NORTHRUP**
> (grasping) They used to raise cattle here.

Shiflett kneels, picks up a SKULL—

> **SHIFLETT**
> Dudn't look like a cow to me.

DUB

Sure is a fuckload of em—

SHIFLETT

And they been dead for a <u>long</u> time.

Northrup reacts to something Billy has picked up, looking frantically over to where the cameraman is kneeling for a close-up of the bones. Dr. Lloyd stands behind him, grinning from ear to ear—

NORTHRUP

Okay— we're gonna have to ask all you folks to leave the premises till we can have this investigated—

DUB

Tell me that's not an arrowhead.

Billy holds the ARROWHEAD up for all to see—

BILLY

Yup. They say the only bad Indian is a <u>dead</u> Indian.

87 EXT. TEMPLE HOUSE — DRIVEWAY — DAY

Reggie stands in front of the Temple house next to a battered FLATBED TRUCK with the coffin on the rear—

88 EXT. TEMPLE HOUSE — BACK YARD

We see Terrell, coming around the back of the house, hunting the sound of a TV PLAYING. The greyhounds, tied up, jump up and down in greeting—

FURMAN (O.S.)

Who's that?

Surprised, Terrell looks up to the rear balcony, where Furman sits morosely facing the sea. The TV plays from inside the house—

> **TERRELL**
> Terrell Wilkins.

> **FURMAN**
> And who is Terrell Wilkins?

> **TERRELL**
> We brung over Miss Delia's box?

> **FURMAN**
> Leave it on the front step.

> **TERRELL**
> Kind of big— we had to borrow a flatbed truck to bring it over.

> **FURMAN**
> What kind of box is it?

> **TERRELL**
> It's a coffin. Made out of pine wood?

> **FURMAN**
> She's gettin ready to plant me under.

> **TERRELL**
> It's for the play she's doing.

> **FURMAN**
> How old are you, son? Don't sound like you can be driving any flatbed truck.

> **TERRELL**
> Naw, Mr.— my daddy drove it over.

He sneaks a look toward the front. No sign of Reggie—

> **FURMAN**
> He's a carpenter, your daddy?

> **TERRELL**
> He works in a hospital. Anesthesiologist.

> **FURMAN**
> He gives people the gas.

                    TERRELL

Yes sir.

                    FURMAN

How old are you?

                    TERRELL

Thirteen.

                    FURMAN

You at the Junior High School—

                    TERRELL

Uh-huh.

                    FURMAN

Where they keep all their trophies, they
still got a picture of two boys holdin
basketballs?

                    TERRELL

They look the same?

                    FURMAN

That was my boys. Dickie and Danny. They set
them some records.

                    TERRELL

Uh-huh.

                    FURMAN

It was segregated then— whole different game
now. You from Delrona or from Lincoln Beach?

                    TERRELL

Lincoln Beach.

                    FURMAN

Got a good spot there, right on the water.

                    TERRELL

Uh-huh.

                    FURMAN

You get out and swim?

                    TERRELL

No.

> **FURMAN**
>
> You don't know how or you just don't get around to it?

> **TERRELL**
>
> There's a undertow.

> **FURMAN**
>
> Course there is.

CU FURMAN

Furman has tears in his eyes, looking out past Terrell toward the water—

> **FURMAN**
>
> There's always gonna be one of those. The trick is, you never want to fight it head on. You got to swim <u>parallel</u> to the shore till the pressure eases up. You struggle against that whole wide ocean, you're a goner.

> **TERRELL**
>
> Uh-huh.

> **FURMAN**
>
> No matter how strong a man is, no matter how much grit he's got, try to fight it head on and it will pull you under.

Terrell is silent—

> **FURMAN**
>
> Miss Delia's off selling my whole life away. You can leave that pine box on the lawn for now. Give the neighbors something to buzz about.

> **TERRELL**
>
> Okay.

Terrell starts away—

                    FURMAN
        Terrell Wilkins?

Terrell pauses—

                    FURMAN
        You can't live on no beach and be afraid of
        the water.

89 INT. RESTAURANT — DAY

Marly and Miss Delia sit across from Greg at a table in
the back of the diner, remains of lunch in front of them—

                    GREG
        Marly tells me you're an actress.

                  MISS DELIA
        More of an impresario than a performer these
        days. Of course, Marly had her own flirtation
        with the theatrical life—

                    MARLY
        Ma—

                  MISS DELIA
        She portrayed a mermaid in a popular roadside
        attraction. Very successfully, I gather.

Marly ignores the condescension, used to it—

                    MARLY
        We should talk money—

                    GREG
        Hey, I'm really relieved that you folks have
        come around to this. Whenever there's an eco-
        nomic shift like what's about to happen,
        somebody gets left holding the bag.

                  MISS DELIA
        Stuck with their property—

                    GREG

After it's been dramatically devalued. If
you'd waited any longer, I'd hate to think—

                  MISS DELIA

Just what are your development plans, Mr.
Forrester?

                    GREG

That's not really my end of the business. I
assume that the whole beachfront area will
undergo some sort of change that— that would
have negatively impacted on your ability to
continue doing business as usual. So the
corporation—

                  MISS DELIA

Out of the goodness of their heart—

                    GREG

We prefer not to destroy anything when we
come into an area, Mrs. Temple. Whether it's
an eco-system or a small businessman.

                  MISS DELIA

That's extremely charitable of you. However,
in view of the fact that we have no crystal
ball to inform us on the scope of your corporation's future activities, I think some sort
of continuing participation would be in order.
On top of your very generous initial offer, of
course.

                    GREG

Continuing—?

                  MISS DELIA

An escalator clause.

                    GREG

I'm not sure—

                  MISS DELIA

Let's say that five years down the line you
have transformed our little beachfront into one

of those cash-generating monstrosities that
grace the coastal areas further to the south—
we'd receive a percentage of the gross proceeds
from all rentals. Or adjusted gross if you
will, depending on our ability to audit.

Greg is speechless. Marly is looking at her in shock—

                    MISS DELIA
          Don't <u>gape</u> at me, darling. I've operated a
          non-profit theater for twenty-five years—

                        GREG
          I'll have to get back to you on this.

                    MISS DELIA
          I imagine you will.

Miss Delia sees a passing Waitress—

                    MISS DELIA
          Cheryl— bring Mr. Forrester a slice of your
          key lime pie.
                       (to Greg)
          People tell me it's exceptional.

90 INT. EUNICE HOME — KITCHEN

Desiree steps in to find Eunice preparing food—

                      DESIREE
          Hey, Mama. What're you cooking?

                      EUNICE
          Lunch.

Desiree sees that her mother is just taking fried chicken
from a KFC box and putting it into the microwave—

                      DESIREE
          You always used to fry your own.

EUNICE

When I was a girl we pulled the feathers off
and threw the feet in a pot for soup. Don't
do that anymore, either.

DESIREE

That's too bad.

EUNICE

When you left here you couldn't boil water.

She pokes a thawing macaroni casserole with her finger—

DESIREE

And a casserole, too?

EUNICE

I'm taking that over to Mrs. Pierce. She
hasn't been feeling well.

DESIREE

You buried the hatchet with Mrs. Pierce after
all these years?

EUNICE

No. But she's my neighbor.

Eunice gathers plates and heads outside—

DESIREE

(following) Mama— if anybody comes to talk to
you about selling this house—

EUNICE

I put all the property in your name.

DESIREE

But you're still alive.

EUNICE

You've got yourself a really good man, there.
Responsible—

DESIREE

You mean unlike _me_.

EUNICE

We can't change how things went, Desiree, but—

DESIREE

(close to tears) Growing up here—the way everybody looked up to you and Daddy— I couldn't just be good, I had to be perfect.

EUNICE

Nobody expected that.

DESIREE

Of course they did. Once I went off the straight and narrow and everybody knew it—

EUNICE

Nobody—

DESIREE

<u>E</u>verybody knows <u>ev</u>erything here. If you didn't know about me and Lee Phillips it's cause you didn't <u>want</u> to. How was I going to come back here and look people in the eye?

EUNICE

Your family was here.

DESIREE

Daddy ran away from his family—

EUNICE

Your father lived in a sharecropper's shack and he was nearly full grown—

DESIREE

He was fifteen, same age as me—

EUNICE

He was a young man and those times were different!

DESIREE

You— both of you— had these ideas about what a decent person was, how they acted.

Desiree is trying hard not to cry—

DESIREE

I let you down. I was— afraid to face that.

EUNICE

You broke your father's heart.

DESIREE

And when you sent me away you broke mine.

Eunice looks at her—

EUNICE

Your father worked so hard to maintain a degree of respectability. Everybody was watching him— white people, black people—

DESIREE

And there I go, showing my color— isn't that what they used to call it?

EUNICE

I thought it would be better for you, for all of us—

DESIREE

Young girls get pregnant and have babies every day!

EUNICE

We were hoping to put an end to that. We were trying for a better life—

DESIREE

Moving up—

EUNICE

Taking care of ourselves. Taking care of each other.

Desiree shakes her head—

DESIREE

Well, talking isn't gonna change what's been done, is it?

A silence. They don't make a move toward each other—

                    DESIREE
          Are you okay, Mama? Dr. Lloyd said—

                    EUNICE
          I will live until I die.

She stirs the casserole, not wanting to face her daughter.

                    DESIREE
          If— if anything should happen, and you're
          worried about money to take care of Terrell—

                    EUNICE
          Baby— what good is <u>money</u> gonna do for Terrell?

91 INT. WATERFRONT BAR — EVENING — TV SCREEN

We watch the TV mounted at one end of the bar—

Yordan stands in front of the excavation while local
ARCHEOLOGISTS spread bones out on squares of canvas—

                  YORDAN (TV)
          Archeologists from the state university say
          the find is of enormous importance, the
          remains almost definitely those of the first
          known Native-American inhabitants of Planta-
          tion Island.

We CUT to Underhill, excited, being interviewed—

                  UNDERHILL (TV)
          The site seems to be a well or cistern of
          some sort. We've discovered quite a few cru-
          cifixes among the bones, and from a forensic
          examination I'd have to say we're dealing
          with a mass burial following a massacre—

We CUT back to Yordan—

> YORDAN (TV)

Plans to expand the Exley Plantation Estates development at the location have been post-poned indefinitely.

> MARLY (O.S.)

That mean you're out of here?

BAR — JACK, MARLY

Jack sits at the bar with a stiff drink, watching the TV, as Marly appears behind him—

> JACK

Hi.

> MARLY

Turn over a rock, there's no telling what you'll find underneath it.

> JACK

I've been shut down by fish, I've been shut down by birds—

> MARLY

Never by people?

> JACK

Not live ones.

> MARLY

So where to now?

> JACK

They're flying me to a site on Vieques Island tomorrow. Puerto Rico?

Marly nods. She waits a beat for Jack to say she has to come with him, that he can't live without her. He doesn't—

> MARLY

So— kind of bad timing, huh? With us.

> JACK

Yeah.

She leans forward, kisses his cheek—

                         MARLY
     You have fun down there.

She exits—

                                        FADE OUT:

92 EXT. HIGHWAY — MORNING

VEHICLES pass by the camera close enough for us to see the
occupants in CLOSE-UP. First comes Scotty Duval, singing
along with a song on the radio, then Jack in a Plantation
Estates company car, bleary-eyed, then Billy in his trailer,
Steve Tregaskis sitting next to him describing the dream
waterslide with his hands. Next comes a hauler with several
pieces of EARTH-MOVING EQUIPMENT on the back. Smoot and his
alligator flatbed bring up the rear as we PAN to watch them
all disappear over the arch of the CAUSEWAY—

93 EXT. EUNICE STOKES' HOUSE — FRONT YARD — MORNING

Reggie and Desiree pose a little uncomfortably in front
of Eunice's house, the rental car already IDLING beside
them. A FLASH—

                         DESIREE
     It's bright daylight out, Mama. You don't
     need the flash.

WIDER

Eunice is taking their picture with an Instamatic as Terrell looks on—

                         EUNICE
     Terrell, get in the picture. Come on—

---

314   JOHN SAYLES

> DESIREE

Stand in between us, Terrell.

Terrell mopily positions himself in between Reggie and Desiree. Desiree puts her arm around him, but all three are uncomfortable—

> EUNICE

That's it— smile now—

FLASH! Terrell immediately steps away—

> EUNICE

That's gonna be a nice one.

Reggie gives Terrell's shoulder a little punch, heads for the car—

> REGGIE

Now I'm serious about those grades, Terrell—

> TERRELL

Uh-huh—

> EUNICE

I'll send you a copy when he gets them.

> REGGIE

You hear that? There's no escape.

He hugs Desiree—

> REGGIE

I'll call you when I get in.

> DESIREE

I won't be too long.

> REGGIE

Take as much time as you need.

He gets in the car, waves a last time, and pulls away. We HOLD on Desiree—

94 EXT. SPRING (UNDERWATER) — MORNING — MARLY

Marly looks at us, framed by a tree over her head. She DIVES straight at us, shattering the surface calm of the crystal-clear SPRING, the camera looking up through water as she swims straight toward it—

95 EXT. FRANCHISE STRIP — MORNING

The foursome are playing through on a franchise strip, using the center road, lined with burger joints and T-shirt shops, as their fairway—

> MURRAY
>
> Before it was land it was gold.

> BIDWELL
>
> Gold.

> MURRAY
>
> That was the dream.

> BIDWELL
>
> To be richer than kings.

> MURRAY
>
> Ponce de Leon wanders ashore, runs into a native wearing a three-pound gold necklace. "Where'd you get all that?" he asks. The native demonstrates in sign language— "I picked it off the ground." Next thing you know the place is lousy with Spanish— they killed off entire tribes forcing them to look for the stuff. Wherever you found a Spaniard you found six Indians with shovels, sweating their asses off— but not one nugget did they find.

> CASH
>
> So where'd the native guy get it?

He picked it up off the beach where it washed
ashore from Spanish galleons that were always
sinking in the neighborhood. Full of precious
metals from Bolivia, Peru— places where they
had mines and an inexhaustible supply of
Indians to work in them.

BIDWELL

Chasing after their own treasure.

MURRAY

Chasing the dream. What do we have today
where you can strike it rich like that,
transform your life in an instant?

CASH

Hap Gordon won the Florida Lottery. Where you
scratch the card?

Murray shakes his head—

MURRAY

It lacks poetry.

BIDWELL

When we lived in Lauderdale I had a metal
detector. Used to work the beaches over every
morning.

MURRAY

And?

BIDWELL

Mostly pop-tabs from beer cans.

MURRAY

We live in impoverished times. What do our
young people dream of? Appearing on quiz
shows. Dating supermodels.

CASH

That's something.

MURRAY

Compared to pieces of eight? There's no

mystery anymore. There are human footprints
on the moon.

BIDWELL.

They say there might be gold on the moon.

MURRAY

There's a thought. Prospecting in outer
space.

Murray hits a three iron. They watch the ball sail away, carom
off a Tastee-Freez, and bounce back down the center road—

SILENT SAM

But what will we do for Indians?

MUSIC — CREDITS

PASSION FISH

BY

JOHN SAYLES

Introduction

THE GERM FOR THE STORY of *Passion Fish* came when I first saw Ingmar Bergman's *Persona* in the late 1960s. I had worked as an orderly in hospitals and nursing homes, and his very dark psychological tale of an actress who stops speaking and the nurse who comes to care for her struck a familiar note. I felt that an American version would be more of a comedy and involve a white patient and a black nurse (though I feel there is no gap harder to bridge than that between the healthy and the seriously ill—I think it's in our genes). The idea percolated for many years, gathering odd bits of detail, until one morning we woke up in a friend's house in Lake Arthur, Louisiana, and Maggie Renzi said, "This is where we should set the movie about the paralyzed woman and her nurse." I had been looking for a place that would seduce her out of her cocoon of self-pity, a culture that still valued the personal and had a complicated racial history, and Cajun country in Louisiana fit visually and in story terms.

Passion Fish can be seen as part of a trilogy about stages of life that includes *Baby It's You* and *Return of the Secaucus Seven*. In *Baby It's You* Sheik and Jill, in their late teens, are just getting the news that everything may not be possible, that there are limits to who they can be and what they can do. The Secaucus Seven are further down the road—the first returns have come in and it's a rough world they're facing out there. The women in *Passion Fish* are forty, and it's clear that bridges have been burned, that there are things they will never do. May-Alice will not become the next Meryl Streep. Chantelle can't be the party girl she used to be and win back control of her daughter. These two very damaged people are thrown together in a power relationship—one has power because she signs the checks, the other because she can walk—that makes the difference in race a minor issue between them (one which grows in importance the few times they go out in public together). By the end of the story I hope it's clear that each at least *wants* to be happy again and is willing to try to do something about it.

These depths of despair naturally bring soap opera to mind, and rather than skirt the issue I chose to attack it head-on by making May-Alice a former soap opera star. The main requirement of soap opera is that it has to be very involving without being too upsetting—who could tune in for true, deep grief, hopelessness, and suffering day after day? This is echoed in the scene where the other soap actresses visit, and one tells the story of auditioning for the one-line science-fiction role stating "I never asked for the anal probe." None of us do, of course, but once it manifests itself, in whatever form, how do we deal with it? May-Alice's first instinct is to roll into a ball and drink herself slowly to death. Given her circumstances, very understandable. But we only get one life, no matter what restrictions are placed on it by birth and circumstance, and what we try to do with it is how we define ourselves.

Language in southwestern Louisiana has a special music to it, one that May-Alice has fought hard to leave behind. It is an extraordinarily photogenic place, which led me to the idea that she might begin her salvation by picking up a camera. Though Chantelle is less entranced by the nature around her, the isolation does serve as a kind of refuge from her previous life and a safe place to meet her estranged father and daughter. What's not so apparent in the script, as usual, is the effect that Cajun and zydeco music had on the film (just as *Baby It's You* makes less sense without its soundtrack). There are things that a screenplay can only suggest but that are essential to the soul of the finished film. So maybe throw on a little Clifton Chenier or Balfa Brothers while you read this.

JOHN SAYLES

PASSION FISH

1 INT. HOSPITAL ROOM — DAY — CU WOMAN'S HAND

It is dark in the room. The hand lies on top of a white sheet, dream-twitching—

ECU EYES

Closed, eyeballs flicking around under the eyelids in the REM state of a dream—

CU OTHER HAND

Trembling, raising off the bedsheet, fingers spreading, touching the bedrail to the side, grasping the metal, the bedrail shaking noisily—

ECU EYES

The eyes pop open, staring straight up. We hear the WOMAN GASP—

CU HAND

Lets go of the bedrail and reaches through it, clawing air, searching for something—

NIGHT TABLE

Glass of water, Kleenex box, some remote-control devices. We hear desperate GRUNTING, off, then the hand appears, groping, knocking the glass of water over with a loud

CRASH. The hand steadies, finds the top of the table, finger-walks till it closes on one of the remotes. We PAN as it grabs hold and brings the device back to the face of MAY-ALICE. She fumbles with the buttons in a panic, breathing rapidly. We hear the STATIC of a TV SET from the foot of the bed. May-Alice hits a button again and again—

MAY-ALICE

Come, Goddammit! Help me! Why don't you come?!

We PAN away from her, TILTING UP as we go, till we see a TV set mounted up in a nook in the wall facing her bed. May-Alice doesn't have a call button, she has the TV controls, and is changing channels rapidly. When we settle on the TV she gives up, the TV is resting on a soap opera. Two WOMEN, one black, one white, sit on a couch in a living room set, talking. The white woman is played by May-Alice (Scarlet)—

RHONDA

(TV) You didn't recognize him?

SCARLET

(TV) No. Do I know him?

RHONDA

(TV) Look, I'm not a doctor, and I don't know anything about your condition, but I think it would be better if I didn't tell you those kinds of things.

SCARLET

(TV) It's all so strange. All I remember is— I wasn't happy, was I?

MAY-ALICE

We are above her, doing a SLOW-ZOOM in at her face as she starts to watch the show with a kind of horror—

                              RHONDA (O.S.)

          (TV) Scarlet—

                              SCARLET (O.S.)

          (TV) You keep calling me that. It sounds like
          some other person—

                              RHONDA (O.S.)

          (TV) Isn't there anything you can remember?

TV SCREEN

We are still ZOOMING IN SLOW on the screen as the soap
camera SLOW ZOOMS into a CU of Scarlet—

                              SCARLET

          (TV) There is something— it's more like a
          dream than anything that really happened. I'm
          walking down a hallway— it's dark— and it's
          so quiet I can hear my footsteps echoing. The
          hallway is very long, it seems never to end—

MAY-ALICE

We HOLD on her face now—

                              SCARLET (O.S.)

          (TV) All the time I'm walking I have this
          feeling that when I reach the end of the hall
          I'll find something—

May-Alice frowns, seeing something wrong—

TV SCREEN

The soap camera PANS OFF Scarlet onto a CU of Rhonda's
face. RHONDA is moved by this reverie, a single tear
rolling down her cheek—

(TV) —it's very frightening at first, but if I
can stand up to it, face it, it could be something wonderful. And then I have this feeling
that even though I can't see anybody or hear anybody, that I'm not alone. Somebody is with me.

MAY-ALICE

Indignant—

                    MAY-ALICE

That's my close-up. He gave her my fucking
close-up!

LIGHTS FLICK ON and May-Alice squints against the sudden
glare. She turns her head and we SHIFT to see the white
hip of NURSE QUICK leaning up against the bedrail. We stay
in May-Alice's POV, never really seeing Nurse Quick's face
as she moves around the bed—

                  NURSE QUICK
    Is something wrong?

May-Alice holds out the control device—

                    MAY-ALICE
    I thought this was the call button.

                  NURSE QUICK
Do you know where you are?

                    MAY-ALICE
Yeah, I'm in the fucking hospital. I was here
yesterday, wasn't I?

                  NURSE QUICK
You've been here for a while.

May-Alice frowns, trying to remember clearly—

> MAY-ALICE

My legs fell asleep. I wanted to get up—

There is a long pause. Nurse touches May-Alice's forehead, lifts one of her eyelids with her thumb—

> NURSE QUICK

Do you know who you are?

> MAY-ALICE

(pissed, nods toward the set) <u>She's</u> the one with the amnesia, not me! Just help me sit up, alright?

> NURSE QUICK

You had surgery yesterday. We put the rods on your spine. Do you remember? (May-Alice shakes her head no) I'm going to call Dr. Miles, he'll give you something to calm you down—

> MAY-ALICE

I don't need to be calmed <u>down</u>, I need to be helped <u>up!</u> You did something to me, didn't you? You gave me a shot and my legs went to sleep.

> NURSE QUICK

I'm going to call Dr. Miles—

> MAY-ALICE

No! You give me a straight fucking answer! What did you do to me?

> NURSE QUICK

(leaving) I think he's on the floor—

> MAY-ALICE

<u>No</u>!

May-Alice holds herself up on her elbows, struggling mightily, tilting and grabbing the side of the bed. With her other hand she yanks at the sheet. We PAN down with her gaze—her legs are pale, feet in cotton boots to keep her flexed, a catheter tube full of bright yellow urine snaking from the side of the bed over her thigh and disappearing up under her hospital gown. We PAN back to her face, arms starting to shake as she looks and Nurse Quick's hands appear just in time to catch her before she bangs her head collapsing backward—

> **NURSE QUICK**
> I'll get Doctor Miles. He'll go over it with you again.

We start to PAN and TILT back up to the TV screen—

> **MAY-ALICE (O.S.)**
> What am I doing here?

> **NURSE QUICK (O.S.)**
> Sometimes the medication makes it hard to remember—

> **MAY-ALICE (O.S.)**
> What happened to my legs?

We reach the screen again. The sound of their VOICES is drowned out by May-Alice, SCREAMING—

> **MAY-ALICE (O.S.)**
> WHAT IS WRONG WITH ME? WHAT IS WRONG WITH ME?!!!

2 INT. SWIMMING POOL — DAY — (OPENING CREDITS BEGIN)

May-Alice is floating on her back in a swimming pool, a THERAPIST'S hands supporting her gently from below. We HEAR but don't see the SWIMMING ACTIVITIES of other patients and therapists around them. The hands let go, letting May-Alice float on her own—

> **THERAPIST**
> Try to hold your position without using your

arms too much— now turn your head to the
left, very slowly—

May-Alice starts to sink sideways, thrashing the water
with her arms, panicking. The therapist's hands hold her—

                    THERAPIST
I'm right here. I won't let you drown.

                    MAY-ALICE
I knew there was a catch.

3 INT. THERAPY ROOM — DAY — (CREDITS CONTINUE)

May-Alice is long-sitting inside low parallel bars, wheelchair beneath her, her legs straight out and suspended at
the calves in cloth stirrups hung by bungie cords from the
bars. She tries to do a dip, pushing her body up with her
arms. Her arms tremble straining, and she gives up. A
therapist pauses, blocking the FG—

                    THERAPIST
It's not going to get any better unless you
keep at it, May-Alice.

                    MAY-ALICE
Then it's not going to get any better.

                    THERAPIST
(points) Look at Carlos— he's doing ten reps
already, with weights on his shoulders.

                    MAY-ALICE
Carlos is a monster. Carlos should be in the
fucking circus.

                    THERAPIST
You're just as good a candidate for rehab as
he is.

                    MAY-ALICE
Right. Can you take me back to my room now?

                    THERAPIST
     No.

                    MAY-ALICE
     My shoulders hurt.

No comment from the therapist—

                    MAY-ALICE
     You're going to make me stay here?

                    THERAPIST
     Go back to your room if you want. You know
     the way.

May-Alice glares, tries to pull herself forward to free
her legs, grimly struggling. But she can't unlock her
knees and almost falls from the chair trying. She leans
back, breathing hard. We hear a MALE VOICE, huffing from
one to ten in Spanish next to her—

                    THERAPIST
     If you had some upper body strength you
     wouldn't have any trouble with that.

                    MAY-ALICE
     (closes eyes) Fuck you. (raises voice) And
     fuck you too, Carlos.

4 INT. THERAPY ROOM — DAY — (CREDITS CONTINUE)

May-Alice is in a hands-and-knees position on a mat, sup-
ported at the waist by a therapist straddling her—

                    THERAPIST
     How are we doing?

                    MAY-ALICE
     I feel like I'm in a live sex show. How much
     longer?

                    THERAPIST
Try to find your center of gravity and work
on keeping your head up—
                    MAY-ALICE
You get off on this, don't you?

5 INT. BEDROOM — DAY — (CREDITS CONTINUE)

May-Alice sits in bed, moping. She glances icily at
someone to her left—
                    MAY-ALICE
So who are you?
                          DR.
I'm Dr. Kline—
                    MAY-ALICE
Shrink.
                          DR.
I'm a psychologist.
                    MAY-ALICE
You've got the voice.
                          DR.
Do I?
                    MAY-ALICE
I was under analysis for seven years.
                          DR.
Well— I'm going to ask you a few questions
about yourself—
                    MAY-ALICE
Are you going to make me walk?
                          DR.
No, May-Alice—
                    MAY-ALICE
You gonna make it so I can pee without
sticking plastic up inside me?

                    DR.

I'm not a urologist.

                 MAY-ALICE

Then go peddle it somewhere else.

                    DR.

You're angry.

                 MAY-ALICE

Oh, Christ—

                    DR.

No, that's good. You're going to need your
anger—

                 MAY-ALICE

Leave me alone.

                    DR.

This isn't just about you, you know. The
other people in your life—

                 MAY-ALICE

There aren't any other people in my life.

A pause—

                    DR.

Well. How did that happen?

                 MAY-ALICE

Look, I feel shitty enough without you rubbing it in, so just <u>van</u>ish, all right?

We hear the Dr. leave. May-Alice goes back to her moping—

6 INT. PT ROOM — DAY — (CREDITS CONTINUE)

May-Alice lies on a mat, surrounded by others who we see
only pieces of. A therapist strolls through the FG and BG
intermittently, calling out instructions to the group.
May-Alice is face-down, struggling—

THERAPIST
Okay, raise yourselves up onto your elbows—
that's it— not too much— side-to-side with
your head— now push your body back till your
elbows are under your shoulders. That will
give you the leverage. That's really good,
Chuck. I want you to roll to the left now,
very slow—under control— that's it— and go
right to the supine elbows post ion, using
your momentum— don't lie back. Now, from the
elbows we extend the arms, keeping balance,
walking up to a sitting position— wonderful.
Now, leaning forward, those of you with your
legs still crossed, leaning forward, keeping
balance—

May-Alice has only gotten to her elbows. She starts to cry—

7 INT. HALLWAY — DAY — (CREDITS CONTINUE)

May-Alice sits on her chair at a pay phone, installed low
on the wall, shooting glances around her as she talks into
the receiver—

MAY-ALICE
No, I don't want you to visit, I don't want
you to sue anybody else. I just want out of
this fucking boot camp— I'll sign anything—
it's like a fraternity here, all these gang
members shot in holdups, motorcycle casual-
ties, hang-gliders, rugby. They have <u>water</u>
fights in the hallway at night— I want to go
home. No, <u>home</u> home. Down there. I still own
it, don't I?— You're my business manager,
you're supposed to know this stuff— Harry,
just square it with the insurance and get me
out of here!

----

8 INT. AIRPORT — DAY — (CREDITS CONTINUE)

We watch a trio of STEWARDESSES pass, seeing them only from the knees down, wheeling their little luggage racks behind. They lead us to a WHEELCHAIR being pushed in the opposite direction. We see dead legs in braces, feet placed on the stirrups. Someone in a blue uniform is pushing, finally parking the chair in a patch of sun by a large window. We see planes taxiing outside—

                    ATTENDANT
          (off) Somebody will come for you when it's
          time to board, Miss Culhane—

We SLOW TILT UP till we see May-Alice, alone, staring blankly. A pair of FAN'S BODIES crowd the screen to either side of her—

                    FAN #1
          SCARLET?

                    FAN #2
          We read all about your tragedy in the *Digest*.

                    FAN #1
          We were so shocked—

                    FAN #2
          You're one of our favorites—

                    FAN #1
          Could you sign this?

May-Alice nods, signs the offered slip of paper, gives them a weak smile as she returns it—

                    FAN #1
          Thank you so much. You're going to make a
          wonderful comeback, I just know it.

                    FAN #2
          Enjoy your flight.

They exit frame. May-Alice searches in a side pocket of the chair, comes up with a pair of sunglasses, puts them on. MUSIC from a slow Cajun fiddle BEGINS. We ZOOM IN tighter, tighter on her sunglasses, till one dark lens fills the frame and we FADE TO BLACK:

MUSIC CONTINUES. OPENING CREDITS END. TITLE APPEARS.

WE FADE UP TO:

9 CU NAMECARD — INT. LOUISIANA AIRPORT — DAY (MUSIC CONTINUES)

The name "CULHANE" handwritten in marker on the card. We PULL BACK to see an older black DRIVER in a livery uniform waiting, holding the sign as PASSENGERS file by. We PAN to see a STEWARDESS pushing May-Alice, still wearing her shades, up to the driver—

> **DRIVER**
> Miss Culhane?

May-Alice nods—

> **DRIVER**
> (smiles) Welcome home.

10 INT. THERAPY ROOM — DAY

A trapeze bar hangs before us. Hands grip it from below, then May-Alice pulls up into the shot, holding her upper body at a forty-five degree angle, straining—

> **LOUISE**
> (off) Hold it there as long as you can.

Not very long. May-Alice's arms shake, she drops out of

frame with a thud. LOUISE, a physical therapist, steps into the shot—

> LOUISE
> That's as much as you can do?

2-SHOT

May-Alice lies back on a training table, the trapeze bar swinging above her. Charts mapping the muscles and nerves of the human body adorn the walls. A section of plastic spinal chord is mounted like a sculpture. Louise looks at May-Alice's legs—

> MAY-ALICE
> I don't have any upper body strength.

> LOUISE
> We gonna get you some.

Louise pulls May-Alice's arm up—

> LOUISE
> Car accident—

> MAY-ALICE
> Fucking taxicab. I was getting out of one when another comes along and sideswipes it. Hit me, took the door right off. Fucking kamikazes.

> LOUISE
> Mmmmn. Don't let me push this down.

> MAY-ALICE
> I was going to have my legs waxed.

> LOUISE
> New York City.

> MAY-ALICE
> (defensive) Yeah.

Louise moves to the other arm—

LOUISE

Says you some kind of actress.

MAY-ALICE

Some kind. I was on daytime.

LOUISE

Daytime?

MAY-ALICE

Soap operas.

LOUISE

(nods) Some my patients watch those.

MAY-ALICE

Right. We always got lots of letters from shut-ins.

LOUISE

I might even have seen you. What bring you down Louisiana?

MAY-ALICE

I heard what a brilliant therapist you were.

Louise gives her a look—

LOUISE

Might not be New York City, but we do all right. Even get you legs waxed here, you want.

MAY-ALICE

I didn't realize the hair would keep growing.

Louise tries to flex May-Alice's foot, frowns—

MAY-ALICE

I have a house here. It belongs to my family.

LOUISE

Vacation house—

MAY-ALICE

I grew up here. Jeff Davis Parish.

LOUISE
(smiles) Could have fool me.

MAY-ALICE
Thank you. I spent a fortune losing my accent.

LOUISE
Okay— there two kinds of therapy I'm going to work on you. One is to strengthen the muscles you still have control over, keep your back lined up right, increase your range of motion. The other is to control the circulation and tone in the areas you've lost the use of.

MAY-ALICE
Don't kill yourself.

LOUISE
Excuse me?

MAY-ALICE
I'm not the wheelchair Olympics type.

LOUISE
(sighs) May-Alice, you're a T-10, complete spinal lesion— whatever movement and sensation you've lost because of that isn't never coming back. But the rest of your body, rest of your life— that's whatever you want to make it.

MAY-ALICE
Right, Coach.

LOUISE
Now I don't know what you were like before the accident—

MAY-ALICE
You mean my "pre-morbid personality?"

LOUISE
(a little smile) You been reading the literature. You got a standing frame at this house?

MAY-ALICE

My business manager says he bought everything in the catalog.

LOUISE

Well you got to use it. I want you to stand one hour a day—

MAY-ALICE

(not interested) Sure.

LOUISE

If you're gonna be my patient—

MAY-ALICE

Look, I know the whole routine and I'm not buying into it. I don't want you coming to my house, I don't want your pep talks— this visit is just something my business manager cooked up with the insurance company.

LOUISE

Am I gonna meet this guy? Business manager?

MAY-ALICE

I'm out of business.

LOUISE

(persevering) All right. But I want you to send your people in, I'll show them the passive exercise routine—

MAY-ALICE

I don't have any "people." Not left alive.

LOUISE

Nobody down here with you? Nobody at this house?

MAY-ALICE

Just me.

LOUISE

We gonna have to do something bout that, aren't we?

11 EXT. LAKE, HOUSE — DAY

A WS of a house set along on a wide expanse of green, facing a calm lake with islands of cypress popping up in the distance. A van pulls up in front—

EXT. HOUSE — CLOSER

A strong-looking woman in a nurse's uniform, DRUSHKA, is wheeling May-Alice down a ramp from the side of the van to the front of the house. She pauses at the door, frowning—

          DRUSHKA
     No ramp.

          MAY-ALICE
     No.

          DRUSHKA
     The house has not been prepared.

          MAY-ALICE
     I figure we'll sort of work our way into it.

Drushka frowns again, takes the side panel off the chair—

          DRUSHKA
     An old house.

          MAY-ALICE
     Not that old.

          DRUSHKA
     Old houses are dirty.

          MAY-ALICE
     I had my manager call to get it cleaned.

Drushka huffs as she picks May-Alice up in her arms—

          DRUSHKA
     There should be a ramp.

12 INT. HOUSE—DAY

Drushka carries May-Alice across the threshold like a new-
lywed, steps in and begins to look around disapprovingly.
We PAN with her gaze to see a new orthopedic bed still
half-assembled, chairs covered in plastic— Drushka passes
into the frame again, still carrying May-Alice. We FOLLOW
them to look into the bathroom—

> **DRUSHKA**
> Is too narrow.

We FOLLOW them back, past some stairs—

> **MAY-ALICE**
> You'll be up there. Have the whole floor to
> yourself. Throw parties, whatever—

Drushka gives her a stony look. They step into a little
living room area. A new TV set, VCR, etc., sit across from
the couch half out of their boxes—

> **MAY-ALICE**
> Why don't you just throw me on the couch for
> now?

Drushka carefully lays her on the couch, a pillow under
her head. She crosses to the TV, runs a finger across the
screen, leaving a slash in the layer of dust—

> **MAY-ALICE**
> There's a guy from the video store in Jen-
> nings supposed to come hook all that up.

> **DRUSHKA**
> (looks at finger) Old houses are dirty.

13 CU REMOTE CONTROL PANEL — INT. LIVING ROOM — DAY

May-Alice's fingers pushing the channel button—

TV SCREEN

Flicking on to the soap we've seen before—

MAY-ALICE

Sitting propped up on the couch, wearing sweatpants and
sweatshirt, holding a white wine spritzer in her hand, the
wine and seltzer bottles on an easily reachable low table,
a bag of sour-cream-and-onion potato chips open on her
lap. We hear a VACUUM CLEANER approaching. May-Alice turns
up the sound with her remote. The vacuum comes closer.
More volume from the remote. The vacuum keeps coming till
Drushka is there pushing it in front of May-Alice. May-
Alice moves her head slightly to try to see around her.
Drushka props the vacuum against her thigh, spreads her
arms wide and shouts—

DRUSHKA

Germs!

14 INT. BATHROOM — DAY

May-Alice is in her chair in the narrow bathroom, struggling with a jerry-rigged bar installed to help her
transfer to the toilet. She finally makes it onto the
seat, resting a moment, when she hears a SQUEAKING NOISE.
We PAN with her gaze to the window. Drushka is outside
with a squeegee on a pole, washing the window. She mouths
the word "germs." We PAN back to May-Alice, who covers her
face with her hands—

15 INT. LIVING ROOM — NIGHT

May-Alice sits staring at the TV. Drushka appears and lays a
tray of food on the low table in front of her. May-Alice

looks at it suspiciously— some thoroughly-steamed vegetables surrounding a smoking pile of what looks like boiled sawdust—

> **DRUSHKA**
> You eat now.

> **MAY-ALICE**
> What exactly is this?

> **DRUSHKA**
> Kasha. Big fiber. Is good for stool.

> **MAY-ALICE**
> Yeah, it looks like it might have something to do with that.

> **DRUSHKA**
> You must eat.

May-Alice pours herself some wine, no seltzer this time—

> **MAY-ALICE**
> Kasha, huh?

16 INT. BATHROOM — NIGHT

May-Alice sits doubled over in a plastic chair in the shower, her face close to her knees, while Drushka, wearing plastic gloves, reaches in to scrub her back hard with a soapy washcloth—

> **MAY-ALICE**
> That hurts.

> **DRUSHKA**
> You must be clean.

> **MAY-ALICE**
> I'm clean enough. It hurts.

> **DRUSHKA**
> You think this is pain? At home, I do one hundred abortion, illegal, no drugs. That is pain.

May-Alice turns her head as best she can to try to get a look at Drushka. Drushka scrubs, sulking—

                    MAY-ALICE
         (quietly) May I please get out now?

17 CU REMOTE CONTROL — INT. LIVING ROOM — DAY

The remote held loosely in May-Alice's hand—

TV SCREEN

The familiar soap is on—

MAY-ALICE

Looking bad, a bit drunk in her rumpled sweatsuit. Her hair is a mess, her eyes bleary. She's drinking wine with ice cubes floating in it from a large Coke glass. Drushka clumps in with a bucket of water and a sponge and a bottle of Murphy's Oil Soap—

                    MAY-ALICE
         Little cleaning?

Drushka ignores her, begins to wash the walls, scrubbing hard. May-Alice looks back to the screen, then back to Drushka—

                    DRUSHKA
         Germs.
                    MAY-ALICE
         It's important that we have clean walls. I'll
         be climbing them soon.

18 CONTROL — INT.LIVING ROOM — NIGHT

Finger on the channel button. We TILT UP to May-Alice's face, blank as she watches. Drushka clears her throat, off. We PAN over to where Drushka stands in her nightgown, arms folded across her chest, eyes angry and tired—

> **MAY-ALICE**
> Can you hear this?

> **DRUSHKA**
> Is three in morning.

> **MAY-ALICE**
> I'll turn it down.

> **DRUSHKA**
> You must sleep.

> **ALICE**
> I'm not tired.

> **DRUSHKA**
> Is night. You must sleep.

> **MAY-ALICE**
> I got the rest of my life to sleep.

Drushka snorts, wheels and clomps away. May-Alice shoots a defiant look after her, then deliberately turns the volume up—

19 CU BREAKFAST TRAY — DINING ROOM — MORNING

Hi-fiber cereal, half a grapefruit, tomato juice, very yellow scrambled eggs. We TILT-UP to May-Alice, looking down at it, bleary-eyed and nauseated by the sight. We PAN from her to Drushka, standing with the remote held hostage in her hand—

> **DRUSHKA**
> Eat.

> **MAY-ALICE**
> I'm not hungry.

                    DRUSHKA
        Is good breakfast. Eat.

                    MAY-ALICE
        I'm not hungry. I'm not even awake.

                    DRUSHKA
        No eat, no TV.

                    MAY-ALICE
        Weren't you in *Ilsa, She-Beast of the Gulag?*

                    DRUSHKA
        Eat.

May-Alice lifts a forkful of egg, looks at it carefully,
looks at Drushka, then flicks it deliberately—

WALL

Splat! The eggs hit the wall making a nice Rorschach
design, then dribble downward. We PAN SLOWLY back to
Drushka, watching the wall, expressionless. She turns to
May-Alice—

                    DRUSHKA
        I call agency. They send new person tomorrow.

She lays the remote on May-Alice's tray as she passes out
of the room. May-Alice pushes the food away, stonefaced,
lifts the remote, and hits the on button—

20 TV SCREEN

The soap we've seen before is on. We hear the PERKY NURSE—

                    PERKY
        (off) —before I found Him I'd get like really
        de<u>pressed</u> and all, you know, like I'd try to
        go on a diet—

As Perky crosses in front of the screen we PAN up and begin to FOLLOW as she paces back and forth in front of May-Alice—

> ### PERKY
> —and I'd starve myself and like throw up a lot and everything but the minute I went off the diet I'd gain back all the weight I lost and then some and I'd feel so <u>weak</u> and worthless and— you know— like— like—

> ### MAY-ALICE
Pudgy?

> ### PERKY
> <u>Pudgy</u>! Yes! And then I found Him and it like clicked in my head that He loves you whether you're like pudgy or skinny or short or tall or really smart or kinda stupid or all healthy and athletic or like— you know, like—

> ### MAY-ALICE
Crippled?

> ### PERKY
> Physically <u>chall</u>enged, you know? And then it clicked in my head that I had like this vocation, this calling, which was like <u>help</u>ing people, and it's all connected because that's what He did on the cross, and if you can give of yourself to His lowliest creatures—

May-Alice holds out the remote and clicks it.

21 TV SCREEN

Same show, days later. We hear WEEPING off, then a new nurse, PHOEBE, passes in front of the screen and we FOLLOW as she paces woefully across the room—

> ### PHOEBE
I'm really sorry.

> You hate this job.

May-Alice is in different sweat pants and shirt, rumpled, her hair stuffed under a baseball cap. She barely shifts her eyes from the screen as she talks to Phoebe—

PHOEBE
> No, it's not that. I mean, I do hate this job, but that's not what's so terrible.

MAY-ALICE
> Problems with your boyfriend?

Phoebe nods, weeping—

MAY-ALICE
> Well, you shouldn't let some big dope get you all hysterical.

PHOEBE
> (defensive) He's not a big dope! He's not even American.

MAY-ALICE
> Ahhhh. What's his name? Derek?

Phoebe shakes her head no—

MAY-ALICE
> Jean Claude?

She shakes no again—

MAY-ALICE
> (snaps) Paolo.

Phoebe nods yes, weeping even harder—

MAY-ALICE
> Have you let this guy borrow money?

Huge bawling. May-Alice sighs, holds out the remote, clicks it—

A22 TV SCREEN

We TRACK BACK from the screen to see LAWANDA, an eager Black caretaker, in a chair in front of May-Alice, flipping through a copy of *TV GUIDE* as she chatters—

LAWANDA

Do you know that Blake?

MAY-ALICE

Different show.

LAWANDA

I just hate her. How about Lucinda?

MAY-ALICE

Lucinda?

LAWANDA

Lucinda on the story. Do you know her?

MAY-ALICE

Different show.

LAWANDA

Raven? Dominique?

MAY-ALICE

Different show.

LAWANDA

It's the same network though. She's on right after you—

MAY-ALICE

There's not like a room where they store us all in between shows—

LAWANDA

What about that Erica? I hate her too. She was here right now I swear I'd slap her face for what she did to that poor little—

May-Alice clicks the remote to change the channel—

22 TV SCREEN

Same show, days later. A new voice, KIT, starts as we
begin to PAN back to the couch—

> KIT
> (off) You wouldn't believe what a fuckhead
> this guy was. Anyhow, he ditches me down in
> Morgan City, this is like the lowest pit of
> Hell, right—

Kit is sitting next to May-Alice on the couch, both
watching the screen. Kit smoking. She takes the bottle
from May-Alice and pours herself a drink—

> KIT
> —and I'm flat out there for a couple weeks
> till I meet this biker, they call him
> Blacktop, and we take off. You like bikes?

> MAY-ALICE

Mmmmmn.

> KIT
> Anyway, he gets disability checks from the
> government— he was in some psychological drug
> experiment thing when he was in the army and
> something went wrong— you know what it's like
> to sleep with somebody with a ten-inch
> hunting knife strapped to his thigh?

> MAY-ALICE

Mmmmmn.

> KIT
> He was an all right guy, though, as long as he
> stayed on the medication. When he'd skip a
> couple doses though—(whistles). Anyway, he had
> to go back in for a refit on the steel plate

in his head and I took up with this musician—
you know heavy metal? This is beyond that— a
guy I know who was electrocuted once working
on the rigs says he sees the same blue flashes
when Duane plays. You ever been electrocuted?

                         MAY-ALICE
Uhn-uh.

                           KIT
He's got this thing about not washing, Duane,
but hey— mu_si_cians, right? You don't mind if
I smoke, do you?

May-Alice clicks the remote. She closes her eyes—

23 EXT. COUNTRYSIDE — DAY — BUS

A bus wipes the frame, leaving CHANTELLE, a black woman in
her 30's standing on the side of the road with a suitcase—

CU CHANTELLE

She looks across a flat stretch of green field—

CHANTELLE'S POV

May-Alice's house, an old car parked in front of it—

24 DOOR

Chantelle's hand appears to KNOCK, wait, KNOCK HARDER.
Nothing. We TILT DOWN as she reaches for the doorknob,
turns it—

25 INT. HOUSE — DAY

A blast of backlight as Chantelle steps in. We FOLLOW her
around, honing in on a STATIC SOUND from the living room.
May-Alice is on the couch, half covered, sweaty, debris
from junk food scattered around, lying with her face covered by her arms. Chantelle crosses to the TV, caught
between stations, searches, then crosses to the couch to
find the remote to turn it OFF. She frowns at the empty
wine bottles on the floor. May-Alice lifts her arms, eyes
red from crying. Chantelle sits on the arm of the couch—

                    CHANTELLE
          I'm Chantelle.

                    MAY-ALICE
          Didn't think they'd send another one.

                    CHANTELLE
          How long have you been without somebody?

May-Alice frowns at the TV—

                    MAY-ALICE
          I dropped the remote. I think it's behind the
          couch.

May-Alice tries to sit up, her arms shaking with the effort.
She barely makes it, seems dizzy—

                    CHANTELLE
          You ought to have a ramp out there.

Chantelle crosses to the far wall to get the wheelchair.
The egg stain is still there. She looks to May-Alice—

                    MAY-ALICE
          Breakfast.

Chantelle brings the chair over—

                    MAY-ALICE
I haven't been taking my Ditropan— had an
accident here—

                    CHANTELLE
I'll help you wash up.

Chantelle helps her into the chair—

                    MAY-ALICE
Listen, Sherelle—

                    CHANTELLE.
Chantelle.

                    MAY-ALICE
If you got any problems? Personal problems?
I don't want to hear them.

Chantelle pushes her out of frame—

26 INT. BATHROOM — DAY

May-Alice is in the bathtub, washing herself, while
Chantelle sits on the toilet lid watching her—

                    MAY-ALICE
You been doing this long?

                    CHANTELLE
No. You?

                    MAY-ALICE
(a small smile) You _are_ a nurse, aren't you?

                    CHANTELLE
Yeah. But I never did this caretaker thing
before. Stay over at somebody's house.

                    MAY-ALICE
Well, I'll tell you Shondelle, it's a snap.

                    CHANTELLE.
Chantelle.

                         MAY-ALICE
         All the things I can't do, you do them for me.

CU MAY-ALICE

We SLOWLY TIGHTEN on her as she speaks—
                         MAY-ALICE
         These days that's almost everything. Can't go
         anywhere by myself, can't cook anymore, can't
         work anymore, can't shit without a supposi-
         tory, can't have sex I can feel unless I
         really get into blow jobs—

She catches herself—
                         MAY-ALICE
         Sorry. You're probably some big Christian,
         right, and I just put my foot in my mouth—

2-SHOT
                         CHANTELLE
         (deadpan) None of my business <u>what</u> you put in
         your mouth, Miss Culhane.

May-Alice almost smiles—
                         MAY-ALICE
         Chantelle, huh?
                         CHANTELLE
         Chantelle.
                         MAY-ALICE
         What did they tell you about me at the
         agency?
                         CHANTELLE
         (shrugs) You're a T-10.

                    MAY-ALICE
What else?

                    CHANTELLE
Said you had your own money so the pay was
better than the state cases.

                    MAY-ALICE
Did they tell you I was a bitch?

Chantelle considers, then plunges ahead—

                    CHANTELLE
On wheels.

27 INT. DINING ROOM — EVENING

May-Alice is parked at the dinner table, watching as
Chantelle lays a TV dinner in front of her—

                    MAY-ALICE
Lean Cuisine. Miss Perky must have left this.
She was the second or third one they sent over.
There any wine in there?

Chantelle pulls out a bottle that is two-thirds empty—

                    CHANTELLE
Just this.

                    MAY-ALICE
The last one was a real sponge. Surprised she
left me anything.

                    CHANTELLE
(pointedly) I don't drink.

                    MAY-ALICE
Well good for you. They'll be holding a
case of this for me at Ernie's in town.
They bill me.

She watches as Chantelle pours her a drink—

> MAY-ALICE
>
> I like it cold.

28 INT. LIVING ROOM — NIGHT — CU REMOTE

The remote in Chantelle's hand, passed to May-Alice—

> MAY-ALICE
>
> Hey, you found my umbilical chord.

May-Alice is tucked into her nest on the couch—

> CHANTELLE
>
> You got a way to call me if you need some-
> thing?

> MAY-ALICE
>
> (waves remote) I turn the volume way up.
> Look, I got no idea what the last one left
> you up there—

> CHANTELLE
>
> I'll be fine. Good night, Miss Culhane.
> (starts to leave)

> MAY-ALICE
>
> Chantelle? I don't usually wet myself.

> CHANTELLE
>
> Don't worry about it.

29 TOP OP STAIRS — NIGHT

Chantelle steps up into the shot, and we FOLLOW her down
the hall and into her room. Her suitcase is on the unmade
bed. She looks around— rock posters, Haitian art, black
candles. She puts her head in her hands, trembling, and
starts to cry—

FADE TO BLACK:

FADE UP TO:

30 INT. UPSTAIRS HALLWAY — DAY

Chantelle is hauling heavy metal posters out of her room. She pauses at the top of the stairs as she sees something out the window, below—

31 EXT. HOUSE — DAY

May-Alice's UNCLE REEVES stands in front of the house, checking it out like a potential buyer. The front door opens and Chantelle steps out—

>   **CHANTELLE**
> I help you?

>   **REEVES**
> I was wondering if May-Alice might be in? Nobody seems to answer your telephone.

>   **CHANTELLE**
> She's asleep.

>   **REEVES**
> Ahhh.

>   **CHANTELLE**
> You know her?

>   **REEVES**
> I'm her uncle. Her uncle Reeves.

32 INT. KITCHEN — DAY

They speak low so as not to wake May-Alice. We FOLLOW Reeves as he casually pokes into drawers and cabinets, searching for something, Chantelle watching him with her back against the refrigerator—

                    CHANTELLE

You don't look old enough to be anybody's
uncle.

                    REEVES

You're so kind. I was something of an after-
thought in the family. May-Alice's father was
already in high school when I was born.

He closes a drawer, not finding what he's searching for—

                    REEVES

What time does May-Alice usually rise?

                    CHANTELLE

Noon or so.

                    REEVES

Sensible girl. Noon would suit me fine. But
as long as there is real estate to be bought
and sold in the Crescent City, I have no
rest. (he smiles ruefully) Real estate. This
is what our dreams come to.

                    CHANTELLE

Can I help you find something?

                    REEVES

I'm poking around, aren't I? I lived here for
a spell— just after May-Alice's parents passed
on. Bachelor days.

                    CHANTELLE

If you're looking for those bottles, I threw
all that away.

                    REEVES

(face falls) I see.

                    CHANTELLE

Wasn't so much left. (sees his shakiness) Got
some white wine cold in here.

                    REEVES

(sighs) That might be pleasant.

He watches Chantelle pull out a bottle and pour him a glass—

> ### REEVES
> My brother— May-Alice's father— was an amateur flyer— he was quite a sportsman, actually. This house was once filled with his trophies, on every wall, until I was compelled to donate them to a local museum of natural history. Their eyes seemed to follow me from room to room.

Reeves watches the glass as Chantelle brings it to him, a disapproving-mother look on her face—

> ### REEVES
> They were flying down to the Keys, for the bonefishing I believe, not the marlin— May-Alice's father was a great admirer of Mr. Hemingway. He flew everywhere, hunting, fishing—

> ### CHANTELLE
> And her mother went along?

> ### REEVES
> May-Alice's mother was a great admirer of May-Alice's father. "Whither thou goest, I shall go."

He sips the wine, makes a face—

> ### REEVES
> At the service at least three people rose to comment on what an excellent <u>pilot</u> my brother was.

Reeves frowns at the wine—

> ### REEVES
> Not my drink, I afraid.

---

33 INT. DARKROOM

DARKROOM LIGHT comes ON as Reeves steps in, followed by
Chantelle. A layer of dust on everything, a few old
photos clipped to an overhead line to dry, curled and
yellowing. Reeves picks up a camera from next to the
sink, looks at it—

                            REEVES
        I built this myself. When I was younger, pho-
        tography was quite an obsession of mine. Have
        you ever seen the work of Mr. E.J. Bellocq?

                          CHANTELLE
        Don't think so.

                            REEVES
        It's very striking— anyhow, photography remained
        an avocation and not a way of life.

He kneels, pulls a nearly full bottle of bourbon from
between dusty bottles of chemical fixer. He smiles and
wiggles the bottle at Chantelle—

                            REEVES
        Improves with age.

34 INT. KITCHEN — DAY

Chantelle busts ice cubes into a Tupperware bowl. We
FOLLOW her to the living room, Reeves and May-Alice
yakking in good spirits—

                            REEVES
        My friend Jason got his first taste of finan-
        cial independence and was gone with the
        proverbial wind.

                          MAY-ALICE
        He inherited money?

> **REEVES**
>
> The only thing Jason is in line to inherit is
> a Naugahide dinette set.

May-Alice is laughing as Chantelle enters and lays the ice
on the table in front of them. May-Alice has her wine
bottle and Reeves his bourbon, half empty now—

> **REEVES**
>
> No, Jason has made his mark in the world of
> commerce.

> **MAY-ALICE**
>
> Jason never worked a day in his life.

> **REEVES**
>
> You remember he was something of a potter?
> Well he came up with a scheme to manufacture
> homoerotic delftware—

> **MAY-ALICE**
>
> (laughing) Go on—

> **REEVES**
>
> Dinner plates with little Dutch boys painted
> in compromising positions—

> **MAY-ALICE**
>
> Nooo—

> **REEVES**
>
> Perversion is rampant in our society.

> **MAY-ALICE**
>
> You're better off without him.

> **REEVES**
>
> I keep telling myself that.

Chantelle steps out, leaving us with May-Alice and her
uncle. A long, sobering pause—

> **REEVES**
>
> I was so sorry to learn about your afflic-
> tion, May-Alice.

May-Alice tries to shrug this off—

REEVES
I always wanted you to be the one who went away and became famous and was always happy.

MAY-ALICE
At least I went away.

REEVES
And now this.

MAY-ALICE
Reeves, if you start to cry I'm going to throw my drink at you.

35 INT. BEDROOM — NIGHT

Chantelle paces back and forth, in and out of the frame. She is agitated, jumpy. She sits on her bed, head in her hands—

36 INT. KITCHEN — NIGHT

Chantelle appears with the bowl of half-melted ice. She scoops her hand into it and rubs a bit on her face, closing her eyes—

37 INT. LIVING ROOM — NIGHT

Reeves is asleep, sitting on the couch, head thrown back. May-Alice is nodding off in her chair. Chantelle enters, crossing to lay a blanket over Reeves, then to wheel May-Alice to her bedroom—

MAY-ALICE
(half awake) That's my uncle Reeves. Idn't he great?

CHANTELLE
He's real— (searches) <u>lit</u>erary.

MAY-ALICE

(laughs) Reeves has been literary ever since
he was a boy. Didn't go down real big in the
family.

CHANTELLE

Takes all kinds.

MAY-ALICE

He gave me his camera. Idn't at sweet?

38 INT. KITCHEN — DAY — CU GRAPEFRUIT

A half grapefruit staring up—

MAY-ALICE

May-Alice staring down at the grapefruit, in the same outfit
she went to bed in, pushed close to the table—

CHANTELLE

Glances at May-Alice studying the grapefruit, then goes
back to looking at a shopping list—

CHANTELLE

You need me to cut that up for you more?

MAY-ALICE

I can't deal with grapefruit in the morning.

CHANTELLE

We don't have any eggs. I got em on the list.

MAY-ALICE

I can't deal with breakfast at all.

Chantelle sits, pulls the grapefruit in front of her,
sprinkles it with sugar and starts to eat—

                    MAY-ALICE
There's still a car out back, isn't there?

                    CHANTELLE
Light brown. Says Buick on the side.

                    MAY-ALICE
Good. The last one took it in to Lafayette a
couple times, afraid she might have sold it.

                    CHANTELLE
Anything you need before I go?

                    MAY-ALICE
I can change the channels myself.

                    CHANTELLE
Should we— should I help you in the bathroom
before—

                    MAY-ALICE
(snorts) I was the best voider in my rehab
group. Thought they'd give me a fucking medal
or something.

                    CHANTELLE
Bathroom's not set up too well—

                    MAY-ALICE
Keys should be in the car.

Chantelle nods, stands with the list—

                    CHANTELLE
I'll try to get back as soon as I can.

                    MAY-ALICE
Don't kill yourself.

Chantelle stops by the door—

                    CHANTELLE
You neither.

39 EXT. ROAD — CAR — DAY

The Buick approaches us on a country road, starts to buck, coughs and dies right in front of us—

40 INT. CAR

                    CHANTELLE

    Damn.

39 EXT. CAR

Chantelle steps out, slams her hand on the hood—
                    CHANTELLE

    Damn!

She looks back the way she came, then down the road. Shakes her head, starts walking in the same direction she was driving—

41 INT. BATHROOM — DAY

May-Alice has just flushed and is wriggling back into her sweatpants, still seated on the bowl. The chair is just in front of her, but there are no special rails built in and the space is very narrow. She tries to do her usual transfer, pulling on the towel rack to the side to begin her swing, but the rack tears right out of the tile and May-Alice falls backward off the bowl onto the floor, landing hard on her hip and shoulder, knocking the air out of her lungs. She wheezes for breath—

42 EXT. ROADSIDE — DAY — SHOES

Chantelle's shoes sit abandoned in the roadside grass. We PAN over to her feet, toes working. We hear a CAR APPROACHING—

SUGAR

SUGAR LEDOUX, a handsome black man about Chantelle's age, sticks his head out of the window of a pickup hauling a horse trailer, and smiles as he comes to a stop—

Chantelle stares back at him—

SUGAR

> SUGAR
>
> I sure hope you need a ride.

43 INT. CAR

Sugar driving Chantelle into town—

> SUGAR
>
> Break down?

> CHANTELLE
>
> No gas. (Sugar smiles) Don't be smirkin at me. Lady I work for left it on empty. Thought I could make it to town.

> SUGAR
>
> You're not from here. I can tell.

> CHANTELLE
>
> (grumpy) Yeah, an you are. I can tell.

> SUGAR
>
> Somebody in a bad mood. Must have walked three, four miles.

No response—

> SUGAR
>
> What you do for this lady you work for?

> CHANTELLE
>
> Take care of her, I guess.

                    SUGAR

White lady.

                  CHANTELLE

Mmmmmmn.

                    SUGAR

Old?

                  CHANTELLE

You a detective?

                    SUGAR

You a nurse?

                  CHANTELLE

I was. Almost.

                    SUGAR

Pay must be real good, get a fine-looking young
woman live out with some sick old white lady.

Chantelle gives him a look—

                  CHANTELLE

Pay's all right.

                    SUGAR

Well, I hope you stay working round here.

                  CHANTELLE

If you're trying to be charming, don't be
wastin it on me. What's that smell?

                    SUGAR

Smell?

                  CHANTELLE

More from the back, but it's up here too.

                    SUGAR

(laughs) That's horse, darlin.

                  CHANTELLE

You got a <u>horse</u> back there?

                    SUGAR

I take care of em. Put shoes on their hooves,
train em for their owners—

                         CHANTELLE

And you givin me grief about I take care of
a white lady? (looks out) This the town?

                          SUGAR

Most of it. Where you want me to leave you?

                        CHANTELLE

Here is fine.

                          SUGAR

You want me to find you some gas, run you
back out—

                        CHANTELLE

I can manage myself.

Sugar stops the pickup, offers his hand—

                          SUGAR

Sugar.

                        CHANTELLE

What?

                          SUGAR

Sugar LeDoux. That's me.

                        CHANTELLE

You gotta be kiddin.

                          SUGAR

Real name is Ulysse. Like Ulysses in the
mythology? Ma mere aime beaucoup les clas-
siques. What's your name?

                        CHANTELLE

(getting out) Chantelle.

                          SUGAR

Chantelle what?

                        CHANTELLE

Chantelle-who's-got-no-time-for-any-French-
talkin-Louisiana-cowboys.

                          SUGAR

(calling) Do you dance, Chantelle?

Chantelle turns, face serious—

CHANTELLE

No. Not anymore.

Sugar watches as she walks away—

41 INT. BATHROOM — DAY

May-Alice is struggling to pull herself up on the toilet
again, pulling on the edge of the sink, but she doesn't
have the strength. She is crying, and when she gives up
pulling and just hangs by her arms she starts to scream—

MAY-ALICE

Shit! Shit! Shit! Shit!

44 EXT. MARINA — DAY — CU GAS PUMP HANDLE

Somebody is pumping gas into a large metal can—

CHANTELLE

(off) Excuse me—

REVERSE — WIDER

We shoot past RENNIE BOUDREAU, a white man around forty,
who is filling several gas cans from pumps next to the
edge of the lake. He looks up to see Chantelle several
feet away—

CHANTELLE

Will that gas work in a car?

Rennie looks at the pump as if it's a tough question—

RENNIE

It's gas.

CHANTELLE

So it would work. That was a stupid question, right?

RENNIE

Question isn't stupid unless you already know the answer. It work fine in a car.

CHANTELLE

I guess I'll need about two gallons. Can I buy one of those cans?

RENNIE

(looks at them) Them're mine.

CHANTELLE

You don't work here?

RENNIE

Don't nobody <u>work</u> here. Old Hebert own the pumps, but he mostly drinks and sleeps and leave the box out for people put their money in. He sleepin now.

CHANTELLE

People just leave their money for what they take?

RENNIE

You not from here, are you?

CHANTELLE

No.

RENNIE

And your car is broke down somewhere thout no gas. You wait one minute, I take you there, put some in.

CHANTELLE

Well— I got all this stuff, sittin at the liquor store—

RENNIE

We run by there, pick him up. (He glances at the pump price) I pump you two gallon, that's three dollar twenty.

Chantelle crosses to a cigar box set on a little stand between the pumps. An old fishing reel serves as a paper-weight to keep the bills from blowing away. She lays the money in—

                    CHANTELLE
          Nobody ever stole some?

                    RENNIE
          Doesn't nobody want to deal with Hebert, he
          hear you been skimmin his bar money. (caps
          the gas can, hangs the pump.) That Ernie's
          liquor store or Lanois'?

45 INT. HOUSE — DAY

May-Alice is on the floor between the bathroom and the living room, dragging herself forward on her elbows with great effort, crying. She stops to rest, laying her cheek flat on the wood of the floor, breathing hard—

46 EXT. ROADSIDE — LATE AFTERNOON

Rennie is funneling gas into the tank of the Buick, his pickup (a general contracting ad and number hand-painted on the side) parked ahead. Chantelle is loading groceries into the back seat—

                    RENNIE
          This used to belong to Mr. Culhane, live out
          by the lake.

                    CHANTELLE
          S'his daughter's now.

                    RENNIE
          May-Alice. Word is she stuck in her bed.

                    CHANTELLE
          Paraplegic.

Rennie frowns, lays the can down, puts the cap on the tank—

                    RENNIE
        How she doing?

                    CHANTELLE
        (shrugs) I just started out there.

Chantelle hefts a case of wine bottles into the seat—

                    CHANTELLE
        Place could use some work— it wasn't set up
        for somebody in a chair.

Rennie reaches into the glove compartment of his pickup
and comes out with a card—

                    RENNIE
        I do carpentry, little plumbing, fix your
        roof—

                    CHANTELLE
        (takes card) I'll talk to her.

                    RENNIE
        You maybe wanna have this old car looked
        at. Doesn't nothing like to sit for twenty
        years.

She slides into the front seat, turns the key. The engine
comes roughly to life—

                    RENNIE
        You find a Evangeline's just north of her
        place on the highway, you can gas up.

                    CHANTELLE
        Thanks a whole lot. I'll tell her you said hi.

                    RENNIE
        (shrugs) She won't remember me. (taps hood)
        Bonne chance.

47 INT. LIVING ROOM — EARLY EVENING

May-Alice has reached the couch and managed to pull herself up into a sitting position at the base of it. She
rests, breathing heavily, then we HEAR the CAR PULLING IN.
She finds the remote control, flicks the TV ON, tries to
compose herself. We hear Chantelle ENTER, lay a box down.
She steps into the room. May-Alice won't take her eyes off
the TV—

> CHANTELLE
>
> I'm really sorry I'm so late—

> MAY-ALICE
>
> I need a glass of wine—

> CHANTELLE
>
> The car didn't have any gas in it, it broke
> down—

> MAY-ALICE
>
> With ice.

> CHANTELLE
>
> I had a terrible day.

> MAY-ALICE
>
> Mine was a scream. If you just bring the
> bottle in I can pour my own.

Chantelle is not in the mood for this. She sits on the
edge of the couch—

> CHANTELLE
>
> (quietly) I'm not your waitress.

> MAY-ALICE
>
> What are you then?

> CHANTELLE
>
> Will you look at me?

Nothing from May-Alice—

                    CHANTELLE
        Will you please look at me?

May-Alice looks, fierce, very close to crying again—

                    MAY-ALICE
        I didn't think you were coming back.

                    CHANTELLE
        Course I was.

                    MAY-ALICE
        How should I know that?

                    CHANTELLE
        Cause I <u>told</u> you I would. I'm going to bring
        in the rest of the groceries. If you want a
        drink it's on the table in the kitchen.

                    MAY-ALICE
        I can't make it out there.

Chantelle looks for the chair, then to May-Alice. Concerned, she kneels by her—

                    CHANTELLE
        You're all sweaty. Where's your chair?

                    MAY-ALICE
        I couldn't get back into it in the bathroom.
        It was easier to come out here.

                    CHANTELLE
        You fell?

May-Alice tightens up, mad again. Chantelle pulls a pillow
from the couch, lays it on the floor, then takes May-Alice
behind the neck and back, and lays her down on the floor—

                    CHANTELLE
        I need to look at your legs—

                    MAY-ALICE
        I didn't hit hard—

                              CHANTELLE
          I need to look at your legs—

                              MAY-ALICE
          No—

May-Alice struggles with her arms as Chantelle tries to
pull her sweatpants down, but has no strength left.
Chantelle backs off—

                              CHANTELLE
          Please. You could be hurt.

May-Alice goes deadpan, lays her arms across her face.
Chantelle gently pulls her pants down, tilts her from side
to side, feels down her legs—

                              CHANTELLE
          You got a big bruise under your hip. I don't
          think anything is broken. We should take you
          in for X-rays.

                              MAY-ALICE
          No.

                              CHANTELLE
          There's no way for me to tell for sure if—

                              MAY-ALICE
          (screams) No! Godammit, it's my fucking body
          and I said no!

Chantelle backs off, sits against the couch—

                              CHANTELLE
          I'm not much good at this, am I?

                              MAY-ALICE
          (musing bitterly) Yeah, I've been thinking
          about a career change myself. Aerobics
          instructor, mail carrier— who knows, maybe
          something on the oil rigs.

                    CHANTELLE
You thought I stole your car?

                    MAY-ALICE
I thought you drove back to the Agency and
told them you were quitting.

                    CHANTELLE
I need this job.

A silence. May-Alice still has her hands over her eyes—

                    CHANTELLE
        (stands) I'll get you some dinner.

                    MAY-ALICE
        (quietly) Could you pull my pants up first?

                                        FADE TO BLACK:

FADE UP TO:

48 INT. STAIRS — DAY

Chantelle sits halfway down the stairs, brooding. We hear
the TV SET below. Chantelle makes up her mind, stands—

                    CHANTELLE
        (to herself) Here I come, ready or not—

49 INT. LIVING ROOM — DAY

May-Alice sits in her chair watching the soap. She turns
to look into the hall—we PAN with her gaze to see
Chantelle step in with a thin exercise mat, dumbbell,
chest expander piled in her arms—

REVERSE

Looking past Chantelle to May-Alice—

> **MAY-ALICE**
>
> You going to toss those?

> **CHANTELLE**
>
> Taking them out with us.

> **MAY-ALICE**
>
> Us?

> **CHANTELLE**
>
> Us. You and me.

> **MAY-ALICE**
>
> Out?

> **CHANTELLE**
>
> Outside.

> **MAY-ALICE**
>
> I don't like the sound of this.

Chantelle lays the equipment down and begins to wheel May-Alice toward the door—

> **CHANTELLE**
>
> Got to get some strength in your arms.

> **MAY-ALICE**
>
> Why?

> **CHANTELLE**
>
> Cause I'm not going to take you to the potty and wipe your butt every four hours and pretty soon you're gonna be too weak to do it for yourself. How's that?

May-Alice squints as the chair is tilted over the threshold and out into the sun, bumping down the few steps. Her eyes adjust slowly and she doesn't like what she sees—

> **CHANTELLE**
>
> When was the last time you were outside?

MAY-ALICE

They used to park us out on the roof at the rehab hospital.

CHANTELLE

You need sun.

MAY-ALICE

Raisins need sun. Al_fal_fa needs sun. You leave people outside they get skin cancer.

CHANTELLE

You swim?

MAY-ALICE

Not willingly.

CHANTELLE

Can you swim in this lake?

MAY-ALICE

You mean with the snakes?

Chantelle checks out the lake as they reach the edge—

CHANTELLE

Maybe I'll find you a pool. (hands her the dumbbell) Let's see what you can do.

May-Alice looks at her, then deliberately drops the weight to the ground beside her chair—

MAY-ALICE

That's what I can do. Now push me back in.

CHANTELLE

Push yourself back in.

MAY-ALICE

Don't pull that motivational crap on me! I want to go back inside!

CHANTELLE

If you do a wheelie it's easier. I'll have some lunch ready when you get there.

Chantelle heads back up to the house—

                    MAY-ALICE
        Get back here! Goddammit, get back here
        and bring me inside! Chantelle! It's
        uphill!

                    CHANTELLE
        (over her shoulder) Yeah, so's life.

                    MAY-ALICE
        Chan<u>telle!</u> (to herself) I can't do it myself.

She turns to look at the water, the dock—

                    MAY-ALICE
        <u>Fuck.</u>

50 SCREENED PORCH

Chantelle sits on the porch rocker, looking out the front
window to the yard. We hear May-Alice calling—

                    MAY-ALICE
        (off) Chantelle! Chantelle! Godammit, get out
        here!

51 EXT. LAKE — AFTERNOON — CU FROG

A big frog stares from the edge of the water—

MAY-ALICE

May-Alice stares back at the frog, morose—

                    MAY-ALICE
        Beat it.

FROG

Staring—

MAY-ALICE

> **MAY-ALICE**
> I said beat it, asshole.

FROG

Gets the drift, darts off into the water—

MAY-ALICE

May-Alice makes a face, looks around—

> **MAY-ALICE**
> Just what I need. Fucking <u>na</u>ture.

52 EXT. LAKE — EVENING

A beautiful sunset colors the water of the lake—

MAY-ALICE

Watching the sun go down. She seems to have chilled out a bit. Chantelle appears behind her with a cup of something, offers it. May-Alice looks at her, takes the cup—

> **CHANTELLE**
> Hot tea.

May-Alice drinks a bit. Chantelle sits on the ground by her and looks over the lake—

> **MAY-ALICE**
> Water gets clear this time of year. I saw some fish.

                    CHANTELLE

Yeah?

                    MAY-ALICE

Couple herons, too.

                    CHANTELLE

There really snakes in here?

                    MAY-ALICE

Were when I was little. We kind of ignored
em. (shrugs) Kids aren't scared of anything.

                    CHANTELLE

I was scared of stuff.

                    MAY-ALICE

Well— at least they're not scared of everything.

                    CHANTELLE

I was watching you. All day.

A silence—

                    CHANTELLE

Am I fired?

                    MAY-ALICE

Don't leave me places.

                    CHANTELLE

Will you do something to get stronger?

                    MAY-ALICE

Why do I need to be stronger?

                    CHANTELLE

Cause the next one you get might not be so
nice as me.

                    MAY-ALICE

Right. And you're Florence Fucking Nightingale.

                    CHANTELLE

You got a telephone. Any time you want you
can get rid of my ass. But if I'm gonna stay
here I got to be able to do my job.

May-Alice scowls, looks away from her—

> ### CHANTELLE
> You gonna try it?

> ### MAY-ALICE
> (evenly) Don't leave me places.

53 EXT. YARD — DAY — CU WEIGHT

A five-pound barbell weight, suspended by a rope tied through the center hole, slowly rises. We TILT UP with it till we see May-Alice, working her forearms by rolling the weight up on a length of broom handle. She reverses her grip to slowly lower the weight, then sees something that makes her drop the whole thing—

MAY-ALICE'S POV

Two women are getting out of a car by the house. One sees her, waves, and calls—

> ### PRECIOUS
> May-Alice!

MAY-ALICE

Stuck in her chair under the shade of a huge tree, the lake behind her, she realizes she is trapped—

> ### MAY-ALICE
> Oh shit.

Approaching. They are TI-MARIE and PRECIOUS ROBICHAUX, SISTERS in their late thirties who have mastered the art of smiling and taking mental inventory at the same time—

> ### TI-MARIE
> We're so glad we caught you at home!

                    PRECIOUS
We've been so naughty about not visiting—

                    TI-MARIE
We weren't sure if you—

                    PRECIOUS
We weren't positive you'd remember us.

                    TI-MARIE
Precious, that's the character she played,
not May-Alice. You remember us, don't you
darlin?

They have reached May-Alice, who looks stricken. Her eyes
shift beyond them— Chantelle coming behind them, a bag
of potato chips and bottle of wine in hand. She slows as
she sees the company. May-Alice makes little jerking ges-
tures with her hand, trying to warn Chantelle of something. The sisters watch, wondering if this is only a tic
or what—

                    CHANTELLE
Hello?

                    MAY-ALICE
(forced smile) Chantelle, these are my old
friends, Ti-Marie and Precious Robichaux.
Chantelle is my— uhm— as<u>sis</u>tant.

                    SISTERS
Hello. Pleased to meet you.

                    CHANTELLE
Would you like to stay for lunch?

May-Alice closes her eyes in defeat—

54 EXT. BACK PATIO — DAY

May-Alice in her chair, the sisters in theirs, around a
small circular table. Things are awkward between them—

TI-MARIE

We've been following your program.

PRECIOUS

Everybody is so proud of you.

TI-MARIE

There are so few people from here to be rec-
ognized on a national level. Unless you read
the sports pages.

PRECIOUS

Edward reads them out loud to me.

TI-MARIE

Edward is her husband.

PRECIOUS

(sparkles) Twenty years next May.

TI-MARIE

Precious has inertia confused with romance.

PRECIOUS

And Ti-Marie changes husbands like Edward
changes automobiles— a new one every four
years.

TI-MARIE

Anthony lasted five.

PRECIOUS

It took you a year to find him to serve the
papers. (brightens, to May-Alice) Of course,
we're very provincial compared to the goings-on
on your television program— what was it called?

MAY-ALICE

The Young and the Stupid.

PRECIOUS

(frowns, to Ti-Marie) Was that it?

TI-MARIE

It's a <u>joke</u>, Precious.

55 INT. KITCHEN — DAY

Chantelle has thrown everything from the fridge and the cabinets onto the table, hoping for inspiration—

> **CHANTELLE**
> Lunch. Damn— what do these people eat for <u>lunch</u>?

54 cont. EXT. PATIO — DAY The SISTERS digging in now—

> **PRECIOUS**
> And you never married, did you?

> **MAY-ALICE**
> Once.

> **PRECIOUS**
> Oh. (pause) And were you blessed?

> **MAY-ALICE**
> Pardon?

> **PRECIOUS**
> Children?

> **TI-MARIE**
> She wants to know if you had children.

> **PRECIOUS**
> I don't need an interpreter, Ti-Marie, I do speak <u>Eng</u>lish—

> **MAY-ALICE**
> I never had children.

> **PRECIOUS**
> What a shame. And now you ca—

> **TI-MARIE**
> Precious, slow down, darlin—

> **MAY-ALICE**
> I thought about having them, but I never really did anything about it.

> **PRECIOUS**
> You were always so ec<u>cen</u>tric at school—

TI-MARIE

She means different—

PRECIOUS

I just knew you'd do something— o<u>rig</u>inal with your life. Didn't we always used to wonder how May-Alice was going to end up?

MAY-ALICE

And now you know.

There is an uncomfortable silence. Chantelle arrives with a 50's-looking tray laden with cream cheese and olives spread on crackers and tomato soup served in three very different bowls. Not even the spoons match. Smiles freeze on the sisters' faces—

TI-MARIE

And what have we here?

CHANTELLE

We haven't unpacked the china yet—

PRECIOUS

Moving is such a bother.

TI-MARIE

You haven't moved in twenty years, Precious.

PRECIOUS

Well I can <u>emp</u>athize, can't I?

MAY-ALICE

Could you bring some more wine, Chantelle?

We FOLLOW Chantelle back into the kitchen, hearing their VOICES as she goes—

PRECIOUS

(off) She is a <u>jew</u>el, isn't she? Wherever did you find her?

TI-MARIE

(off) Did her people work for your parents?

                    MAY-ALICE
(off) She works for an agency.
                    PRECIOUS
(off) Ahhh—
                    TI-MARIE
(off) You don't see as much colored help
these days.
                    PRECIOUS
(off) It was the Sixties. Those riots up
North—
                    MAY-ALICE
Right. How you gonna keep em down on tho farm
after they've burned Chicago.
                    PRECIOUS
Did they burn Chicago too?
                    TI-MARIE
It's a joke, Precious.
                    PRECIOUS
Well ours down here have certainly caught the
attitude.
                    TI-MARIE
Precious and Edward have a Guatemalan woman—
                    PRECIOUS
Spanish—
                    TI-MARIE
She speaks Spanish, darlin, she's from
Guatemala.

May-Alice pulls a pad from the pouch on her chair and
scribbles something on it. Precious reacts to her first
taste of soup—
                    PRECIOUS
Oooh. It's warm.

They look at her—

> **PRECIOUS**
> I thought it was gazpacho. I wasn't expecting—

> **MAY-ALICE**
> Campbell's.

> **PRECIOUS**
> (breathless apology) Just a little sur<u>prised.</u>
> Excuse me. My husband, Edward, can't tolerate
> truly hot soup. He's very sensitive—

> **TI-MARIE**
> Edward? Sensitive?

> **PRECIOUS**
> You are so <u>crit</u>ical of him! Just because he's
> faithful and steady—

> **TI-MARIE**
> Steady? He's practically comatose.

> **PRECIOUS**
> Edward is in perfect health—

> **MAY-ALICE**
> It's a <u>joke</u>, Precious.

Chantelle appears to set a bottle of wine and three mis-
matched glasses on the table—

> **MAY-ALICE**
> Chantelle? I just thought of something else
> we need at the market.

Chantelle takes the note from May-Alice, exchanging a look.
We FOLLOW her into the house as she unfolds it—

> **PRECIOUS**
> (off) I remember when we were here last. Your
> parents, God bless them, were still with us.
> Some sort of soiree—

> **MAY-ALICE**
> (off) A slumber party.

> PRECIOUS

(off) Oh, yes. I remember now—

56 CHANTELLE'S POV — CU NOTE

The note reads—"Help! Get them out of here!"

54 EXT. PATIO — DAY

Reminiscing—

> PRECIOUS

Laurel Pettibone was there, and Stacy Lee
Ellis, and who was that girl? The one with the
hair?

> TI-MARIE

We all had <u>hair</u>, Precious—

> PRECIOUS

No, this is the one with the <u>hair</u>. Who we were
so awful to? She wore it in that enormous <u>braid</u>
down her back like some sort of peasant woman—

> MAY-ALICE

(quietly) That was me.

> PRECIOUS

May-Alice, it couldn't have been <u>you</u>—

> MAY-ALICE

There was a picture I had of Joan Baez, took
me hours to get the same effect—

> PRECIOUS

Perhaps I misremember. I'm thinking of somebody we just <u>tortured</u>—

> MAY-ALICE

(smiles) That was me.

An awkward silence. It's about to get heavy, but Chantelle
arrives in the nick of time—

> **CHANTELLE**
>
> Miss Culhane, it's 2:15— it's time for your
> injections.

> **MAY-ALICE**
>
> (picks up) Right. My injections.

> **PRECIOUS**
>
> Oh dear— have we overstayed our welcome?

> **MAY-ALICE**
>
> If I don't have the spasms they only take
> about an hour—

> **TI-MARIE**
>
> (rising) We were just passing through, anyway—

> **PRECIOUS**
>
> And now that we know where you are—

> **MAY-ALICE**
>
> (to Chantelle) You think I'll need the
> restraints today?

> **CHANTELLE**
>
> I've got them set up. (to sisters) Excuse
> us, please—

May-Alice gives a brave little wave as Chantelle sweeps
her away on the chair. We HOLD on the sisters, their
smiles slowly fading. Finally—

> **PRECIOUS**
>
> That <u>was</u> her with the strange hair, wasn't it?

57 INT. KITCHEN — AFTERNOON

May-Alice wheels into the kitchen to find Chantelle
replacing all the food she pulled out that afternoon—

> **MAY-ALICE**
>
> I feel like I've been picked clean by buzzards.

CHANTELLE
You hadn't seen them for a while—

MAY-ALICE
Since I boarded with them at Grand Couteau.
I thought the soup bit was brilliant.

CHANTELLE
Opened the can and heated it up. What's so
brilliant about that?

MAY-ALICE
I thought— you know— you were trying to help
me get rid of them.

CHANTELLE
I can't cook.

MAY-ALICE
Sure you can.

CHANTELLE
There some rule, all black people got to know
how to cook?

MAY-ALICE
Darlin, down here there's a rule _every_body
got to know how to cook.

58 INT. LIVING ROOM — NIGHT

May-Alice is watching something with a creepy suspense
score. She sees Chantelle wandering out in the hall,
unsettled about something—

MAY-ALICE
You want to watch with me?

CHANTELLE
What is it?

MAY-ALICE
Bette Davis and Joan Crawford pretending
they're the Robichaux sisters.

Chantelle comes in and stands next to May-Alice, arms folded across her chest. She reacts to a sudden zing on the screen—

CHANTELLE

Whew.

MAY-ALICE

Yeah. And you thought I looked bad.

Chantelle sits in the wheelchair a few feet from May-Alice, half-watching the show—

MAY-ALICE

Chantelle? Do you have to wear that uniform all the time?

CHANTELLE

I thought you wanted it on.

MAY-ALICE

I thought <u>you</u> wanted it on.

CHANTELLE

The agency said I should wear it.

MAY-ALICE

Fuck the agency. It's so— <u>nurs</u>ey.

CHANTELLE

I am a nurse. Not an "assistant."

MAY-ALICE

I don't know what else to call you. You're not my servant—

CHANTELLE

Thank you.

MAY-ALICE

And you're not my housekeeper, or my babysitter—

CHANTELLE

And I'm not your friend—

An awkward pause as the truth of this sinks in—

> MAY-ALICE

Caretaker?

> CHANTELLE

Chantelle. Just tell em— "This is Chantelle."
Let them figure out the rest.

They watch the show for a moment—

> MAY-ALICE

You know, you can go out at night if you
want.

> CHANTELLE

Outside?

> MAY-ALICE

Into town. You know— Lafayette, whatever.

> CHANTELLE

I'm fine out here.

> MAY-ALICE

It must be so boring for you.

> CHANTELLE

It's a job, it's supposed to be boring.

> MAY-ALICE

(smiles) "Oh no, Miss Culhane, it's <u>never</u>
boring working for <u>you.</u>"

Chantelle gives her a flat look—

> CHANTELLE

You want me to be that way, I can try.

> MAY-ALICE

No. You have to be totally straight with
me, okay? Whatever you got on your mind, I
want to hear it.

> CHANTELLE

Yeah?

> MAY-ALICE

Yeah.

                    CHANTELLE
You sure?

                    MAY-ALICE
Positive.

                    CHANTELLE
(considers, then—) You drink too much.

                 MAY-ALICE
No I don't.

A long pause. May-Alice takes a deliberate sip of wine—
                 CHANTELLE
This the one where she feeds her sister a rat?

                                        FADE TO BLACK:

FADE UP TO:

59 INT. LIVING ROOM — DAY — CU MAY-ALICE

May-Alice asleep on the couch. Daylight spills on her
face. We HEAR a HAMMER BANGING outside. May-Alice opens
her eyes, raises her head slightly to look around—

MAY-ALICE'S POV

Chantelle sits in the wheelchair, by the window, looking
out moodily—

MAY-ALICE, CHANTELLE
                    MAY-ALICE
Chantelle?

                    CHANTELLE
You woke up.

MAY-ALICE

Somebody's pounding on my house with a large blunt object. Of course I woke up.

CHANTELLE

He's been doing it for a long time now.

MAY-ALICE

He? Who's he?

CHANTELLE

Guy I hired to build a ramp, fix up the bathroom. You told me you wanted to, and I think he's giving a good deal—

MAY-ALICE

Why'd he have to start so early?

CHANTELLE

It's past noon, Miss Culhane.

May-Alice pulls herself to a sitting position, still groggy—

MAY-ALICE

Would you call me May-Alice?

CHANTELLE

You mean when your friends aren't here?

MAY-ALICE

All the time.

CHANTELLE

(shrugs) Whatever you want.

May-Alice looks toward the hammering, looks at her wrinkled, crumb-littered sweatpants and T-shirt—

MAY-ALICE

How long have I been wearing these?

CHANTELLE

Since Monday.

MAY-ALICE

What's today?

                         CHANTELLE
Thursday.

                         MAY-ALICE
I kind of gross you out, don't I?

                         CHANTELLE
Is this a trick question?

May-Alice smiles. Chantelle pushes the chair over by her—
                         CHANTELLE
Come on. He hasn't started on the bathroom yet.

60 EXT. HOUSE — DAY

Rennie pushes the beginnings of a ramp flush with the
front doorsill, the door propped open, then closes it to
check the clearance. When he opens it again May-Alice sits
there in her chair, fresh clothes, hair brushed, amazed
to see who it is—
                         MAY-ALICE
Rennie?

                          RENNIE
Hi.

                         MAY-ALICE
It's Rennie, right?

                          RENNIE
Yeah. It's me.

                         MAY-ALICE
Hi.

                          RENNIE
Hi.

                         MAY-ALICE
Uhm— wow. How are you?

                          RENNIE
I'm fine. Older. How are you?

                    MAY-ALICE
I'm uh— so you're a carpenter?

                     RENNIE
Some of this, some of that.

                    MAY-ALICE
Uh-huh. Oh— Chantelle wondered if you wanted
to come in for something to drink— lemonade,
iced tea—

                     RENNIE
Sure.

                   MAY-ALICE
Great. (can't get over it) Rennie.

                     RENNIE
(smiles) May-Alice.

61 KITCHEN

May-Alice is subdued, shy around Rennie. Chantelle sits
by the fridge, sipping iced tea, watching them at the
table—

                   MAY-ALICE
You have a family, I guess.

                     RENNIE
Mmmmn.

                   MAY-ALICE
How many kids?

                     RENNIE
Five.

                   MAY-ALICE
Wow. I didn't know people had that many anymore.

                     RENNIE
(shrugs) Us coon-asses do.

                   MAY-ALICE
You still go out in your father's boat? I
suppose you got your own now—

                    RENNIE

That's mostly what I do. Take tourists into
the bayou, point out the gators and snakes.
Beats chasing around the oil patch like my
father.

                 MAY-ALICE

(nods) Five kids. I know your wife?

                    RENNIE

Don't see how you'd of met. (stands) Well—
thanks. Later you might want to show me what
you need in the bedroom.

Chantelle snorts a laugh and May-Alice shoots her a
dirty look—

                 MAY-ALICE

We got all these rails and things from the
gimp catalogue but I never got round to
having them installed.

                    RENNIE

I'll take a look. (leaving) That's a nice
boat you got sitting out front.

                 MAY-ALICE

Hasn't been run for twenty years.

                    RENNIE

Ought to somebody check it out some time.

He's gone. May-Alice turns to Chantelle—

                 MAY-ALICE

Why didn't you tell me it was him?

                 CHANTELLE

He somebody special?

                 MAY-ALICE

At least he's not in jail.

                 CHANTELLE

You know him from school?

MAY-ALICE

From before I went off to Grand Couteau He was real wild— we all had crushes on him, but he was— you know— his father wore alligator teeth around his neck and had all these tattoos. Rennie'd come over and sell fishbait to my father.

CHANTELLE

White trash.

MAY-ALICE

It's more complicated than that. Dey was de real swamp Cajuns, darlin. De vrai chose. Rennie Boudreau— five kids. Jesus.

May-Alice catches sight of herself in the reflection of her glass—

MAY-ALICE

I look like shit, don't I?

62 INT. KITCHEN — NIGHT

Chantelle sits at the table, reading a letter she's just written. We hear the TV PLAYING from the living room. Chantelle folds the letter, puts it in an envelope, starts to address it. Halfway through she loses heart, pushes it away from her—

63 INT. LIVING ROOM — NIGHT

May-Alice sits on the couch, wearing sweatpants and a T-shirt, the TV playing a LOCAL CAR COMMERCIAL. She drinks wine out of the bottle. She puts the bottle down, thinking. She puts her hand between her legs, watching it studiously, then puts it under her T-shirt to hold one of her breasts. She holds it there, and looks forlornly back at the TV set—

64 INT. LIVING ROOM — DAY

May-Alice is loading Reeve's camera with film while next to her Chantelle fools with an answering machine she has just pulled from the box and set up—

MAY-ALICE
Reeves used to let me mix chemicals for him in his first darkroom. That was a big deal, him taking me seriously—

CHANTELLE
(into machine) Hi. May-Alice isn't here right now. If you'd like to leave a message, wait till after the beep and leave your number.

MAY-ALICE
May-Alice is <u>al</u>ways here— they know that. And what if it's for you?

CHANTELLE
Won't be anybody calling me. Listen, what if the car's gonna take more than a day to fix?

MAY-ALICE
(shrugs) Stay over, I guess. Be a nice break from me.

CHANTELLE
I should tell em to leave the time they called, huh?

May-Alice pushes the message button, speaks into the machine—

MAY-ALICE
May-Alice has crawled into a hole to die. If you'd like to leave a message, forget about it.

65 INT. DINER — DAY

Chantelle sits at the counter of the diner. There are

horsey things on the walls around her, menu items like "Backstretch Burger" on the menu listed above her. We PAN to include Sugar, paying for something at the register. He sees her, comes over—

> **SUGAR**
> It's Chantelle-who-don't-have-time—for-me.

> **CHANTELLE**
> Sugar.

> **SUGAR**
> Only thing good here is breakfast, and that's long over.

> **CHANTELLE**
> What you doing in here then?

> **SUGAR**
> (raises thermos) Coffee machine's bust over to work. Come on with me, get some real food.

> **CHANTELLE**
> I got to be somewhere.

> **SUGAR**
> You got time to burn, girl. I seen that old car of your white lady's sitting over by the Bourgeois Brothers garage. Them boys slower than a three-legged mule.

Chantelle looks around the diner as if considering—

> **SUGAR**
> Can't tell you what to do with the rest of your life, Chantelle, but I know you don't want to be spending no five hours of it in here.

66 EXT. YARD — DAY

May-Alice is on her chair by the edge of the lake, taking pictures with the camera Reeves gave her. She puts the camera to her eye, pans it—

MAY-ALICE'S POV — THROUGH LENS

We PAN from the lake toward the house, till we STOP with
a man staring between the cross-hairs, May-Alice reflex-
ively tripping the shutter—

MAY-ALICE

Startled, she lets the camera down—

MAY-ALICE'S POV — LUTHER

LUTHER, a black man in his forties who looks like he's been sick
for a while, stands looking at her a few feet away, eyes hidden
behind shades— May-Alice is scared, tries not to show it—

> **MAY-ALICE**
> Hello?

> **LUTHER**
> (steps closer) Chantelle here?

> **MAY-ALICE**
> Uhmm— (considers lying)— no. She went to town.

> **LUTHER**
> You the lady she's working for?

> **MAY-ALICE**
> Yes.

He nods, looks back toward the house—

> **MAY-ALICE**
> I'm not sure when she's going to be back.

He steps almost next to her, looks out over the lake, then
glances at May-Alice—

> **LUTHER**
> You afraid of me?

                        MAY-ALICE
(lying) No.

                          LUTHER
Don't be. (frowns) She okay?

                        MAY-ALICE
Chantelle? Sure. She's fine.

                          LUTHER
Happy?

                        MAY-ALICE
Well, happy I don't know. I mean— she seems
okay. She lives— you know— upstairs. I don't
really know what goes on upstairs. I don't
know if she's happy. (shrugs) I don't know
Chantelle.

                          LUTHER
No reason you would.

                        MAY-ALICE
I just live with her twenty-four hours a day.
(sighs) Was she expecting you?

                          LUTHER
Don't think she wants to see me.

                        MAY-ALICE
Oh.

Luther steps closer to the water, pulls his shades to rub
his eyes—

                          LUTHER
Nice to live near water.

                        MAY-ALICE
Yeah, I suppose it is.

He turns and looks at her carefully—

                          LUTHER
You can't feel anything in your bottom half?

                    MAY-ALICE
That's the general idea.

                      LUTHER
I felt that once. Started in my feet, then up
to my knees— I remember thinking how when it
reached my heart I'd be dead.

                    MAY-ALICE
What happened?

Luther puts his shades back on—

                      LUTHER
Oh, I did some more of whatever it was I was
messed up on— shot me right past into somewhere
else. (turns) She finished with the de-tox?

                    MAY-ALICE
(surprised but hiding it) Uhm— yeah. I guess so.

                      LUTHER
(nods) She makes up her mind to do something
you don't want to be in her way, Chantelle.

                    MAY-ALICE
I've noticed.

                      LUTHER
Well that's good, she's keeping straight.
(sighs) I don't think I'm going to wait
around.

                    MAY-ALICE
Don't mind me—

                      LUTHER
I can't do this yet. You tell Chantelle I'm
sorry. (starts away)

                    MAY-ALICE
Who do I say came to call?

He turns to answer, walking backwards—

Bad news. She'll know who you mean.

We HOLD on May-Alice. She takes a picture of him leaving—

67 EXT. EVANGELINE DOWNS — DAY

Chantelle and Sugar are eating courtbullion and rice at trackside. Horses are being exercised on the turf—

SUGAR

How's that for you?

CHANTELLE

It's fine.

SUGAR

That on top is courtbullion. Made that myself.

A silent pause—

SUGAR

So all the women up north so hard to get next to, or is it just you?

CHANTELLE

Just me. You bet on these horses or just take care of em?

SUGAR

Sometimes I bet em. Only for the fun of it.

CHANTELLE

What's fun about losing your money?

SUGAR

If you win that's fun cause you make the money and if you lose that just show you how much you don't already know bout horses. You learn something, which is always fun. But if you don't risk nothing you can't get nothin.

Chantelle just shakes her head. Sugar smiles—

                         SUGAR
          Come see my office.

68 INT. /EXT. STABLE

A girl of about fifteen, ALBERTINE, is brushing down a
quarter horse. She nods to Sugar as he steps in with
Chantelle—

                         SUGAR
          Hey, darlin. Albertine, say hi to Chantelle.
                       ALBERTINE
          Lo.
                       CHANTELLE
          Nice to meet you.
                         SUGAR
          Albertine's my first girl. She stays with me
          most of the summer.
                       CHANTELLE
          You got more?
                         SUGAR
          Let's see— by Albertine's mama, which was my
          first wife, I had her and a boy, Henri. Henri
          got him a basketball scholarship to LSU—

As Sugar talks he stoops by an unshod horse, lifts its
foreleg, and holds a horseshoe against the hoof to check
the shape—

                         SUGAR
          Then with my second I had Cecile and Eugenie,
          they live out by Breaux Bridge now. Don't see
          enough of them. Then let's see— Rosalynn—
                       ALBERTINE
          Rosalynn—

                          SUGAR

Yeah, by Rosalynn there was Andre, Delia and
Lorenzo. Lorenzo just startin up school now.

                       CHANTELLE

Whose horse is this?

                          SUGAR

Man who's gonna put his top stallion on one
of my mares.

                       CHANTELLE

You let him do that?

                          SUGAR

That's how I'm gettin <u>paid</u>, darlin. Kind of
bloodline his stallion got, cost me a fortune
to pay for that semen.

                       CHANTELLE

(makes a face) Seems like a shame to buy when
there's so much of it out there that's free.

Sugar laughs, begins to pound the shoe against his anvil
to shape it—

                       CHANTELLE

You really do that, huh? Like in the cowboy
movies.

                          SUGAR

I'm a blacksmith.

                       CHANTELLE

(bit of a smile) You a black somethin, all
right.

69 INT. CLUB — NIGHT

We TRACK through a fairly large club, crowded, most all of
the patrons black. A ZYDECO BAND PLAYS in the center, and
dozens of couples are up and dancing. We find Chantelle
sitting at a table alone, watching. She looks to her right—

CHANTELLE's POV — SUGAR

Talking and laughing with a couple who stand at the edge of the dance floor—

CU CHANTELLE

Considering him—

CHANTELLE'S POV — SUGAR

He turns and meets her eyes. He smiles, comes over, bringing Chantelle back into a 2-shot. He bends and says something we can't hear because the MUSIC is so loud. He leads her out onto the floor and we FOLLOW. Sugar starts to show Chantelle how to dance to this music, Chantelle checking out the others on the floor and slowly getting into it. She allows a smile to cross her face—

70 EXT. PARKING LOT — NIGHT

Chantelle and Sugar sit on the hood of Sugar's car out in the club parking lot. We hear MUSIC from inside, VOICES and LAUGHTER from people coming out to their cars—

> SUGAR
> You move real nice. I wish I could dance with you and sit and watch you at the same time.

> CHANTELLE
> You don't ever stop, do you? Pouring that stuff on.

> SUGAR
> (serious) I don't say nothin I don't mean.

> CHANTELLE
> (looks away) Alright. Sorry.

JOHN SAYLES

                    SUGAR
Don't be sorry. Just don't be so suspicious.

                  CHANTELLE
Man been married twenty-five times, got himself more children than a field got clover—
how'm I sposed to trust you?

                    SUGAR
I never ast you to <u>trust</u> me, darlin. I just
want you to <u>be</u> with me. Have some fun.

                  CHANTELLE
I already had enough fun to last me a lifetime.

A pause. He looks at her seriously, then smiles—

                    SUGAR
Would you spend the night with me? You don't
have to like it.

Chantelle laughs. They look at each other for a long
moment. Sugar kisses her. Chantelle sighs, scared that
she's so interested—

                  CHANTELLE
You probably live in the swamp, right? Got
dead raccoons and shit hanging in your house—

71 INT. MAY-ALICE'S LIVING ROOM — NIGHT

May-Alice drinking wine, on the couch watching TV. She
sighs, turns the set off. She sits brooding for a moment,
then yells—

                  MAY-ALICE
Aaaaaahhhhhh!

Alone. She reaches over for her chair—

----

72 EXT. HOUSE — NIGHT

A floodlight illuminates the wet grass of the lawn. May-Alice wheels into the shot, stops. The bottle of wine she was drinking is in her lap. She listens to the night around her, then yells again—

                    MAY-ALICE
          Aaaaaaaaaaaaaaaaahhhhhhhhhhhhh!

A slight echo from the lake. May-Alice takes the bottle and finishes it off. She drops it on the ground, pushes on out of the shot—

73 INT. DARKROOM — NIGHT

TOTAL BLACKNESS. We hear WHEELCHAIR CLUNKS, DOORS OPENING—

                    MAY-ALICE
          (off) Dammit—

CLICK. The RED DARKROOM LIGHT comes ON and we see May-Alice wheel into the room. There is just enough room for her to maneuver around the tables and sinks. May-Alice wheels over to where the chemicals are stored. She smiles, grabs a bottle of bourbon from a lower shelf—

                    MAY-ALICE
          Reeves.

May-Alice puts the bourbon on the table behind her, then hoists a large bottle of chemical up onto her lap, palming a layer of dust off the label to read it—

74 INT. BEDROOM — NIGHT

Chantelle and Sugar are making out hot and heavy on the

---

bed, still with most of their clothes on. Sugar kneels and starts kissing his way up Chantelle's leg, pushing her dress up as he does. Chantelle strokes his head, into the passion, then tears come and in a moment she is weeping. Sugar leaves off and comes up to hold her. She breathes deep, trying to get control—

                    CHANTELLE
          Sorry.

                    SUGAR
          I made love to women who weren't <u>sat</u>isfied,
          but you the first that come out and cried
          about it—

                    CHANTELLE
          Naw. It's just me.

Sugar kisses her cheek, takes a finger and rubs a tear from her face, licks it off—

                    SUGAR
          I been wonderin what you taste like.

                    CHANTELLE
          Yeah?

                    SUGAR
          More salt than sugar, so far.

                    CHANTELLE
          (smiles) I'm not— I don't think this is gonna
          happen. Not tonight.

Sugar looks down towards his dick—

                    SUGAR
          Yeah. You kind of took the wind outa my
          sails, there.

                    CHANTELLE
          Poor baby.

                    SUGAR
          It got feelins too, you know.

> CHANTELLE

That right?

> SUGAR

If I'm lyin I'm dyin.

Chantelle puts her head on his chest—

> CHANTELLE

Can I sleep right here tonight?

> SUGAR

Mmmmn-hmmm.

> CHANTELLE

What's that name of yours? The real one?

> SUGAR

Ulysse. Like the guy in the story went off to fight in the Trojan wars with an army, and he's the only one makes it back alive.

> CHANTELLE

A survivor.

> SUGAR

Yeah. He was that.

> CHANTELLE

You know the whole story?

> SUGAR

It's a long one.

> CHANTELLE

Tell it to me?

75 INT. MAY-ALICE'S LIVING ROOM — DAY

Early morning sun slanting into the empty room—

> CHANTELLE

(Off) May-Alice? MAY-ALICE?

Chantelle steps into the room, searching—

CHANTELLE

>   Damn.

76 EXT. HOUSE — DAY

Chantelle outside on the lawn, calling toward the lake—

CHANTELLE

>   May-Alice!

No answer. Chantelle looks to the side, sees—

CHANTELLE'S POV — RACKS

Wheel tracks in the grass lead toward the shed that houses
the darkroom. We TILT till we see the discarded wine
bottle. Chantelle steps into the shot, scoops up the
bottle, heads for the shed—

77 INT. SHED

DARKNESS. The outside door opens, spilling light, and
Chantelle steps in—

CHANTELLE

>   May-Alice?

MAY-ALICE

>   (inside) Don't come in.

CHANTELLE

>   You all right?

MAY-ALICE

>   (inside) Shut the outside door first. I'm
>   printing.

Chantelle shuts the outside door, plunging us into TOTAL
DARKNESS again—

> MAY-ALICE
> (inside) Are you in the dark?

> CHANTELLE
> I can't see a thing.

> MAY-ALICE
> (inside) You can come in then.

> CHANTELLE
> I can't see the doorknob.

> MAY-ALICE
> (inside) Down to your right, about as high as
> your hip.

We hear FUMBLING, then a door opens on the RED LIGHT of the darkroom. We FOLLOW Chantelle in. May-Alice sits with tongs in hand, a timer clicking on the table next to a printing tray full of fixer, a large print starting to form beneath it—

> MAY-ALICE
> You get in late?

> CHANTELLE
> It's morning.

May-Alice looks up—

> MAY-ALICE
> Really?

> CHANTELLE
> I stayed in town. They're not finished with
> the car.

> MAY-ALICE
> (shakes her head) No sense of time in here.

Chantelle lays the empty wine bottle down on the table, lifts the bourbon bottle, nearly empty—

> CHANTELLE
> I see you've been busy.

                         MAY-ALICE
I don't need a sermon.

                         CHANTELLE
You think you could get through a day without
a drink?

                         MAY-ALICE
Sure.

                         CHANTELLE
Okay. Today. Twenty-four hours, starting
right now. You got enough problems with your
liver and kidney without—

                         MAY-ALICE
Hey, you're the addict, not me!

Chantelle is taken totally off balance. She speaks quietly—

                         CHANTELLE
What do you mean by that?

The timer goes BING! May-Alice lifts the print out of the
tray with the tongs and turns it toward Chantelle. The
photo is of Luther when he first surprised May-Alice—

                         CHANTELLE
He was here?

                         MAY-ALICE
In the afternoon.

                         CHANTELLE
Hope he didn't scare you. He wouldn't hurt
anybody, Luther.

                         MAY-ALICE
I'm glad to hear it. He didn't seem too
healthy. Turn the light on, would you?

WHITE LIGHT snaps on. The photo hasn't fixed, its image
darkening till the whole print is black. May-Alice looks
at it—

MAY-ALICE

This is the only part I can't remember how to do.

CHANTELLE

I cleaned up. Finished detox a month ago.

MAY-ALICE

Or maybe the fixer is worn out—

CHANTELLE

Am I fired?

MAY-ALICE

Fired? For what?

CHANTELLE

Lying.

MAY-ALICE

I told you when you came here I didn't want to hear about your problems.

CHANTELLE

I lied to the Agency. Gave them my records from back in Chicago, told them I'd been off in Europe for two years. (sits) Luther had some restaurants, owned a big car— it was fun living high. Exciting. Then we got to free-basing, and everything else kind of fell away. Luther lost his business, and I lost—well—

MAY-ALICE

What stopped you?

CHANTELLE

I guess I didn't want to die.

May-Alice takes this in—

CHANTELLE

(hesitant) I need this job.

MAY-ALICE

You're not fired.

May-Alice wheels back from the table, looks at the bourbon bottle—

>   MAY-ALICE
> And if I'm not gonna drink today, I might as
> well go to bed.

                                    FADE TO BLACK:

FADE UP ON:

78 INT. LIVING ROOM — DAY

May-Alice on the couch with her head in her hands. We hear Chantelle come in—

>   CHANTELLE
> How you feeling?
>   MAY-ALICE
> Like shit.

Chantelle sits by her—

>   MAY-ALICE
> How did you do it?
>   CHANTELLE
> At first I was in a hospital. No place to
> score. It's back in the real world that's hard.
>   MAY-ALICE
> This isn't the real world.
>   CHANTELLE
> I know.

79 EXT. LAWN — DAY

May-Alice lies on her back on a mat, working out with handweights—

CU MAY-ALICE

Her face tight and determined—

80 INT. LIVING ROOM — DAY — CU REMOTE CONTROL

May-Alice's fingers punching channels impatiently—

CU MAY-ALICE

Frowning at the TV. She shuts it off, looks back toward
the kitchen—

81 INT. KITCHEN — REFRIGERATOR

The refrigerator door opens. We PAN around, looking for
booze. All gone—

MAY-ALICE

In her chair, disappointed—

82 EXT. HOUSE — DAY

May-Alice wheels down to the dock, camera in her lap. She
pauses to pull a bottle of seltzer from a pouch on the
chair, drinks—

83 EXT. YARD — DAY — VARIOUS-SHOTS

May-Alice shooting pictures of whatever moves and some
things that don't. We see some of them THROUGH THE LENS.
Finally she hears the sound of a MOTOR KICKING and DYING—

84 EXT. YARD — VIEWFINDER POV

Looking through the camera we PAN around till we HOLD on
the dock, where a man squats by an old boat tied up there.
SNAP! The shutter falls to capture the moment—

CLOSER — VIEWFINDER POV

We can see now that the man is Rennie, tinkering— SNAP!

CLOSER — VIEWFINDER POV

Right behind him now. Rennie turns— SNAP!

85 EXT. DOCK — DAY

Rennie stands in the old flatboat, his tools spread out
on the dock beside him. He has the housing off the motor
as May-Alice wheels up—

> **RENNIE**
> People been cuttin your grass all these years
> had sense theyd've brought this inside. You
> got you some rust. Couple three parts I can
> have her running, though.

> **MAY-ALICE**
> Chantelle ask you to fix this?

> **RENNIE**
> Just thought I'd do it.

> **MAY-ALICE**
> (wary) Oh.

> **RENNIE**
> Live on the water, you want a boat.

A pause as she watches him work—

MAY-ALICE

So how's your father these days?

RENNIE

Dead.

MAY-ALICE

Oh.

RENNIE

Started him a fight in Smokey's over to Port Arthur, couple roughnecks put him away in the parking lot. (shrugs) That's the way he lived it. (points to boat) Some day I get her runnin, I take your friend and you out, see the neighborhood.

MAY-ALICE

Sure.

RENNIE

You never did like it much down here.

MAY-ALICE

The place was alright— I just had a problem with who people expected me to be.

RENNIE

I know how that is. You miss up there?

MAY-ALICE

(thinks) No. You're going to be alone you can do without forty million people reminding you of it.

RENNIE

Are you okay? (she frowns) You seem a little upset or somethin—

MAY-ALICE

I'm fine. I just started— a diet. Makes you cranky, your blood sugar and all that. (tentative) So— did you ever get away from here?

RENNIE

Drafted. Sent me to the Philippines, guard ammunition on its way to the war. The work

part was boring. The rest was like Port
Arthur on payday night.

A silence—

                         RENNIE
Everybody here was real proud how you did on
the TV.

                        MAY-ALICE
Sure.

                         RENNIE
I never did see your program. Arlene won't
have it in the house.

                        MAY-ALICE
A critic.

                         RENNIE
No television, no radio, no liquor, no card
playing— won't sing a song less the Lord's
name is in it.

                        MAY-ALICE
That's serious.

                         RENNIE
She took religion between the second and
third babies. Her people were like that but
she'd run off from them when I met her.
(shakes his head) She got the kids in it with
her now. They pray for me a lot.

                        MAY-ALICE
I was married for a little bit. An actor.
That should have been the tip-off right
there. Finally told him "There's only room
for one child in this apartment, and that's
me." (looks at Rennie) So was I snotty to you
when we were kids?

                         RENNIE
(thinks) You weren't much of anything to me.
We just kind of looked at each other. I think

you were real nice to the people you knew.
Different— you know— but real nice.

                    MAY-ALICE
          Then how'd I get like this?

Rennie isn't sure what she's asking. He steps onto the
dock, scooping up his tools—

                    RENNIE
          I'm layin cement today over at Landry's. I be
          by in a couple days.

                    MAY-ALICE
          Bye, Rennie.

We HOLD on May-Alice, watching Rennie walk away toward the
house. She pulls out the seltzer, looks at it, drops it
on the ground—

86 INT. DARKROOM — DAY

May-Alice desperately searches the lower shelves, pulling
each bottle of chemicals out and laying it on the floor,
searching for more of Reeves' stash—

87 INT. KITCHEN — DAY

Chantelle is working on the letter again. She gives up,
tears it and the envelope in two, crosses to toss them in
the trash. She is not in a good mood. May-Alice rolls in
from outside, agitated and sweaty—

                    MAY-ALICE
          Alright, the game's over.

                    CHANTELLE
          What game?

                    MAY-ALICE

Where'd you put all the liquor?

                    CHANTELLE

Threw it away.

                    MAY-ALICE

It's in the trash?

                    CHANTELLE

I poured it out, put the bottles in the bin.

                    MAY-ALICE

You poured it <u>out</u>?

                    CHANTELLE

(coolly) The recycle people don't want nothin
left in the bottles.

                    MAY-ALICE

Look, Chantelle, I'm not ready for this. When
I get stronger—

                    CHANTELLE

You keep drinking you won't get any stronger.

                    MAY-ALICE

Okay— the deal was twenty-four hours, right?
Ernie's closes at nine— if you're going to
have any here by early tomorrow morning—

                    CHANTELLE

I'm not getting you any more.

                    MAY-ALICE

What?

                    CHANTELLE

You want it you can get it yourself.

                    MAY-ALICE

I can't drive.

                    CHANTELLE

Well that's something to work toward, isn't
it?

                    MAY-ALICE

(pissed) Don't hand me that condescending

bullshit, just go in and get me some fucking
wine!

CHANTELLE

Just listen to yourself—

MAY-ALICE

<u>No</u>! <u>You</u> listen to <u>me</u>! I want you to do what
I tell you—

CHANTELLE

(moving away) Dream on, girl—

MAY-ALICE

Who made you the fucking warden?

CHANTELLE

(turns on her) And who made you the queen of
the whole damn world? Sit around feeling
sorry for yourself, TV-watchin dried-up mis-
erable old witch! You can't keep from
drinking one lousy day and you not even a
<u>drunk</u> yet, you're just <u>spoiled</u>! Girl, I wake
up most days and I want to get high so bad I
can't even <u>breathe</u>—

MAY-ALICE

Cocaine is different—

CHANTELLE

Bull<u>shit</u>! What do you know about it?

She starts out of the room—

MAY-ALICE

Where are you going?

CHANTELLE

I can't be around your shit, you understand
that? I'm going away from <u>you</u>!

We HOLD on May-Alice as Chantelle slams out. May-Alice is
angry and scared. She grabs the dish-drying rack, filled

with plates and silverware, and flings it across the room.
SMASHING and CRASHING—

                    MAY-ALICE
          (screams) Ahhhhhhhhhhhhhhh!

88 EXT. HOUSE — EVENING

A WS of the house as the sun sets—

89 INT. KITCHEN — EVENING

We start on the floor, broken bits of plate still scattered about. The wheelchair wheel bumps over one—

CU SKILLET

The lid is pulled off with a wash of steam to reveal a col-
orful jambalaya finished in the skillet. We WIDEN to see
May-Alice pull it off the burner, then dish it into a
serving platter with a wooden spoon. She wheels it over to
the table. Beyond her we see the counters crowded with
boxes and wrappers and utensils, cabinet doors open, things
spilled. The table is set for two, steaming soup in the
center, cornbread, red beans— a real feast. Chantelle steps
in in the BG, looking down as she steps in broken crockery,
then looking around to survey the scene. Both she and May-
Alice are subdued, embarrassed about their outbursts—

                    CHANTELLE
          You been cooking.

                    MAY-ALICE
          Gotta do something to keep busy.

                    CHANTELLE
          Smells good.

                    MAY-ALICE
          Sit.

Chantelle considers, then takes a place at the table. She examines the china—

                    CHANTELLE
        Nice plates.

                    MAY-ALICE
        I broke most of the other stuff.

                    CHANTELLE
        You did a number on em—

                    MAY-ALICE
        (points) That's okra gumbo there. You start
        with some of that.

                    CHANTELLE
        Thank you. (looks around) We'll have to get
        Rennie over to lower the cabinets.

                    MAY-ALICE
        I was going to make biscuits but I couldn't
        reach the flour.

She rolls over to the refrigerator, opens it and stares in, sighing—

                    MAY-ALICE
        Chantelle?

                    CHANTELLE
        Yeah?

                    MAY-ALICE
        Iced tea or Kool Aid?

90 INT. DARKROOM — DAY

Under the red DARKROOM LIGHT we see the picture of Rennie turning around at the dock starting to develop in a tray— Watching it, tongs in hand. There is a KNOCK—

                    CHANTELLE
        (off) May-Alice?

> **MAY-ALICE**

Yeah?

CHANTELLE

(off) We got company.

MAY-ALICE

Damn. Who is it?

CHANTELLE

(off) They say they're from Daytime.

91 EXT. PATIO — DAY

May-Alice wheels out to find DAWN, KIM and NINA standing awkwardly on the patio. Dawn is black, Kim and Nina white. Dawn and Nina are roughly May-Alice's age, while Kim is just beyond ingenue. Chantelle hangs back by the door to watch. Dawn steps forward to hug May-Alice—

MAY-ALICE

Dawn—

DAWN

Hi, baby. So good to see you.

KIM

May-Alice—

Kim kisses her cheek—

MAY-ALICE

You tracked me down.

KIM

We're on a junket. They expanded it to New Orleans this year.

Dawn sees that Nina is hanging back shyly—

DAWN

May-Alice, this is Nina Crosley—

MAY-ALICE

Hi.

                              NINA
(shakes her hand) Hi.

                              KIM
She's playing you.

                              DAWN
Scarlet.

                          MAY-ALICE
I'm back in the story?

                              DAWN
Vance thought it was time.

                              NINA
I'm pregnant.

                          MAY-ALICE
Oh— sorry— have a seat, please—

                              NINA
No. Scarlet's pregnant. On the show.

                          MAY-ALICE
Oh. Wow.

                              NINA
I've been auditing Lamaze classes. Me personally. For— you know— preparation.

                          MAY-ALICE
I had a hysterectomy.

                              NINA
Oh, I'm sorry—

                          MAY-ALICE
On the show. Scarlet. In my third season.

                              NINA
(worried) A hysterectomy—

                              DAWN
(idly) Took the crib and left the playpen.

Chantelle laughs. Dawn is suddenly a self-conscious, and
gets back her somewhat regal manner—

                              DAWN

(smiling) Something my mother used to say.

                               KIM

Was she southern?

                              DAWN

(shrugs) She was from the south <u>side</u>—

                              NINA

(sitting) Maybe that's why the baby had to be
by Zon-Dar.

                           MAY-ALICE

I haven't been keeping up lately— Zon-Dar?

                              NINA

He went back to his planet.

                           MAY-ALICE

Ah. Well. This is— uhm— a great surprise. Why
don't you all have a seat. Would you like
something to drink?

Kim looks to Chantelle—

                               KIM

Do you have sassafras tea?

Chantelle looks to May-Alice who looks to Dawn—

                              DAWN

She read it somewhere.

                              NINA

(to Chantelle) Wine spritzer?

                           CHANTELLE

(looks to May-Alice) We don't have anything
alcoholic. I'll just bring a bunch of stuff
out—

Chantelle retreats into the house—

MAY-ALICE

She's uhm— Chantelle— isn't really my maid or
anything.

NINA

Oh, I'm sorry—

KIM

I thought she was like a family retainer.

MAY-ALICE

Right— so— you all drove over together?

KIM

May-Alice, this country is so— it's so laden,
you know?

MAY-ALICE

Laden? With what?

KIM

Oh, just— atmosphere. Portent. It's like the
air is thick with— with— what is it thick
with?

DAWN

Humidity.

KIM

Right. It's liquid and heavy with history and
tradition. It's— fecund.

May-Alice looks to Dawn for help—

DAWN

Must be great for the soil.

92 EXT. PATIO—DAY (LATER)

Kim steps out onto the lawn, drink in hand, gazing roman-
tically into the distance—

KIM

"This land, deep and inviolate, paid for in
blood, infused with the life spirit of those

who would endure on its face, standing in mute
and eternal reproach to the cheap intransi-
gent babble of the towns that fester in its
nether parts; this land, whispering with
overripe breath its tale of original sin."

WOMEN — PATIO

Chantelle has cleared the refrigerator of drinks— pitchers
and bottles cover the table. They are a bit stunned by
Kim's outburst—

                    NINA
    That's amazing. Who wrote that?
                    KIM
    (turning) I forget.

May-Alice, orange soda in hand, shakes her head—

                  MAY-ALICE
    That's why I never had kids. After surviving
    me as a mother they'd grow up and write more
    of that twisted gothic shit.

                    DAWN
    You'd be a great mother.

                  MAY-ALICE
    Dawn, I couldn't keep a pet <u>tur</u>tle alive. And
    then when I was married it was to that— that
    <u>act</u>or—

Chantelle steps out with more ice for drinks—

                    DAWN
    He was on the show.

                  MAY-ALICE
    Jamie? On a soap?

                    NINA
    He played Zon-Dar.

MAY-ALICE

He got you pregnant? He's got a sperm count
of two—

NINA

So you didn't stay friends?

MAY-ALICE

The only good thing about this fucking accident is I don't have to pay alimony to the
little creep anymore.

NINA

Oh. Wow.

KIM

(drifts back) Does this place have a name?

MAY-ALICE

You mean Lake Arthur?

KIM

Author?

CHANTELLE

Arthur. Like the King. May-Alice turning back
into a cracker down here.

KIM

Actually, I meant the house. Does your family
have a name for it?

MAY-ALICE

You mean like Belle Rive?

KIM

Well—

MAY-ALICE

Does your apartment in New York have a name?

KIM

14G.

MAY-ALICE

Right.

DAWN

(standing) Jeffrey calls our place in the

Hamptons "Uncle Tom's Condo," but that's
just to be perverse.

Dawn heads for the house—

> **NINA**
>
> I feel terrible.

Kim and May-Alice turn to look at her—

> **NINA**
>
> Here I am sitting having a nice time in your
> backyard and I'm the one who stole your part
> and had an affair with your ex-husband and now
> I'm carrying his baby.

> **MAY-ALICE**
>
> An affair?

> **NINA**
>
> Oh no— not in real life— he was— he was
> taken.

May-Alice looks to Kim, who looks back sheepishly—

> **MAY-ALICE**
>
> Taken?

> **KIM**
>
> He's grown a lot since you knew him. That's
> what I thought, anyway.

> **MAY-ALICE**
>
> You poor baby. How did it come out?

> **KIM**
>
> (shrugs) He went back to his planet.

93 HOUSE — DAY

Dawn comes back through the kitchen. Chantelle is assem-
bling BLTs—

DAWN

Can I help you with anything?

CHANTELLE

I'm fine.

DAWN

Uhm— Kim doesn't eat meat. And Nina's gonna
open it up and scrape out that mayonnaise.

CHANTELLE

How bout you?

DAWN

Oh, I'll eat anything.

Dawn leans on the counter, shy—

DAWN

You from around here?

CHANTELLE

(shakes her head) Chicago.

DAWN

Yeah? Me too. Cooley High.

CHANTELLE

Du Sable.

DAWN

Where'd you live?

CHANTELLE

Euclid Street.

DAWN

Pill Hill. Father must be a doctor. I come
out of Cabrini-Green.

CHANTELLE

That's a long way up.

DAWN

Yeah. So— how is she?

CHANTELLE

See for yourself.

                    DAWN

I don't think I'd be able to handle it.

                  CHANTELLE

You and her good friends?

                    DAWN

We spent a lot of time together. Work—you
know.

                  CHANTELLE

Yeah.

                    DAWN

You two seem to get on pretty well.

                  CHANTELLE

(considers) We spend a lot of time together.

94 EXT. PATIO—LATE AFTERNOON

Chantelle sits with the others now, remains of lunch lying
in front of them, a more reflective mood settling in—

                     KIM

I did Blanche, I did Laura, I did Alma in
Summer and Smoke, I did Frankie in *Member of
the Wedding*—

                    DAWN

Where was this?

                     KIM

Minnesota. In school.

                    DAWN

Minnesota, huh?

                     KIM

One more year on daytime, save my money, I'm
gonna quit and go back to class. Do some theater.

                    DAWN

I heard that one before.

                  MAY-ALICE

I <u>said</u> that one before.

NINA

I didn't ask for the anal probe.

The others look at her. She is deep in thought—

NINA

Four years starving in New York, doing show-
cases that I had to pay for myself, that was
my first big break. My first feature. This
like zero-budget movie about people who are
taken up into alien spaceships and given physicals against their will? I go in to the audi-
tion and the director is really like in<u>tense</u>
and mysterious and he has me sit with my eyes
closed and like free-associate, right? We do
these improvs about the aliens representing
all our primal fears and it's great, finally
some real <u>act</u>ing, and they tell me before I
leave that I've got the part only I don't know
what it <u>is</u> yet, but I'm so <u>thrilled</u> it's this
<u>fea</u>ture, you know, not a student film or any-
thing and my agent gives me a script and I go
through looking for Margaret, the part they
say I have, with my yellow underliner marker
in my hand and it's drying <u>out</u> and finally I
find only this one page with the corner folded
over. I'm in a therapy group of these people
who have had these alien physicals against
their will and I've only got one line. "I
didn't ask for the anal probe."

Nobody laughs. This is the story of somebody's life—

MAY-ALICE

Not much to build a character on.

NINA

But I'm a pro<u>fess</u>ional, right? I pre<u>pared.</u> I
had back-story for this woman, I knew that

she'd been to the hairdresser just before the therapy group, that she didn't trust the guy who sat next to the fuchsia, that she turned the TV set on the minute she got back to her apartment just for the sound of it, I even had my boyfriend at the time— you know— with a thermometer—

MAY-ALICE

We get the picture.

NINA

For the sense memory, right? I was loaded for fucking <u>bear.</u> Then it comes time to shoot the scene and they do one take of the wide shot, and they stop just before my line. I was terrified they were going to cut it. They move in for close-ups, reaction shots, mostly things that mean I have to go sit outside cause the camera is set up where my chair is? By the time they get to me it's late and the crew is grumpy cause they're non-union and don't get paid extra for overtime and the lead actor is <u>gone</u>, he's got his shrink appointment, so I'm al<u>one</u> staring at a piece of tape on a stand next to the camera and the director says, "Let's try it a few times without cutting, and give me some different colors."

DAWN

(smiles) Colors.

NINA

I didn't <u>ask</u> for the anal probe.

<u>I</u> didn't ask for the anal probe.

I didn't ask for the anal <u>probe.</u>

I didn't ask for the <u>anal</u> probe.

A silence as they contemplate this. May-Alice breaks the ice—

> MAY-ALICE

And to think you ended up with Zon-Dar.

95 EXT. DRIVEWAY — NIGHT

The women are getting into their car. Dawn driving, as May-Alice wheels out to see them off. Chantelle hangs back a little—

> KIM

I won't forget this, May-Alice. I really won't. The light and the water and the smell of the honeysuckle—

> MAY-ALICE

That's fertilizer, darlin—

> KIM

—the whole thing. It's been—

> DAWN

Atmospheric.

> KIM

—tran<u>scend</u>ant.

Dawn makes a face and sits in the car. She reaches out to take May-Alice's hand—

> DAWN

You come back up, you tell me right away. You promise?

> MAY-ALICE

Promise.

> NINA

(calling from rear) Bye Chantelle!

CHANTELLE

Waving as we hear the CAR REV, then PULL AWAY. She steps
forward to stand by May-Alice, watching them go, brooding—

                    MAY-ALICE
          I need a drink.

                    CHANTELLE
          Too bad.

May-Alice looks at her—

                    MAY-ALICE
          When you think I'll be strong enough to have
          just a little?

                    CHANTELLE
          Never.

May-Alice scowls, looks after the departing car—

                    CHANTELLE
          You miss it much?

                    MAY-ALICE
          Drinking?

                    CHANTELLE
          Acting.

                    MAY-ALICE
          (considers) It's the only thing I was ever
          good at.

                                        FADE TO BLACK:

FADE UP TO:

96 INT. BEDROOM — DAY

May-Alice is long-sitting on her bed, surrounded by
clothes—

                    MAY-ALICE
        Chantelle? Chantelle?

Chantelle enters—

                    CHANTELLE
        Yeah?

                    MAY-ALICE
        I think I need help dressing. Do my legs look
        weird?

                    CHANTELLE
        (shrugs) Bit pale.

                    MAY-ALICE
        More than the rest of me?

                    CHANTELLE
        Naw. I guess not.

May-Alice holds up an expensive-looking dress—

                    MAY-ALICE
        What about this?

                    CHANTELLE
        (shakes head) Shorts. S'what I'm wearing.

                    MAY-ALICE
        Do you have some I can borrow?

                    CHANTELLE
        Yeah.

May-Alice looks across into her mirror, grabbing a handful
of hair—

                    MAY-ALICE
        Look at this. Think you can do anything with this?

                    CHANTELLE
        I'm not a hairdresser.

                    MAY-ALICE
        You had <u>friends</u>, right? Friends, women
        friends, help each other with their hair?

JOHN SAYLES

CHANTELLE
My friends don't have your kind of hair.

MAY-ALICE
Right.

CHANTELLE
And we don't have time for any cornrows.

MAY-ALICE
What am I doing this for? Why do I give a shit?

CHANTELLE
He likes you.

MAY-ALICE
You think he does?

CHANTELLE
He asked you to go out on his boat.

MAY-ALICE
He asked you out too.

CHANTELLE
He's not after me.

MAY-ALICE
He's not after me, either. He just asked us out to be nice.

CHANTELLE
He asked you out. He asked me to come along. Now if you don't want me to—

MAY-ALICE
No. You have to come. (looks at hair) I feel like I'm fucking thirteen years old. I'm pathetic.

CHANTELLE
You're not pathetic.

MAY-ALICE
He's just asking us out to be nice.

CHANTELLE
Sure.

MAY-ALICE

Or he just wants to show us his boat. Men get
off on that, showing women their machines.

CHANTELLE

Yeah.

MAY-ALICE

Or maybe he really *is* after you.

CHANTELLE

You're pathetic.

97 EXT. BAYOU — DAY

May-Alice sits in her chair lashed down on the front of
the flatboat. Chantelle sits beside her, and Rennie steers
with the motor in the rear. He cuts the motor down to an
idle and they drift, deep in a mangrove bayou—

CHANTELLE

Are we lost?

RENNIE

No.

CHANTELLE

How can you tell?

RENNIE

(shrugs) Been comin in here all my life.

MAY-ALICE

(points) Look—

THEIR POV — HERON

An enormous blue heron flaps up ahead of them, gathering
speed over the water till it lifts and soars over the
treetops—

BOAT

JOHN SAYLES

RENNIE

Saw one of those take off with a two-foot mud snake in his mouth. My papa almost swallow his tobacco.

MAY-ALICE

It meant something to him?

RENNIE

Everything meant somethin to him. Had alla them coon-ass superstitions. Catch something in his traps, whatever it was, turtle, gator, possum— he cut the stomach open, see what was inside. Tell the future.

CHANTELLE

There lots of snakes in here?

RENNIE

This Cottonmouth Heaven in here. I find some for you.

CHANTELLE

Don't go out of your way.

98 EXT. BAYOU — DAY — VARIOUS SHOTS

The boat moving through the trees. Animals appearing alone the shoreline— snake, armadillo, gator, nutria, birds. May-Alice, Chantelle, and Rennie pointing, reacting.

99 SHORE — DAY

The boat is pulled up on the little beach of a small island. We are getting near the Gulf, wider stretches of water between mangrove islands. We PAN to see Chantelle and May-Alice lying on a blanket by the water. Rennie standing beyond them, fishing—

MAY-ALICE AND CHANTELLE — CLOSER

Chantelle is poking the skin on May-Alice's legs to see
if she's gotten too much sun already—

CHANTELLE

I never went out on any boat. Not my
father's style, nature stuff. Course maybe
if he had boys—

MAY-ALICE

You had sisters?

CHANTELLE

Naw. He wanted sons, all he got was me.

MAY-ALICE

Tough on your mother.

CHANTELLE

I lost her when I was fourteen. Diabetes.

MAY-ALICE

You still close to your father?

CHANTELLE

(frowns) I married right out of high school
and he didn't want me to. When we split up
it was like "I told you so" and who needs
that, right? Then later, when I took up with
Luther—(sighs) We don't talk anymore.

Chantelle covers May-Alice's legs with a towel—

MAY-ALICE

I wasn't talking with mine when they crashed.
I'd just gone up North against their will. My
mother would sneak in my room at night and say
how she could see my side of it but she was
in this po_si_tion, and couldn't I just help
keep the peace? She never stood up for me. Or
for herself. She hated flying. But she went
along.

Rennie squats next to them with a big catfish in his hand—

                              RENNIE
              Lunch.

                            CHANTELLE
              Ooooh. Nasty-looking.

                            MAY-ALICE
              She's from Chicago.

Rennie slices the fish's belly—

                              RENNIE
              Let's check out what the future got in store
              for us.

CU FISH

Rennie's knife probes out the stomach, slices it open— two
little silver fish, intact, slip out—

SHORE

                            MAY-ALICE
              What's that mean? Is it good?

                              RENNIE
              Passion fish. Hold out your hands.

                            CHANTELLE
              Whoah—

                              RENNIE
              It's real bad luck not to.

They gingerly hold out their hands and he places a fish
in each palm—

                              RENNIE
              You squeeze that little fish tight now and
              think bout somebody you want some loving
              from.

May-Alice and Chantelle look at each other, make a disgusted face, then squeeze their fish—

> CHANTELLE
>
> You're makin this shit up, right?

> RENNIE
>
> Ever since there been Cajuns they been squeezin the passion fish. Some says you got to swallow em raw—

> CHANTELLE
>
> I don't need it that bad.

100 CU FISH SKELETON — LATE AFTERNOON

Lifted on a stick. We WIDEN to see Rennie taking the fish carcass to wedge it between some half-submerged rocks. Chantelle is packing up the remains of the picnic—

> RENNIE
>
> Leave this baby for the crawfish.

> MAY-ALICE
>
> What is this island, Rennie? Does it have a name?

> RENNIE
>
> Despair.

> CHANTELLE
>
> Nice.

> RENNIE
>
> Story is, there was a slave woman went crazy out here. Lost her only daughter to pnuemonia, run off from her people and holed up here.

He dips to one knee by May-Alice. She puts her arms around his neck and he scoops her into his arms, standing—

> RENNIE
>
> Trappers come by in their pirogues, they hear

her moanin and cryin bout her lost baby.
Despair.

Rennie places May-Alice in her chair. Chantelle adjusts her legs and slides the side panel in—

                    CHANTELLE
          (slaps a mosquito) What did she live on?

                    RENNIE
          Oh— bird's eggs, fish— everything that walks,
          flies, hops, or crawls out here got a use.
          It's all good eatin.

Rennie gives the motor cord a pull. The engine sputters and dies. Tries again. Dies. Again. Nothing.

                    CHANTELLE
          (swats again) Something broke?

                    RENNIE
          Yeah.

                    CHANTELLE
          Can you fix it?

Rennie pops the cowling off the motor—

                    RENNIE
          Gonna take a little time. I'm real sorry.

                    MAY-ALICE
          No hurry.

                    CHANTELLE
          (waving bugs away) Sure. We'll just feed the
          bugs while you fix it.

Rennie bends and scoops a double handful of mud from the bank, dropping it on deck next to May-Alice. He starts to rub it on her legs—

                    RENNIE

     Here. Better do this, keep them skeeters off
     you—

                  CHANTELLE

     (teasing) That looks like fun.

Rennie tosses a handful of mud toward Chantelle—

                    RENNIE

     Help yourself.

Chantelle makes a mock insulted look to May-Alice over
Rennie's head, then silently mouths "He likes you"—

                  MAY-ALICE

     Shhhhhhh.

101 EXT. BAYOU — NIGHT

Rennie steers with the motor running slow, pointing a flashlight to see ahead as they wind through the narrow bayou—

                  CHANTELLE

     Now are we lost?

                    RENNIE

     (shrugs) No matter where you at, there you is.

                  CHANTELLE

     Great.

                  MAY-ALICE

     (happy) Your kids must love being out here
     with you.

                    RENNIE

     Arlene won't let em come. Says the devil
     lives out here. That's why the trees won't
     grow straight.

                  MAY-ALICE

     That's too bad.

> RENNIE

You getting cold up there?

CLOSER — MAY—ALICE AND CHANTELLE

Chantelle is worried that they're lost, but May-Alice is having a great time—

> MAY-ALICE

We're fine up here.

A low-hanging branch scrapes across the deck. Chantelle starts and grabs May-Alice's hand—

> MAY-ALICE

Just fine.

102 EXT. BAYOU — NIGHT — VARIOUS SHOTS

The moon through the tops of the mangroves.
The flashlight playing on the trees and water ahead.
Rennie steering, searching.
Chantelle watching for snakes.
May-Alice smiling, taking in the night.

103 EXT. DOCK — NIGHT

Rennie stowing gear from the boat as Chantelle unlocks the wheels to push May-Alice back to the house—

> RENNIE

I'll take care of all this. I'm really sorry.

> MAY-ALICE

I loved it. It was wonderful.

> CHANTELLE

A thrill a minute.

                    MAY-ALICE
You want to call from the house? Your wife—?

                    RENNIE
She knows where I am. She's not worried.

                    MAY-ALICE
Right. Well— good night.

                    CHANTELLE
Night.

                    RENNIE
Good night.

We TRACK AHEAD as Chantelle wheels May-Alice away—

                    MAY-ALICE
His wife's not worried.

                    CHANTELLE
Should she be?

                    MAY-ALICE
Why worry about some cripple, got a freezer
compartment for a pussy—

                    CHANTELLE
Don't be that way.

                    MAY-ALICE.
Look at me. Pitiful.

She holds her hands in front of her face—

                    MAY-ALICE
My palms are all sweaty. (makes a face) And
they smell like fish.

                    CHANTELLE
(smiles) Passion fish.

She pushes May-Alice out of the shot—

104 SUN — DAY

There is NO SOUND. We TILT DOWN from a bright sun in a blue sky to see Rennie, soundlessly pounding nails into the dock in front of the house. We watch his back muscles move for a moment, then PAN across to where May-Alice sits, wearing a sundress, her legs hanging over the edge of the dock. She is watching Rennie, smiling. She stands, walks over, kneels behind him, touching his back. He turns, smiles— they kiss. We hear Chantelle's VOICE, off, from some distance—

> CHANTELLE
> (off) May-Alice! May-Alice!

May-Alice looks out across the lake, shielding her eyes from the sun—

105 ISLAND, CHANTELLE AND GIRL — DAY

NO SOUND but Chantelle's VOICE. Chantelle stands waving from the shore of a little island across the water, holding onto a LITTLE GIRL with her other hand—

> CHANTELLE
> May-Alice, it's okay! I found her! I found her!

Chantelle's VOICE, much closer, FADES IN—

> CHANTELLE
> May-Alice May-Alice.

106 INT. LIVING ROOM — DAY

May-Alice starts awake on the couch. She is dressed in shorts and a sleeveless t-shirt. Chantelle is sitting next to her—

> CHANTELLE
> You okay?

> MAY-ALICE
> I was dreaming. You were in it. You were

on that island— and you had a little girl
with you—

Chantelle tightens—

>   **CHANTELLE**
>   Don't dream that anymore, okay?

>   **MAY-ALICE**
>   It's a dream. How can I control that?

>   **CHANTELLE**
>   Try. (stands) It's time to go.

107 EXT. CAR, TOWN—DAY

May-Alice's car back on the road, her wheelchair folded
and roped into the trunk, moving through town—

108 INT. CAR — DAY

Chantelle driving, May-Alice strapped into the passenger
seat—

>   **CHANTELLE**
>   We got to get you a car with hand controls—

>   **MAY-ALICE**
>   I never learned to drive. Before, even—

Chantelle gives her a look—

>   **MAY-ALICE**
>   Hey, I lived in New York. I took taxis—(sees)
>   Jesus— there's Rennie—

109 THEIR POV — STORE

Rennie steps out of the Pic'n'Pay with his arms full of

---

groceries, preceded by his WIFE and a mess of CHILDREN—
Chantelle watches May-Alice for a moment, gauging her
reaction—

> ### CHANTELLE
> Anything you want me to pick up while you're
> at the session? May-Alice?

> ### MAY-ALICE
> (still watching, distracted) Maybe some
> more film.

They drive on, May-Alice looking into the side mirror to
keep an eye on Rennie as they leave

110 INT. THERAPY ROOM — DAY

Louise is working May-Alice's arms and trunk as she lies
on the exam table—

> ### LOUISE
> This seems better. Don't let me move you.

> ### MAY-ALICE
> She's moody, you know? I mean she's very pro-
> fessional, it doesn't get in the way of my
> life—

> ### LOUISE
> Which is?

> ### MAY-ALICE
> What?

> ### LOUISE
> Activities of daily life? What do you do all
> day?

A long pause, May-Alice trying to think what she's been
doing—

> ### MAY-ALICE
> I've started taking pictures.

LOUISE

Uh-huh. Reach your arms over your head.

MAY-ALICE

Outside, mostly. She wants me to buy a sports chair, one of those ones that's like a trail bike. She's into high tech, Chantelle. Not to make her job easier or anything, just, you know— for me. (sighs) I wish she'd open up a little more. She's carrying a lot of weight around, but she won't let anybody close.

LOUISE

You've gotten a little more flexible.

MAY-ALICE

What?

LOUISE

Especially in your neck and shoulders. Reach forward—

MAY-ALICE

She's been all over me about my drinking.

LOUISE

Give me some resistance.

May-Alice tightens her arm and Louise tries to push it down—

MAY-ALICE

I used to have a few glasses of wine with dinner, another while I learned my lines for the next day, then fall asleep. The rest of the time I was working.

LOUISE

Now the other one.

MAY-ALICE

Then when I had the whole day to face—

LOUISE

You're getting stronger.

MAY-ALICE

If I ask her for a drink now she won't give it to me. Like she's the boss.

LOUISE

You think it's something you can handle on your own?

May-Alice thinks for a long moment—

MAY-ALICE

No.

Louise presses on May-Alice's belly, looking for swelling—

LOUISE

How's your bowel function?

MAY-ALICE

Fine if I eat at the same time every day. I almost feel like we could be friends, only there's so much garbage in between us.

LOUISE

Any shortness of breath? Pain in the lungs?

MAY-ALICE

(shakes head) So what do you think?

LOUISE

I'm not done yet.

MAY-ALICE

I mean about her. Chantelle.

LOUISE

(sits against table) I'm a physical therapist, May-Alice, not a marriage counselor.

MAY-ALICE

Right.

Louise takes her legs and stretches them back toward her head—

> **LOUISE**
> You been doing your standing?

Louise flexes May-Alice's knee—

> **MAY-ALICE**
> Doc?

> **LOUISE**
> Call me Louise. Little bald guys with glasses who smoke cigars and play poker are called Doc.

> **MAY-ALICE**
> Did you ever fall in love with a married man?

111 INT. SUGAR'S BEDROOM — DAY

Chantelle sits on Sugar's bed, putting her clothes back on. We hear the SHOWER from the adjoining bathroom. She calls—

> **CHANTELLE**
> Sugar? I got to go! Sugar?

112 INT. KITCHEN — DAY

Albertine is laying her lunch out on the table as Chantelle steps in. Chantelle is surprised. Albertine is used to this—

> **CHANTELLE**
> Oh! Hi—

> **ALBERTINE**
> Hi.

> **CHANTELLE**
> I'm Chantelle—

> **ALBERTINE**
> I remember.

Chantelle smiles, watches Albertine sit to eat—

> **CHANTELLE**
> Sugar said you were at the track—

> **ALBERTINE**
> Workouts are over. Post time not till five thirty.

Chantelle sits against the counter, searching for words—

> **CHANTELLE**
> Albertine— when your parents split up—and Sugar wasn't around— were you mad at him?

> **ALBERTINE**
> (shrugs) Both of em.

> **CHANTELLE**
> You stay mad long?

> **ALBERTINE**
> Naw. I figure they just people. They got their problems, I got mine.

> **CHANTELLE**
> You got problems? At your age?

Albertine gives her a shy smile—

> **ALBERTINE**
> I'm working on some.

113 INT. BEDROOM — DAY — VARIOUS SHOTS

Impressionistic shots of Chantelle and Sugar making love—

114 INT. CAR—EVENING — CU CHANTELLE

Daydreaming as she drives—

> **MAY-ALICE**
> (off) Chantelle? Chantelle?

SIDE ANGLE 2 — SHOT

May-Alice is watching the road ahead, a little worried—

                    CHANTELLE
        Yeah?

                    MAY-ALICE
        Could we drive on the right side of the road
        for awhile?

Chantelle swerves—

                    CHANTELLE
        Sorry. Spaced out.

                    MAY-ALICE
        So what did you do while I was with Louise?

                    CHANTELLE
        Oh— just killed time.

115 INT. HOUSE — NIGHT — CU ANSWERING MACHINE

May-Alice's hand appears to punch the Message button. The VOICE
of DR. BLADES, deep and stern, comes on. We WIDEN to see May-
Alice, then Chantelle entering through the doorway beyond her—

                    DR. BLADES
        Hello, I'm calling for Chantelle— This is her
        father speaking. It's five o'clock on
        Thursday. Denita and I would like to visit
        you this weekend. Please give me a call.

May-Alice clicks the OFF button. She looks back to
Chantelle, frozen in her tracks—

                    MAY-ALICE
        Denita?

                    CHANTELLE
        (quietly) My daughter.

---

116 EXT. ROADSIDE — DAY

We see the same bus Chantelle got off of her first day
pull away, leaving DR. BLADES, a stern-looking man in his
sixties, and DENITA, a little girl of ten. We SHIFT to
include Chantelle in the FG, watching them from our side
of the road—

SIDE VIEW — ROAD

Denita moves first, looking both ways and then starting
across. Dr. Blades lifts their big suitcase and follows
more cautiously—

117 INT. KITCHEN — DAY

May-Alice is wheeling around fixing an elaborate lunch. She
hears the CAR APPROACH, does one last touch, takes a deep
breath, and hurries out of the shot—

118 INT. DINING ROOM — DAY

May-Alice sits at the table with Denita and Dr. Blades as
Chantelle brings in the food. May-Alice is being very
southern and charming—

> **MAY-ALICE**
> Chantelle is such a wonder in the kitchen.

Chantelle shoots her a look—

> **MAY-ALICE**
> I was never much of a cook to begin with,
> then with my misfortune— well— (to Denita)
> You like that, darlin?

> DENITA

It's got rice in it.

> MAY-ALICE

That's what makes it boudin.

> DR. BLADES

We've never had somebody in the family work
as a cook.

May-Alice senses the disapproval—

> MAY-ALICE

Oh, we do share the cooking. Mine just
doesn't taste like much.

Chantelle sits stiffly between her father and daughter,
on trial—

> MAY-ALICE

Denita, it's just so nice to finally have you
here in person. (looks to Chantelle)
Chantelle talks about you so much I feel like
I already know you.

119 EXT. PATIO — DAY

Dr. Blades stands watching as May-Alice wheels around tapping wooden stakes into the ground with a croquet mallet,
making a rectangle—

> MAY-ALICE

You ever do any gardening, Dr. Blades?

> DR. BLADES

Can't say that I have.

> MAY-ALICE

Me neither. Don't think anybody in my family
ever put a thing in the ground that wasn't a
drill pipe.

                    DR. BLADES
My grandfather was a farmer.

                    MAY-ALICE
Yeah?

                    DR. BLADES
Sharecropper. Alabama.

                    MAY-ALICE
(nods) He must have had some stories.

                    DR. BLADES
None that he cared to pass on.

May-Alice lets this one lie. She moves to the next corner—

                    DR. BLADES
Do you think you'll continue to employ my
daughter?

                    MAY-ALICE
As long as she'll have me.

                    DR. BLADES
She told you I have legal custody of Denita.

                    MAY-ALICE
(careful) She never got into the details.

                    DR. BLADES
The court gave her to me when Chantelle was—
when Chantelle was unfit to be a mother.

                    MAY-ALICE
Right.

                    DR. BLADES
Denita has got some school left this year.
But for her vacation— there seems to be a
stable work situation here. A house—

                    MAY-ALICE
Well I'm not going anywheres. I got this
garden to deal with.

120 EXT. LAKE — DAY

Chantelle sits on the tethered flatboat with Denita—

> CHANTELLE
>
> It's not really a swimming lake, baby. People
> fish in it, look for animals—

> DENITA
>
> Animals?

> CHANTELLE
>
> All kinds of things. Raccoons, alligators—

> DENITA
>
> Real alligators?

> CHANTELLE
>
> Yeah, they're real. I even saw the nest of
> one out there.

> DENITA
>
> They have eggs.

> CHANTELLE
>
> That's right. There's a man, a friend of
> ours, he knows all about where they live.
> Maybe some time he'll take you out and see
> all that.

> DENITA
>
> How big is it?

> CHANTELLE
>
> The lake? Oh, this one spreads all the way
> out to the ocean. You never seen the ocean,
> have you?

She shakes her head no—

> CHANTELLE
>
> Well, that's something we'll have to do.

Chantelle gets up her courage—

> CHANTELLE
>
> I been missing you so much.

Denita tightens, knowing heavy stuff lies ahead—

> ### CHANTELLE
> I just messed up. Grownups can do that. I got
> caught up in something bad, and I lost you.

Denita struggles not to cry—

> ### CHANTELLE
> You didn't forget about me, did you?

Denita shakes her head no—

> ### CHANTELLE
> You remember what I was like when I was sick?

> ### DENITA
> Yes.

> ### CHANTELLE
> Well, you're not ever gonna see me like that
> again. That's a promise.

121 EXT. PARISH PICNIC GROUNDS — DAY

A mixture of black and white people stroll, eat, talk and
dance at an outdoor dance. We shoot past the food tables
where ladies are selling their homemade étouffée toward
the back of the bandstand on which a zydeco band is
playing—

FOLDING CHAIRS

Chantelle sits her father and her daughter down in seats
in the first row of folding chairs that face the dance
area and bandstand. She turns to check the band out—

BAND

We TRACK in past a kid playing a washboard, past the accordion player to the drummer. It is Sugar, who winks at Chantelle—

CU CHANTELLE

Uncomfortable to have her past and present in the same place. She gives a surreptitious wave—

MAY-ALICE

Sitting in her chair a bit removed from the audience, watching the dancers, tapping time with her hands. She has her camera in her lap. Rennie appears behind her, puts a hand on her shoulder, then sits on the grass beside her. He nods to the band—

                    RENNIE
     Devil's music.

                    MAY-ALICE
     I love it.

                    RENNIE
     Last time I saw you before you went north was
     at one of these.

                    MAY-ALICE
     Yeah? I must have sneaked over with Marcella
     DuChamps. My father didn't approve.

                    RENNIE
     I never got up the nerve to ask you to dance.

                    MAY-ALICE
     Right.

                    RENNIE
     And then I heard you'd gone away for good.

                    MAY-ALICE
     Well— my dancing days are over.

The band finishes their number, the leader announcing the next band to play. May-Alice applauds. Rennie looks at her. She looks back and they get locked in that longing for a moment before May-Alice breaks it—

                    MAY-ALICE
        How's your family?

                    RENNIE
        (looks away) They're fine.

They sit in silence a moment, May-Alice feeling bad about rubbing it in—

                    RENNIE
        I get you something to drink?

                    MAY-ALICE
        Rennie?

                    RENNIE
        Yeah?

                    MAY-ALICE
        You don't have to have a job to do or some-
        thing to fix to come over and visit.

                    RENNIE
        Yeah?

                    MAY-ALICE
        Yeah.

                    RENNIE
        I'll maybe do that, then.

May-Alice looks away, a little shaky—

                    MAY-ALICE
        Do it soon, okay?

Rennie takes hold of the arm of her chair as they watch the new band start to play— Chantelle, Dr. Blades, and Denita watching. Chantelle sees something, tightens—

SUGAR

Sugar is approaching, looking good, a big smile on his
face—

CU CHANTELLE

She signals sideways towards her father and daughter with
her eyes, gives her head a warning shake—

SUGAR

Slowing only slightly, he reads the signal—

SEATS

Chantelle worried as Sugar steps into the FG, looking down
on them—

                              SUGAR
          Excuse me—

REVERSE ANGLE

Sugar offers his hand to Denita—
                              SUGAR
          Could I have this dance, young lady?

CU ACCORDIAN PLAYER

Singing and playing—

DANCE AREA

Sugar gallantly showing Denita the steps. She is embarrassed and thrilled at the same time—

CHANTELLE AND DR. BLADES

We shoot between them toward the band, seeing Sugar and Denita dance. Dr. Blades sneaks a look at his daughter—

CU ACCORDION PLAYER

Playing and singing—

122 EXT. PATIO—NIGHT

May Alice sits out under the light, looking out at the stars. Chantelle steps out by her—

> **MAY-ALICE**
> They asleep?

> **CHANTELLE**
> I think so.

> **MAY-ALICE**
> Denita is beautiful.

> **CHANTELLE**
> Yeah. Listen, thanks— for today—

> **MAY-ALICE**
> Your old man is a tough nut.

> **CHANTELLE**
> Growing up I didn't have to be good, I had to be <u>per</u>fect. What are those?

WIDER

We shoot toward them through the stakes May-Alice pounded in earlier—

> MAY-ALICE
>> Oh— props.

CU MAY-ALICE

Musing—

> MAY-ALICE
>> A good actress can improvise on a bare stage,
>> but sometimes it's nice to have props.

123 EXT. LAKE — MORNING

The sun coming up to burn off the mist on the water—

124 INT. DARKROOM — DAY — CU PRINT

Under the RED LIGHT of the darkroom, we look at a blank sheet of print stock lying in its chemical bath—

> MAY-ALICE
>> This is the part that's like magic.

The print begins to darken into shape. It is a shot of Denita dancing with Sugar the night before. The timer goes BING!

INT. DARKROOM

Denita stands by May-Alice as she pulls the wet print out of the tray and puts it on the drying roller—

> MAY-ALICE
>> Cute guy. You get his phone number?

Denita giggles. She looks at the dry prints laid on the table—

                    DENITA
        You got pictures of alligators?

                   MAY-ALICE
        No, but I'm gonna get some. Great subjects—
        they'll hold still for hours if they're not
        hungry.

Denita has picked up a photo of Chantelle—

CU DENITA

Looking at the photo—

                   MAY-ALICE
        (off) That's nice, isn't it?

                    DENITA
        Uh-huh.

2-SHOT

                   MAY-ALICE
        (off) Course it's easier to get a smile out
        of an alligator than it is to get one from
        your mother. You keep that, darlin.

125 EXT. ROADSIDE — DAY

Chantelle stands with Dr. Blades by the side of the
idling bus—

                   CHANTELLE
        I'm fine now. I really am.

                  DR. BLADES
        I'll be calling you and your lady at the end
        of the school year—

CHANTELLE
Can't I come up?

DR. BLADES
I don't think you should be back in Chicago—

CHANTELLE
You're not the damn parole board!

DR. BLADES
I am Denita's legal guardian, for as long as
I think it necessary.

Chantelle looks away, trying to control her anger—

DR. BLADES
This seems like a good place for you. You
show me you can hold on here, we'll make some
plans for Denita. (steps into bus) Goodbye.

CHANTELLE
(resigned) Bye, Daddy. Thanks for bringing
her down.

The door closes and as the bus pulls away Chantelle finds
the window Denita waves from. She follows a few steps,
waving back, then stops. She is suddenly furious, kicking
the ground, hurling a stone, swearing, whirling to go back
home. A shiny big rental car slowing as it approaches her
from behind. It stops on the road by Chantelle and VANCE,
a smiling TV producer, leans out of the window—

VANCE
Excuse me— where can I find Lake Arthur?
Chantelle points across the road—

VANCE
Right under my nose, huh? Actually, I'm
looking for somebody. May-Alice Culhane?

126 INT. KITCHEN — DAY

Chantelle sits by the counter, a half-prepared plate of sandwiches next to her, eavesdropping. We hear LAUGHTER from the patio—

> VANCE
>
> (off) I don't know if it was the hysterec-tomy thing that threw her or what, but she comes back up and a week later she gives us notice—

Chantelle stands to look out the window, worried—

> MAY-ALICE (O.S.)
>
> Was she good?

CHANTELLE'S POV — PATIO

May-Alice is wheeling around pulling up the stakes she laid out before. VANCE stands nearby with a drink in hand—

> VANCE
>
> Well— yes. Not like you of course—

> MAY-ALICE
>
> Of course.

> VANCE
>
> It leaves quite a gap on the show.

> MAY-ALICE
>
> If you're hiring people like my ex-husband you got worse problems.

> VANCE
>
> Right. Uhm—can I use the head?

> MAY-ALICE
>
> (points) Be my guest.

We PAN away from the window as Chantelle busies herself with the sandwiches. Vance steps in, looks at her, clears his throat—

                              VANCE

Chantelle, right?

                            CHANTELLE

Uh-huh.

                              VANCE

She really seems good, don't you think?

                            CHANTELLE

I guess so.

                              VANCE

I mean she hasn't gained a lot of weight or
anything. (confidential) You think I have a
shot with her?

                            CHANTELLE

A shot?

                              VANCE

Talking her into coming back to the show. You
think she's ready?

                            CHANTELLE

(shrugs) Ask her.

                              VANCE

I might need an ally on this, Chantelle. She'd
have to come up right away.

                            CHANTELLE

It's her life.

                              VANCE

We can't have her going to seed down here,
can we?

We HOLD on Chantelle as Vance exits to the bathroom. She
snaps open a tray of ice cubes with a loud CRACK,
thinking—

127 EXT. SKY — HERON — DAY

A huge blue heron flaps over the islands—

128 EXT. DOCK — DAY

May-Alice sits in her chair at the edge of the dock, looking up at the heron, Vance standing behind her. She has her camera in her lap and occasionally snaps a picture as Vance pitches—

MAY-ALICE

You want me back on the show?

VANCE

(grins) You're going to love what Edna has come up with for you. A whole new direction—

MAY-ALICE

I'm still Scarlet—?

VANCE

We do a big blitz about in response to the flood of mail May-Alice Culhane is returning to daytime—

MAY-ALICE

What about Nina?

VANCE

She's been gone for weeks. We sent Scarlet to the Mayo Clinic for observation. And we've hatched a great plan to bring you back in. We've found a scene from before where you leave Rhonda in the living room set and you actually walk over to the door—

MAY-ALICE

So we shoot a couch scene on the set—

VANCE

Right— you're back from the clinic, no improvement, then we cut to the tape of you actually walking to the door, and you go outside and we cut back to her watching from the doorway—

MAY-ALICE

I still have amnesia? _And_ I'm pregnant?

Bear with me a second—we hold on Rhonda's
face, and then there's the sound—

The sound of screeching brakes.

Vance's face drops—

VANCE

Edna called you.

MAY-ALICE

No, no. I'm just guessing. Go ahead.

VANCE

There's a screech of brakes, Rhonda screams.
Cut. Monday's show, first thing, there you
are on a stretcher, flashing lights all
around you, and the <u>dri</u>ver of the car that
hit you steps forward—guess who it is?

MAY-ALICE

Max.

VANCE

Edna did call you.

MAY-ALICE

No, really. Keep going. Max ran me over—

VANCE

And he says "Scarlet, my God—"

MAY-ALICE

But I don't recognize him because of the
amnesia—

VANCE

No, you recognize his <u>voice</u>, see, because the
impact of the <u>car</u>—

MAY-ALICE

Ahhhhh—

VANCE

—cured the amnesia. A traumatic blow like that—

MAY-ALICE

—can reverse the effects of what happened when I fell down the elevator shaft.

VANCE

Exactly. So Max is there—

MAY-ALICE

And I remember him, but now I'm paralyzed.

VANCE

Right. That, and— well, Edna had to go beyond that.

MAY-ALICE

Go beyond.

VANCE

See, they're doing a wheelchair thing with Brenda St. Glair on *Santa Fe* so we thought— you've lost the amnesia, and you recognize Max's <u>voice</u>, but

MAY-ALICE

I'm blind?

VANCE

It works like as a metaphor for Scarlet's—

MAY-ALICE

I'm paralyzed and I'm fucking <u>blind</u>?

VANCE

It opens up so many possibilities—

MAY-ALICE

Sure. I can run into walls in my chair, knock over props, have Max take me back so that twit Jessica can get it on with him while I'm in the <u>room</u>—

VANCE

None of this is chiseled in stone yet—

She whirls her chair to head toward the house, Vance hurrying to keep up with her—

MAY-ALICE

Why not put me in a coma, total fucking veg, so you can shoot a few angles of me in bed, then I can come back here and phone in <u>voiceover</u>, Vance? Brain death— think of the metaphoric possibilities in that—

VANCE

(sarcastic) I'd have to check with Edna—

MAY-ALICE

You do that!

VANCE

May-Alice!

The tone in his voice stops May-Alice. She lets him catch up with her—

VANCE

This is a chance that's not going to come around again. You'd better think about it. I'm at the Ramada in Lafayette. Call me.

We TIGHTEN and HOLD on May-Alice as we hear Vance walk away—

129 INT. LIVING ROOM — LATE AFTERNOON

Chantelle sits on the floor in a pool of light. May-Alice has converted the living room into a little gallery—photos she had taken are everywhere, taped to the walls, spread out on the couch, even one propped over the TV screen. Chantelle looks around at them—

CHANTELLE'S POV

PANNING over the photos of the house, the yard, nature shots, till we come to one of Denita, in front of the house, smiling—

CU CHANTELLE

Looking at the photo. We hear a CAR START OUTSIDE, then PULL AWAY. Chantelle frowns, looks toward the window—

130 EXT. DOCK — EARLY EVENING

May-Alice is on her chair by the ramp Rennie has built to get her on board the flatboat. Chantelle joins her—

> **CHANTELLE**
> Guess he isn't staying for dinner.

> **MAY-ALICE**
> Help me on board, okay? I want to go out.

131 EXT. LAKE — EVENING

The boat chugs towards us. Chantelle cuts the motor and they drift—

132 ON BOARD

May-Alice looks out over the water, thinking. Chantelle comes to sit beside her—

> **MAY-ALICE**
> We have to talk.

> **CHANTELLE**
> Yeah.

> **MAY-ALICE**
> Plans.

Chantelle is silent, waiting for the verdict—

> **MAY-ALICE**
> Vance asked me to come back to daytime.

CHANTELLE

You could do it.

MAY-ALICE

Yeah. I could.

She looks at Chantelle, trying to gauge what she's thinking—

MAY-ALICE

So what did your father say?

CHANTELLE

(shrugs) He thinks you're a good influence on me.

MAY-ALICE

(snorts) That's how much he knows.

CHANTELLE

I can't believe I still have to do what- ever he says— like I'm thirteen years old!

MAY-ALICE

I was the faithful daughter in *Lear* once— whatsername— Cordelia. Not much you can do but play it straight till it's over. (looks at lake) Haven't spent a July down here since I lit out. Gets pretty steamy.

CHANTELLE

I bet it does.

MAY-ALICE

Think he'd let Denita stay with you this summer?

CHANTELLE

I have to have a job.

May-Alice looks at her for a long moment, decides—

MAY-ALICE

You've got a job.

CHANTELLE

(shakes her head) New York City? He wouldn't go for that.

MAY-ALICE

What's New York got to do with it?

CHANTELLE

Your show—

MAY-ALICE

What, are you kidding? Back to daytime? Darlin, it's either Friday nights at ten or nothing. One of those lawyer shows where they have hot sex with everybody in the office.

CHANTELLE

You turned him down?

MAY-ALICE

If I'm gonna be here I need you to stay working for me.

CHANTELLE

Bullshit-

MAY-ALICE

Girl, if I'm lyin I'm dyin.

They look at each other. The deal is struck—

CHANTELLE

So we're stuck with each other.

MAY-ALICE

For the time being.

They watch the sunset for a moment—

MAY-ALICE

Chantelle?

CHANTELLE

Yeah?

MAY-ALICE

You <u>are</u> gonna have to learn how to cook.

---

133 LONG SHOT — EARLY EVENING

Two women sitting on a boat in the middle of the lake as
the sun goes down—

CLOSING CREDITS

SILVER CITY (2004)

Original Cast

DANNY O'BRIEN	DANNY HUSTON
DICKIE PILAGER	CHRIS COOPER
CHUCK RAVEN	RICHARD DREYFUSS
TONY GUERRA	SAL LOPEZ
NORA ALLARDYCE	MARIA BELLO
MADDY PILAGER	DARYL HANNAH
MORT SEYMOUR	DAVID CLENNON
CHANDLER TYSON	BILLY ZANE
SHERIFF JOE SKAGGS	JAMES GAMMON
WES BENTEEN	KRIS KIRSTOFFERSON
MITCH	TIM ROTH
VINCE ESPARZA	LUIS SAGUAR
LUPE	ALMA DELFINA
PITO	AARON VIEYRA
RAFI	HUGO E. CARBAJAL
DEPUTY DAVIS	BENJAMIN KROGER
GRACE SEYMOUR	MARY KAY PLACE
KAREN	THORA BIRCH
SENATOR JUDSON PILAGER	MICHAEL MURPHY
HENRY	CHARLES MITCHELL
LLOYD	CAJARDO LINDSEY
PHIL ROSS	PAUL ROHRER
CASEY LYLE	RALPH WAITE
CLIFF CASTLETON	MIGUEL FERRER
CONTRERAS	LARRY GALLEGOS
DEWEY	STEPHEN BRACKETT
DIRECTOR	JOHN C. ASHTON
FOREMAN	DAVID RUSSEL
FREDDY MONDRAGON	RICHARD BEALL
HILARY	ROSLYN WASHINGTON
ELLIE HASTINGS	MAGGIE ROSWELL
KIT	JEFFERSON ARCA
LEO	MICHAEL SHALHOUB
LESLIE	ELIZABETH RAINER
MARCY	AMIE MACKENZIE
PREACHER	GARY SIRCHIA
REBECCA ZELLER	MARE TREVATHAN PHILPOTT
REPORTER #1	JAN VAN SICKLE
REPORTER #2	PATTY CALHOUN
REVEREND TUBBS	DENIS BERKFELDT
YANEZ	RODNEY LIZCANO
LAZARO HUERTA	DONEVON MARTINEZ

SUNSHINE STATE (2002)

Original Cast

MARLY TEMPLE	EDIE FALCO
DELIA TEMPLE	JANE ALEXANDER
FURMAN TEMPLE	RALPH WAITE
DESIREE PERRY	ANGELA BASSETT
REGGIE PERRY	JAMES MCDANIEL
EUNICE STOKES	MARY ALICE
DR. LLOYD	BILL COBBS
EARL PINKNEY	GORDON CLAPP
FRANCINE PINKNEY	MARY STEENBURGEN
JACK MEADOWS	TIMOTHY HUTTON
LEE "FLASH" PHILLIPS	TOM WRIGHT
SCOTTY DUVAL	MARC BLUCAS
TERRELL	BERNARD ALEXANDER LEWIS
TODD NORTHRUP	SAM MCMURRAY
GREG	PERRY LANG
LESTER	MIGUEL FERRER
LORETTA	CHARLAYNE WOODARD
BUSTER BIDWELL	CLIFTON JAMES
JEFFERSON CASH	CULLEN DOUGLAS
MURRAY SILVER	ALAN KING
SILENT SAM	ELIOT ASINOF
STEVE TREGASKIS	RICHARD EDSON
CHAIRWOMAN	VI BENNETT
DICK YORDAN	KYLE MEENAN
MRS. PIERCE	BARBARA YOUNG
BUYER	TIM POWELL
BUYER #2	BRETT RICE
QUARLES	RHYNELL BRUMFIELD
LYLE SHIFLETT	DAN BRIGHT
"CHIEF" BILLY TRUCKS	MICHAEL GREYEYES
DUB	RAND D. BURNS
KRISSY	AMANDA WING
NURSE GWEN	DEBRA BRACEY
OFFICER BRYCE	JON COEN
PARK EMPLOYEE	JAMES BROWER
SOCIAL WORKER	KAREN GARRETT
JUDGE	PATRICIA CLAY
PROSECUTOR	LAIRD STUART
ROSELLEN	BROOKS ANNE HAYES
BOY	JOHN MORRISSEY
SMOOT	JOEY GRIFFIN

APRIL	ASHLEY BRUMBY
UNDERHILL	JAY SMITH
OLNEY	DENNIS NEAL
REVEREND SUTCLIFF	CHARLES ALBERT JR.
TOURIST MAN	DAVID PREUSS
TOURIST WOMAN	MAUREEN PREUSS
CHURCH WOMAN	MAPLE PRATT

PASSION FISH (1992)
Original Cast (in order of appearance)

MAY-ALICE	MARY MCDONNELL
RHONDA/DAWN	ANGELA BASSETT
NURSE QUICK	LENORE BANKS
MAX	WILLIAM MAHONEY
THERAPIST #1	NELLE STOKES
THERAPIST #2	BRETT ARDOIN
DR. KLINE	MICHAEL MANTELL
THERAPIST #3	DANIEL DUPONT
ATTENDANT	CHUCK CAIN
FAN #1	SHANA LEDET QUALLS
FAN #2	PAULA LAFLEUR
LOUISE	MAGGIE RENZI
DRUSHKA	MARIANNE MUELLERLEILE
JESSICA	VICTORIA EDWARDS
PERKY	AMANDA CARLIN
PHOEBE	ELAINE WEST
LAWANDA	LINDA CASTLE
KIT	LEIGH HARRIS
CHANTELLE	ALFRE WOODARD
SUGAR	VONDIE CURTIS-HALL
RENNIE	DAVID STRATHAIRN
REEVES	LEO BURMESTER
PRECIOUS	MARY PORTSER
TI-MARIE	NORA DUNN
LUTHER	TOM WRIGHT
ALBERTINE	JENNIFER GARDNER
KIM	SHEILA KELLEY
NINA	NANCY METTE
DENITA	SHAUNTISA WILLIS
DR. BLADES	JOHN HENRY REDWOOD
VANCE	MICHAEL LASKIN